# The Clash of Civilizations

# The Clash of Civilizations

*War-Making and State Formation in Europe*

Victor Lee Burke

Polity Press

First published in 1997 by Polity Press
in association with Blackwell Publishers Ltd.

2  4  6  8  10  9  7  5  3  1

*Editorial office:*
Polity Press
65 Bridge Street
Cambridge CB2 1UR, UK

*Marketing and production:*
Blackwell Publishers Ltd
108 Cowley Road
Oxford OX4 1JF, UK

*Published in the USA by:*
Blackwell Publishers Inc.
238 Main Street
Cambridge, MA 02142, USA

ISBN 0-7456-1198-2

A CIP catalogue record for this book is available from the British Library and
the Library of Congress.

Typeset in 10½ on 12½ pt Sabon
by Wearset, Boldon, Tyne and Wear
Printed in Great Britain by Hartnolls Ltd, Bodmin, Cornwall

This book is printed on acid-free paper.

# Contents

# Acknowledgments

I would like to thank the many people whose kind and generous efforts helped me with this project.

This book started as a sort of distance-learning postdoctoral research project in social theory with Anthony Giddens, after I had completed my doctorate studying historical and political sociology with Charles Tilly and Mayer Zald at Michigan. Giddens's unwavering and subtle way of communicating that the modern sociologist should not shy away from the difficult classical theoretical problems, in what C. Wright Mills has referred to as the classic tradition, was a source of inspiration throughout the writing of this book. The invaluable support, criticism, and guidance I received from Giddens began before this project was even at the book prospectus stage, and continued through the final draft of the manuscript.

Charles Tilly gave me a top-to-bottom critique with his characteristic verve and creativity. He helped me to come to terms with the concepts of civilization and warfare – in particular how these concepts have been treated by other sociologists and historians in the history of thought – and gave me suggestions for remedies for the conceptual and empirical shortcomings of the book. Randall Collins gave me a deep, thoughtful, and eye-opening reading of an early draft of the manuscript. William Gamson helped me to examine the linkages among political history, women's history, social history, and political sociology and their relationship to this project. William Form helped me with an excellent critique of issues at the macro and supermacro range, particularly regarding the class and institutional levels of analysis. An anonymous reviewer greatly improved all aspects of this book and made it more readable than it would otherwise have been. The historian Raymond Dominick, who teaches Western Civilization, saved me from many factual and interpretive errors from prospectus through early draft stage. André Gunder Frank helped me to examine the economic foundations of my argument. J. Craig Jenkins, Thomas Foster, Elias Khalil, and Ted Dahlstrand gave me helpful early feedback at the prospectus stage.

Thanks as well to Sing Chew, Richard Hamilton, Lowell Hargens, Glenn Hartz, Gisela Hinkle, Steven Joyce, Wen Li, Delwin Lindsey, Barbara McGovern, Robert Merton, Krishnan Namboodiri, Michele Osborne, Barbara Reskin, Catherine Ross, Kazimierz Slomczynski, Arthur Stinchcombe, Verta Taylor, and Mayer Zald for their advice, guidance, counsel, conversations, correspondence, criticisms, and suggestions that directly or indirectly had a bearing on this research, and its completion as a book.

Thanks for the help and patience of Head Librarian Sherri Edwards at Ohio State University at Mansfield, and her faithful assistants, as they had to deal with the technical and logistical problems that I presented in literally breaking the historical record (at least that is my understanding) for the number of books ever checked out to an individual in the history of the Ohio State University library system on any of its campuses.

Also thanks to my research assistants Kerry Baker, Adam Burke, Victoria Burke, Amy Close, John Coleman, Glenn Delong, Chad Flory, Kerri Mellick, Rachel Oktavec, Ty Pritchett, Todd Roston, Heidi Shoup, Jared Thew, Dianna Weber, and Felicia Williamson for their help. Thanks to Yolanda Allen and Marna Utz for their secretarial assistance.

I would also like to thank John Riedl, Dean and Director at the Ohio State University at Mansfield, and Elizabeth Menaghan, Chair of the Sociology Department in Columbus, for their general support of quality research. I would like to thank my colleagues at the Ohio State University both in my sociology department on the Columbus campus, and my interdisciplinary colleagues of the Mansfield campus, for their intellectual stimulation. Thanks to Ann Bone, my desk editor, for her conscientious effort to make this a better manuscript.

Special thanks to Anna Celeste Burke for her support, encouragement, her excellent targeted criticism and her many Flamingos.

Since I did not always follow the wise counsels of my colleagues, the responsibility for this research is of course, mine.

# Introduction

This study has two broad objectives. First, I want to explore a theory that explains how a Germanic tribal structure in the eighth century developed into a world-dominating state system by the seventeenth century. Second, with this theory I will examine empirically the way that war and other aspects of civilizational interaction facilitated the development of governments in Western Europe.

In these explorations I use certain assumptions about the nature of society and social change. I draw on Tony Spybey's elaboration of Anthony Giddens's structuration theory. Like Giddens and Spybey, I examine the way in which *human agency* makes a difference to the structure of society, and the manner in which structure in turn constrains human activity. I examine the roles made by different individuals, classes, and groups in the civilizations under analysis, and their impact on the European state system.

This study concurs with Giddens's ideas regarding evolution in social change: that there are no evolutionary steps or irreversible patterns that each society must move through, and no discernible uniform stages in the human history examined. This idea differs from the evolutionary theories of Auguste Comte, Herbert Spencer, and Karl Marx. Instead, I use Spybey's development of Giddens's idea of *episodes*. This approach, of course, does not mean that humans cannot learn from their mistakes. Nor does it ignore the progress that humans can make in reducing suffering and inequality. It simply asserts that this learning process does not *necessarily* occur in uniform and immutable stages, but transpires in diverse ways in various episodes in human history.

As Giddens points out, a theory on the origins of states must approach this problem in the context of intersocietal systems. Likewise, drawing on Spybey's exploration of Giddens's structuration theory, the emphasis in this analysis is on Europe's development of a state system. States form, exist, and change in these intersocietal systems. David Held, moreover, has pointed out that although at a very abstract level we can talk about something called "the state" as a unified entity, at another level "the state" is in fact a group of highly complex interactions and processes, involving power relations.

The pioneering theoretical and empirical works on the state produced by Charles Tilly and Giddens have shown the advantages of examining the manner in which external events fashion the internal structures of states. The predominance of war in state transformations became evident in their work. This book borrows from Tilly and Giddens the importance of war in forming the mighty structures of European states.

The master of historical sociology, Max Weber, focused on the Protestant ethic as the cause of the origins of the modern world. Weber did not, however, explore the reasons for the origins and success of the Reformation. In this book I critique Weber for his emphasis on the Protestant ethic as a causal variable in the rise of capitalist Europe. Nonetheless, Randall Collins provides a compelling argument that it is wrong to judge Weber by his earliest efforts at understanding the origins of capitalism. Instead, Collins emphasizes the contribution made by the mature Weber in Weber's *General Economic History*. Collins calls these lectures Weber's "last theory of capitalism." My analysis has much in common with that of the mature Weber.

In Weber's last theory of capitalism, Collins argues, politics is tied first and foremost to the external realm of international relationships. Weber argues that societies cannot be understood alone as independent functional units, cultures, or arenas delimited for the convenience of analysis. Collins goes on to argue that from Weber's perspective the key to external dynamics is not economic exchange but military force.

This analysis takes seriously Collins's advice that, in the study of the state and politics, social scientific advances will come from improving geopolitical analysis. In particular he advocates studying the causes and consequences of military interrelationships among states. Again, Collins argues that this effort is worthwhile because of the reverberations between internal politics and interrelations in the external arena. I follow Collins's dictum that the guiding analysis of societies is at the level of a larger international status system that is not reducible to internal interests and resources of local political agents. Arnold Toynbee's vision of civilization is offered in this work as a way of operationalizing Collins's guiding principles.

In addition, like Collins, I tie the fate of capitalism to the fate of the papacy and Christendom. I also follow Collins's lead in arguing that developments in the Middle Ages created the institutional forms within which capitalism could emerge. The Protestant Reformation, which so captivated Weber, was just a particular crisis at the end of a long-term cycle.

In short, besides their own distinctive internal dynamics, European governments changed through their political, economic, military, and cultural interactions with each other. The development of states as complex organizations occurred in a sometimes stable but often chaotic set of political systems. This is true with the linkages of states to internal sources of power as well as with the arrangements they set up with other states (and emerging states) even outside of their own geographical vicinity. This development created webs of influence and systems of social, economic, cultural, political, geographical, military, and linguistic gestalts – sets of exchanges, conflicts, and barriers to exchanges among the various polities in the emerging European state system.

To the ideas of emerging state systems and warfare as key transformational principles I bring in Toynbee's notion of *civilization*. Toynbee and William McNeill have pointed toward the pivotal role that other civilizations have played in the development of the West. In a similar vein Janet Abu-Lughod, drawing on and expanding the work of Immanuel Wallerstein and André Gunder Frank among others, has shown that a number of economic systems existed independently of the West.

The analysis of the role of civilizations in the transformation of states in the past is living history. Civilizations continue to exert a great influence on contemporary states and societies. According to Samuel Huntington, who borrows from Toynbee, the conflict among civilizations will be the latest phase in the evolution of conflict in the modern world. Largely, this new phase has been a product of the collapse of Cold War hostilities. The Cold War, from Huntington's perspective, had partitioned the world stage into various competing groups. In the post–Cold War world there will still be conflicts in which nation states are the primary agents; these conflicts, however, will expand beyond the confines of the nation state, and enlarge into conflicts of civilizations. This clash of civilizations, an expression I borrow in turn from Huntington, will come to dominate global politics. In the new post–Cold War world, civilizations will be the structures in which we will examine the divisions of the globe.

According to Huntington, the divisions that the superpowers brought on in the Cold War – the first, second, and third worlds – are becoming less and less meaningful. Huntington analytically divides civilizations into their atomic parts. At the *micro* level are villages, regions, ethnic groups, nationalities, and religious groups. All of these groups have distinct cultures at different levels. As one moves up the scale from micro to *macro*, however, eventually a particular group is no longer a part of any broader cultural entity. According to Huntington these are the elements that culminate in civilizations. A civilization, according to Huntington, is the highest cultural grouping of people on the broadest level of cultural identity that people have.

From Huntington's perspective, civilizations are not all the same size. Civilizations may be either small or large. There are relatively large civilizations such as Western and Islamic civilizations. On the other hand we can find relatively small civilizations such as Japan. There may also be subcivilizations. Islamic civilization is so complex that it includes Arab, Turkish, and Malay subdivisions. Civilizations may also blend with each other, and civilizations may overlap. Huntington argues that civilizations are the most fundamental forms of social organization. Civilizations have centuries-old, sometimes millennia-old histories, languages, cultures, traditions, religions, and governments. Civilizations all have differing assumptions regarding deities or no deities. They also shape people's ideas regarding marriage or the absence thereof. They supply its members with formulas regarding the role of children, and with the differing notions of the rights and responsibilities of its members. They provide ideas regarding issues of freedom, what constitutes an authority, and what are the appropriate hierarchies.

Giddens argues that civilizations typically bracket large segments of time and space. Fernand Braudel distinguishes between civilizations and *cultures*. To Braudel a culture is a civilization that has not yet achieved maturity, its greatest potential; nor has it consolidated its growth. Moreover, he defines civilizations as entities with relatively dense populations possessing multiple assets and advantages: domestic animals, swing plows, plows, carts, and towns.

Thus civilizations are enduring political, economic, geographical, historical, and cultural entities. They may comprise a large amount of territory and a great variety of peoples. Civilizations may contain empires, vassal states, societies, city states, and tribes. Widely shared cosmologies may support the social relations and states within civilizations. These civilizations have market, exchange, extraction, and/or plundering systems, which often give the economic and institutional core of the civilization its resources. There is also a strong political component in civilizations, where civilizational elites, rulers, or institutions control populations. Most civilizations have written languages. Although the Mongol civilization did not have a written language, scribes were still used from other civilizations.

There are also relational and network dimensions to civilizations. Often civilizations come into existence when a set of political, cultural, economic, military, and social forces forms in a particular area. After this fusion in a particular geopolitical area, the civilizational powers expand and force their cultural patterns on a population that is foreign. At other times trade and cultural networks spread the civilization's products and culture from the emanating core to other societies and civilizations.

Sometimes civilizations may take the form of an imperial structure. This was the case with the Byzantine, Ottoman, early Mongolian, and early Carolingian systems examined here. At other times civilizations may contain or transcend empires and show no imperial structures, as was the case with late Carolingian, medieval, and modern European civilizations, as well as the Viking and later Mongolian and Eurasian civilizations I will explore.

There is a variety of reasons why civilizations clash. The clash of civilizations, from Huntington's perspective, can occur at both the micro and macro levels. Civilizations may struggle over the control of international organizations, and try to influence those states that lie outside their civilizational sphere of influence. In this book civilizations clash for various economic, political, religious, geographical, and military reasons. The final clash between Western and Byzantine civilizations shows that misunderstandings and bad luck also play their part. As I will show, in the case of the Ottoman and Habsburg dynasties the clash of egos between the Sultan and the Emperor led to the clash of civilizations.

Civilizations also have a tendency to clash because of their different *identities*. As Huntington points out, the idea of a civilization consciousness is also another power in the modern world. The renewed Asian identity movement, the new Islamic movement, and the movement of Hinduization of India, all are expressions of civilizational consciousness. To the extent that these civilization consciousness movements become militant or experience oppression, they may engage in war and conflict.

A large episode in this book canvasses the tension among Byzantine, Western, and Islamic civilizations, tensions that also have ramifications into the present. The tension among Islamic, Orthodox (developed from Byzantine civilization), and Western civilizations has led to civilizational earthquakes throughout the centuries, and still creates tremors and social earthquakes in the latter twentieth century; it will continue to do so in the twenty-first century. The tension among the Western, Islamic, Orthodox, and Eurasian civilizations is evident in the atrocities and slaughters in the former Yugoslavia. Likewise, according to Huntington, civilizational clash dynamics continue in the explosive nature of the Middle East, with its intersection of Islamic and Western civilizations.

The battles of the future will occur on what Huntington calls "the fault lines" that separate these civilizations from one another. These civilizational fault lines, from Huntington's perspective, are replacing the ideological political boundaries of the years of the Iron Curtain. Groups near to each other at different parts of the fault lines may fight in the attempt to gain or maintain territory in the general vicinity of those fault lines. Because of rapid communications and transportation, civilizations are colliding in a renewed and unprecedented manner. These new interactions and the ease of these interactions may have negative side effects. There may be conflict over new and unusual customs alien to another civilization. This book deals with the origins of many of these fault lines which will prove to be such a fateful force in the future of this planet.

In covering so much ground in so few pages I have only provided a panoramic view of the ways and means of wars, civilizations, European state-making, and state transformations. I discuss many things very briefly. A single causal strand has been pulled out and examined from the multicolored carpet that is history. The references and citations I provide are only suggestive, not comprehensive. I have compressed this history somewhat mercilessly, and in the process have no doubt missed some important factors, and overlooked some connections and events.

The term *civilization* has the same limitations as any ideal-typical formulation. As Giddens observed, too often in traditional civilizational treatments researchers presume that civilizations are more complex and civilized than oral tradition or so-called "barbarian" cultures. Even Toynbee was guilty of this error. Thorstein Veblen in all his works pokes fun at this elitist perspective. Like the terms *society* in sociology, and the expression *the atom* in physics, these constructs are only focal points for organizing observations. They are not the phenomenon itself. Words are not able to capture into a strict definition such complex processes. Atoms at any given time do not even have a definite structure, and societies are too complex for any definition to capture what they are. Yet ideas such as atoms, civilizations, and societies are useful to the extent they help focus attention on important scientific phenomena.

I pursue a line of research that has an ancient tradition. Indeed, this book puts warfare in the forefront, and I pursue a goal not too different from that of Herodotus when he examined the transformation of ancient Greece. Researchers in the late twentieth century have the good fortune to possess historical sources and scientific methodology that Herodotus would surely have been pleased to have had in ancient Greece.

In a related manner, my emphasis on the civilizational level leaves out the details of how specific political and other organizational structures developed. Likewise I have devoted only limited attention to the social organization of bureaucracies, armies, international agreements, and interinstitutional relationships. My attention to stratification is only suggestive. I provide snapshots of stratification within nation states, and only sketch the relationship between internal stratification systems and interstate systems. Likewise, I have not designed this book to test comprehensively all the theories addressed. Instead, I take an approach similar to Talcott Parsons's strategy in *The Structure of Social Action*, or that of Giddens in *Capitalism and Modern Social Theory*. Like Parsons, I use existing theories in a synthetic manner to develop new theories. Like Giddens's research, this is more an expository and comparative work than a critical study; my goal is not to identify the strengths and weaknesses of world-systems theory, or Michael Mann's ideas, but instead to draw on these ingenious theories in the theory that I am presenting. I definitely pursue an "on the shoulders of giants" approach to theorizing, in contrast to the slash and burn technique. Nonetheless, I shall attempt to show how I have drawn on existing theoretical works, and how these works differ from the theory that I offer in these pages.

Putting states and wars at the center of social change has a venerable heritage, but I aim to approach this tradition with renewed vigor. To some social historians this emphasis on the role of elites in history may seem to have a very old-fashioned flavor. With the arrival of social history, or history from the bottom, or herstory, my approach may even seem like a throwback to early times. For sociologists, however, political and historical sociology is still a new frontier.

C. Wright Mills may have founded modern political historical sociology with the classic work *The Power Elite*. Before this work, after the deaths of Marx, Weber, and Veblen, many sociologists shied away from studying the rich and the powerful. Some have argued that sociologists wanted to "stake out their own turf" distinct from history, economics, and political science. Others have argued that sociologists were reluctant to study political elites because so much of sociology's funding and legitimation came from the state. The new-found sense of security of sociologists within academia (however illusory this may be) has given them the courage to examine this formerly taboo area.

Finally, let me note that this work differs from political histories in significant ways. First, it is theory-driven history. The fact that historians have accumulated centuries of political histories finds the historically inclined social theoretician in an enviable position. The *Clash* has a much more explicit conceptual architecture than is found in most political history. Likewise, because of my training as a sociologist, I rarely argue that events in these pages are the result of a Great Person acting in a social vacuum. I argue against the very idea that the rise of Europe was the product of the Greatness of European Leaders, culture, or civilization. I examine few great people in these pages. More often than not, state-builders are products of the *Zeitgeist* and are more like leaves in a hurricane than the hurricane itself. They are as much products as producers of social structure. Waves of history often wipe out these "*Zeitgeist* surfers." Unfortunately, state-builders often harm thousands of people in their effort to ride the waves of circumstance. Indeed, it is the greatness of non-European civilizations that led to the rise of Europe. Certainly this idea would have been anathema to the political historians of earlier ages.

That I examine political events does not mean that I neglect an exploration of social history. At the meso and micro levels I keep in touch with the interaction between the state and society. The interactions of the faceless individuals whose follies and heroics, as both Giddens and Erving Goffman recognized, are both the products and producers of the structure of society are important features of this research.

Likewise, because I study state-making and elites it does not mean that I ignore herstory. If sociologists have devoted little research attention to studying middle- and working-class women, we have devoted even fewer resources to studying upper-class women. This book encounters numerous women elites and rulers, from the Roman empire through the Age of Exploration and the Counter-Reformation.

For me to explore all the issues listed above would require a much bigger book, or volumes of books, with far different research objectives. As I am a social scientist, this work is primarily for other social scientists and their students. Historians and humanists with theoretical and social scientific leanings will also find this work of interest to themselves and their students. Some researchers may find value in this map I have provided for them, and join in the adventure of exploring civilizations and state transformations.

A strength of this approach is that I question the simple idea of societies and nation states as the largest unit of analysis when thinking of both internal and global affairs. The study of social change involves much more than the analysis of a particular society. This is especially true when one begins an inquiry into political change. Accordingly, there is a broader reach of human history: that of the histories of states and civilizations. In this book I look at the manner in which the clash of civilizations and war created and transformed the European state system.[1]

# 1

# A Theory of the Modern European State System

There are important questions which sociology can help to answer: What creates the development of governmental systems? How is it that huge state systems of domination arise that play central roles in the historical trajectory of humankind? How exactly do great world phenomena such as Mesopotamia, Egypt, India, China, and the Islamic state systems come into existence; what laws govern their maintenance; what dynamics cause their decline? What this problem asks of the sociologist is to unravel the riddle of history. Pitirim Sorokin, Comte, Toynbee, Oswald Spengler and others have attempted studies on this scale and each has offered explanations for the origins of these state systems.

For sociologists interested in the sweep of modern history, the central question revolves round Western European states: How did they come into existence and how did they come to occupy a dominant position in the world's political economy? We have had several centuries of reflection and research on this problem, and yet explaining the origins of the modern European state system remains an intriguing puzzle and an important research problem. From a political standpoint, the European state system is one of the most significant forces in history, its rise to dominance spanning the period between the origins of the Carolingian empire around the eighth century AD to at least the beginning of the twentieth century. The penetration of European political ways and means into all human life makes it crucial to understand how a force of this sort has exerted such an inexorable effect on the human race.

This investigation seeks to uncover the reasons for the dominance of the European state system in the space-time continuum we call history. Of particular importance to this project is understanding the emergence of what I have labeled the binary system: the modern system of state and capitalism.

The model I develop draws heavily on Toynbee's ideas. Just as Einstein needed an anchor when he realized that Newton was dealing with relative laws, not absolute ones, so a corresponding social constant is necessary in order to understand social phenomena that are in flux. For Einstein's physical universe it was light; for Toynbee's social universe it was civilization. I will draw on Toynbee's insight in this analysis. Wilkinson, as Frank and Gills show in their interdisciplinary survey of research, also argues for the importance of a central civilization that he identifies as the "central world system." There is no claim that this or other civilizations are more "civilized" than other societies; only that these entities have a significant impact on world history and that these civilizations typically, but not always, contain a number of societies or city states. Recognizing the importance of civilizations, I examine modern Western civilization, perhaps the most fateful force in the modern world, while moderating Toynbee's view of civilizations as constants. Civilizations move; but not very quickly.

The civilization struggle model that I develop incorporates the Tilly–Giddens principle regarding the primacy of warlike behavior as a central engine in the rise of the Western states, an approach that has found support and development in a number of works that examine war's relationship to the rise of the West.

The approach I use is also sympathetic with Mann's power network analysis, Wallerstein's and Frank's world system/dependency theory synthesis, and the non-Eurocentric view of the development of the modern world taken by Abu-Lughod and Eric Wolf. The research offered here emphasizes the role played by other civilizations in the rise of the European state system, and perceives that the rise of the European state system was in large part the result of the military failure of its excursions to the east. This current research, like the work analyzed by Frank and Gills, argues that there have been numerous and repeated instances of hegemony and rivalry throughout history. Along with these rivalries have come changes in hegemony and periphery–hinterland structure. In addition, adapting their analysis of Abu-Lughod, the East was a causal variable in the rise of the West. War, moreover, is so constant a dynamic in the events that follow that we may do well to turn Clausewitz on his head by stating that politics appears to be war by other means; violence is so pervasive that we see war as a fundamental organizational factor in the origins of the modern Western European state system.

The purpose of this book, then, is to explain the development of that Western state system between the eighth and the seventeenth centuries. The eighth century represented the period after the collapse of the Roman empire when the Carolingian Franks absorbed or destroyed all other Germanic bands, creating the most powerful state system in Western Europe. By the seventeenth century, the outline of the modern state system had crystallized, emerging from the collapse of the feudalism of Western Christendom that was the dominant form of social organization of the Middle Ages in the West.[1]

## Overview of Theories

Many classical theorists explored the rise of the modern binary system of the state and capitalist economy. Sorokin's basic hypothesis is that various civilizations are the products of one of three principles. First, ideational principles create civilizations that embrace religious revelation, one such example being classical Indian civilization. This system created beliefs that the material world was an illusion, or what Hinduism terms the dance of Maya. Real truth, from the Hindu perspective, exists in the Universal Mind, since the material world is the creation of this Mind. In sensate society, however, only senses convey true reality. An ideal type of this form of sensate society is the materialistically based civilization current in the West. Finally, idealistic civilizations are a synthesis of sensate and ideational cultures. In metaphysical outlook, idealistic civilizations are both sensory and supernaturally based, the prime example of this type of society being the medieval period in Western Europe. Change occurs when the civilization collapses from within, almost through ennui or boredom, a process Sorokin calls immanent change.

The rise of Western civilization from Sorokin's perspective, in his magnum opus *Social and Cultural Dynamics*, was created by the exhaustion of the creative potential of the Middle Ages; out of this collapsed civilization came the modern materialistic, sensate culture. The modern secular state system of Europe was the product of this change. In due time, sensate culture will also exhaust its creative potential and a new civilization will emerge from the ashes of the West.

Spengler also addresses the problem of the origins of civilizations, but argues that a civilization is a morphological conclusion or solidification of a previous culture. Spengler presents a cyclical view of history, where civilizations occur as a crystallization of the previous culture, and where, like living organisms, civilizations have life cycles. Civilizations go through youth, maturity, and decline. History, though cyclical, does not precisely repeat itself, but analogous morphologies recur. This means that certain events in history resemble other events. For example, there may be morphological analogies between the roles of Charlemagne and Alexander the Great. In addition, civilizations share a certain holistic coherence in their architecture, science, art, and politics. Hence the state system that developed between the rise of the Carolingian empire and the modern European state system shares certain morphological similarities with the previous state systems found in the city states of Rome and Greece.

In contrast to Spengler's argument, modernization theory of the 1950s and the 1960s links the origins of the modern world, and the European state system, to the industrial revolution. Critics have challenged this perspective for its US and Eurocentric perspective and its technological determinism.

The strength of modernization theory, however, is that it reminds social scientists to be cognizant of the importance of technology in social transformation and of the important linkage between industry and social change. Marx was the master of exploring the linkages between the ways that people earn a

living, the ownership of the industrial process, and social transformation. Indeed modernization theory might not have taken
hold in sociology save through Marxist analysis through Émile
Durkheim. Gerhard Lenski and Jean Lenski, though not a part
of modernization theory, have masterfully explored the importance of technology in social transformation, and I use their
insights in this research.

In contrast to these later theories, statist theories see the rise
of states as a result of properties within the states themselves.
These theories place less of an emphasis on the role of societal
dynamics as a causal variable in state transformation, but
instead see the central shaper of governmental transformation
as the government itself. From this perspective, the political
state-builders' decisions result in the success or failure of their
initiatives. Huntington has done the most influential work
along these lines. In terms of internal state-building within
societies, Theda Skocpol has developed the most comprehensive and original work in this area. I draw from the state-
centered perspective particularly the variation that stresses the
importance of war-makers in the transformation of states.

The modes of production analysis ties the structure of states
to the underlying development of class and the relations of production. From the perspective of that analysis, capitalism
developed states as a by-product of its own development. My
study also examines the manner in which capitalism interacts
with states in the context of an exploration of how civilizations
and states' networks interact with the modes of production in
the rise of the European state system.

A central idea of world systems and dependency theory is
that the rise of the West occurred because of the ability of the
core to oppress a less powerful periphery. The wealth for the
advancement of Western objectives came from the ability of
this core to extract surplus labor from the periphery. As Daniel
Chirot points out, however, it was not so much an absolute
increase in profits and wealth that made the big difference, but
the opportunities that Europe gained from the expansion overseas. The result was the development of a new type of mer-
chant-based capitalist world where the states reflect the class
position of the state in the world economy: core, periphery, or
semiperiphery. I also adopt the general contour of dependency

theory and world-systems analysis, but look at civilizations, states, and war as critical variables in the rise of the modern European state system.[2]

## The Civilization Struggle Model

The central argument of this civilization struggle model is that the origins of the European state system were the product of the collisions among great civilizations; the impact of these collisions works downward and shapes political structures. Likewise, developments at what I will define below as the supermacro, macro, and micro levels work upward to the civilizational and intercivilizational levels, impacting the fates of civilizations. These interactions transformed the political structures of Europe. Without understanding the dynamic and open-ended nature of this entire linkage of activity, from the micro through to the universal level, it is difficult to understand historical motion as outlined by Marx and Weber. The dynamics and statics created by both the success and limitations of dealing with these other civilizations led to the origins and transformation of governments within the West. With the maritime explosion that occurred during the age of exploration, Europe's collision with civilizations of the American Indians created the second wave of capitalist development and colonial state-building.

The civilization struggle thesis is that between the eighth and the sixteenth centuries, competing civilizations were successful in constraining the Western European state system. In this period this success created a pulsar-like epoch of governmental centralization and decentralization as this activity gradually established a centralizing dynamic in Europe that created the modern Western binary state civilization and its subsequent expansion to the west. The Western European capitalist state system was the dependent variable in this civilizational conflict.

The civilization struggle model relates the origins of the Western state system to the social conflict among many civilizations. The conflicts among the European, ancient Roman, Islamic, Viking, Byzantine, various Steppe warrior, Ottoman,

Native American, Eurasian, and Mongol civilizations occur at what I call the *intercivilizational* or *universal plane*. The intercivilizational or universal plane includes the power dynamics of civilizations on a global scale. Lower down the scale of geographical magnitude is the *supermacro level*. At this level are civilizations, society, societies, and networks of societies. Society, societies, and networks of societies are the molecules of the supermacro scale and are the building blocks of civilizations. Within each society at the *macro level* are the dynamics of classes, genders, institutions, states, social structures, economies, and people within these societies. Intercivilizational and supermacro events work downward to transform gender, economic, state, and class relations, while events occurring at the macro level can work upward and permeate other societies and other civilizations at the supermacro and intercivilizational levels. Within the macro scale, the processes of historical change as discovered by Marx and Weber come into play. Class conflict, as Marx predicts, and the Reformation, as Weber argues, affected the historical trajectory of Europe and with it the European state system. These developments are special macro events derived from the universal-level dynamics, most specifically, the struggles among civilizations.

At the *micro level* are the interactions of individuals; they feature importantly as both the products and producers of the structure of society. Together with the behavior of the unknown individuals who create the social tapestry of history, this level also includes powerful charismatic individuals whose actions at the micro level they leverage from the universal-level platform. Throughout these pages, I explore how powerful individuals, through good luck and bad fortune, ability and incompetence, make decisions that for better or worse influence the fates of nations.

Turning from social statics to social dynamics, at the most general level of causality, and utilizing the Tilly–Giddens principle on warlike behavior as an engine, there are *universal struggles* that involve struggles among civilizations (see figure 1). The dynamics of this plane include the interactions of civilizations on a global scale. Drawing on Mann's perspective, among civilizations we see military, political, economic, and

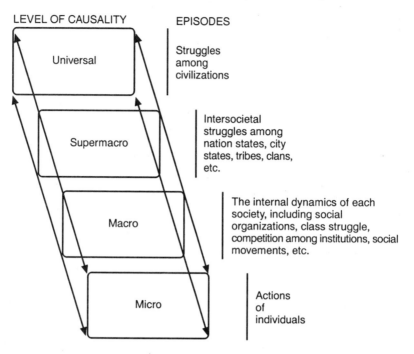

**Figure 1** *Levels of causality and episodes associated with them*

ideological sources of social power. In addition, struggles at this level transform the social structures, psychological makeup, cultural products, geographical location, linguistic characteristics, and communication among the civilizations involved, as well as the rise of states within these civilizations. At this level we see Sorokin's cosmologies existing and his principles in action. Rather than sorting civilizations by these various principles, we can see elements of idealistic, sensate, and ideational principles at work in most of the civilizations that we will examine, with the pure types of the expressions of these principles difficult to find.

Using the work of Wallerstein and Frank, we find that various world systems emerge if one civilization develops a system of hegemony over other civilizations. At other times, rival civilizations create partitioned or simultaneous or overlapping world systems, particularly if there is a balance of power among them, or if political and historical circumstances are such that one civilization is unable to make inroads into the markets and political systems of others. Also, world systems may fail to emerge because the civilizations are decentralized and out of touch, for various reasons, with the lines of trade or conflict of other civilizations. In addition, creating a variation on the ideas of world systems and dependency theory, I track the trajectory of economic flows and the way that core civilizations and their economies come into existence, and show how these civilizations are able to subordinate a less powerful peripheral civilization. Drawing on insights offered by the modes of production analysts, throughout this book I examine how the conflict among civilizations altered the modes of production and the development of capitalism. Influenced by both Abu-Lughod and Frank, I point out that the particular internal dynamic of a civilization has a lot to do with whether a particular rival civilization is generating a world system of its own. We will explore some universal conflicts that even involve multiple world systems. Multiple hegemonies may exist that affect the whole known world, but they may or may not overlap for centuries.

Applying Lenski and Lenski's ideas to the context of civilizations, I will show how technological and cultural features of a civilization also play a role in the conflict among civilizations. As in their work I am interested in the role that technological advantages gave to various civilizations in the conflicts under examination. In particular I inspect the development of military, transportation, and social technologies, including stratification structures, banking and market breakthroughs, that states used for conquest or defense, and examine the advantages that these technological breakthroughs gave to one civilization over another. I also examine those cases where a particular civilization, while having access to a particular technology, refuses to adopt a new technology and the ramifications for this decision on the fates of civilizations.

Under the umbrella of greater civilizational struggles are *supermacro struggles* that are lower down the ladder of geopolitical magnitude, where nations struggle against each other either to defend themselves or to advance their power over other societies. I will also use the Tilly–Giddens principle to organize my observations at this level. Civilizations may radically transform social structures by militarily absorbing previously external societies, altering the social structure of these societies as well as the civilization's own stratification system. An important issue at this level is the degree of centralization. There are internal dynamics within the types of civilizations. Within each we see differing patterns of social structure. We see that economic systems vary by the types of civilizations. The states that emerge within a civilizational conflict generate certain cultural patterns, repress others, and influence the degree of diversity tolerated within a civilization. When examining the internal dynamics of civilizations, as Sorokin argues, we often see a variety of approaches to religion, reality, and cosmologies. There are defining moments when a particular civilization can take on one particular character, or conversely assume various social and cultural principles. Considering Sorokin's work, we look at how war-making activities interact with particular cultures. As Mann would hypothesize, among these societies there are power networks, including military, political, economic, and ideological networks. Socially there are networks related to geographical proximity, or networks maintained through kinship, and other networks that extend further afield.

In a transposition of the work of Wallerstein and Frank to the analysis of civilizations, we discover that within the civilization proper the type of lifestyle and material well-being of a civilization is often determined by the location of its core economy. It is important to identify whether the civilization is in fact an emanating core civilization or a peripheral one. This is also true internally within a civilization. In other words, it is important to explore whether a society is a vassal society within the civilization, or is indeed part of the core. This makes a huge difference in terms of the affluence of the civilization in general.

On the technological front, I argue that within a particular civilization a technological core or a cluster of technological developments may alter the historical path of an entire civilization. In some cases these developments may be of a purely technological nature, or there may be other changes that are in the nature of social technologies in response to military threats. Sometimes, due to desires for external expansion, states may develop military and other forms of technology. At other moments, wars do not generate military technologies but states use technological developments already in existence. In addition, there may be technological advances deriving from economic influences. These create new forms of social technologies, due to shifting military alliances within a particular civilization, or because of conflicts with other civilizations in terms of banking and commercial developments.

Within a civilization the manner in which the mode of production develops may be fashioned by external stimuli, particularly war-making, which affect the development and alteration of the modes of production. In addition I examine how warfare and trade disperse the particular mode of production, or how this mode of production is captured, ignored, or is borrowed by other civilizations.

*Macro intranational struggles*, within each society, are still lower down the scale of geopolitical magnitude, where class struggle, competition among institutions, social movements, social organization, and the internal dynamics of each society exist. The Tilly–Giddens principle shapes society at this level too. Elites attempt to maintain their macro power while engaging in supermacro and civilizational level conflict through political, economic, and military means. If these elites and structures dominate their macro plane, the dynamic is to maintain this domination and expand into other societies and other civilizations at the supermacro and universal levels. If these classes and structures are dominant at all levels in a given geographical area, then this represents a *world historical civilization*.

Within the macro societal level, Marxist dynamics come into being where the successions of classes occur. Even here, however, civilizational level configurations come into play. The history of Western binary civilization is not only the transformation of state structures by one successive class after another. The conflict of civilizations through war-making, as Tilly and Giddens would propose, in a more general way, imposes exogenous classes on to other structures.

The macro dynamic of class conflict interacts with the supermacro dynamics of classes attempting to extend their national domination into international domination. National elites from outside attempt to graft their systems of domination on to other societies, networks of societies, and other civilizations. Civilizations, societies, and societal networks incorporate, drive off, or hold in stalemate these external classes. At other times, these external classes conquer the enemy civilization, societies, and societal networks.

The processes of historical change as discovered by Marx, particularly the importance of class conflict, and by Weber, particularly the importance of forms of ideologies, cultural patterns, bureaucracies, organizations, and institutions, come into play at this level and expand upward and downward to other levels. In addition, we see the various sources of social power and the networks that evolve from these structures. Thus each society has its own particular configuration of political, economic, and ideological sources of social power. The types of social norms and type of stratification system are also a part of each society and within each society there are distinct forms of social organization and networks. Clearly climate, proximity to natural resources, and the like play a role in shaping the society itself and the kinds of struggles or defenses that are open to it. Distinct variations or differences in languages are born and transformed, and these may vary from the language of the dominant core of the civilization. Differing psychological developments linked to the religions, ideologies, and worldviews occur within these societies. At this level the clearest forms of Sorokin's principles may be found in societal trends. Within the societal level, a society's position in a particular civilization, or its relationship to an external civilization, may cause the most intense alteration of existing cultures.

The world systems emanating through core portions of the civilization, and/or from other civilizations, may have a powerful impact on the macro societal level. This is particularly true through warfare. The external civilization's world system may also change a society. Altering the position of another civilization as a rival, a subordinate, or a partner may indirectly alter the society, passing through the whole cluster of societies that make up a civilization. Also within this level we often see states develop, as Bruce Porter shows, where the political core is at war with the political periphery of a particular society.

It is important to track the political developments within a particular society and to see if the point of origin is in its own or another world system. In other words, a society is not to be interpreted just in terms of one particular political system. Depending on the manner in which various civilizations have competed, other world systems may intercept a society. It is important to trail developments within the society and examine the reverberations up to the civilizational level, as well as the intercivilizational or universal level. This is crucial for those civilizations that start off as small societies but expand into world-dominating civilizations. We will see this pattern in a number of cases throughout this study.

A society may internally generate technological developments, or at other times absorb and institute developments by way of the host civilization or external civilizations. The geographical location of a particular society also has a bearing on the types of technologies and cultural and economic systems that develop. Sometimes new technological innovations may occur that a particular society rejects for religious or other reasons. Again it is important for us to follow the multilevel nature of all of these changes.

At the societal level, following the lead of the modes of production analysis, distinct forms of production may develop. In these pages I try to understand the way that universal and supermacro level wars change these modes. In addition, I attempt to discern the manner in which these modes reverberate up through the supermacro and universal levels.

Since the scope of this research is focused on a broad subset of global social and political mechanics, I will pay only scant attention to the mechanics of behavior at the micro level. This is due more to the nature of the research design and the span of centuries I am covering than to any lack of importance of this line of research. Face-to-face routines structure civilizations, societies, and networks of societies, as these structures shape face-to-face behavior, as Giddens has argued. These micro interactions are both the products and producers of the structure of society.

Structuration theory has explained how individuals interact within traditions that shape their everyday behavior. In this sense, these interactions are important features of this research. At the micro level the interaction between members of families, clans, or even individual soldiers who fight each other on a road are influenced by the civilization conflict at the universal level. Indeed the folkways of a group of people may be products of interactions in face-to-face behavior that have worked their way down from the universal level conflicts, or may also be the result of exchanges among members of the upper classes or the interaction of classes among civilizations.

As Mann argues, various power networks can influence all parts of society and I would argue that this is also true at the micro level. Military adventures often mean changes in customs that are quite evident in face-to-face behavior. Political and military events at the universal, supermacro, and macro levels may drastically alter the micro actions of particular individuals. Political and military developments at the very top of the civilizational hierarchy have profound consequences for the degree of spatial, political, cultural, gender, or economic freedom that any particular individual enjoys. As we will see, the religious practices of an individual may be determined or altered by the outcome of a war, and conversely the religious fates of nations and civilizations may be altered when at the micro level individuals alter their own religious beliefs, through some form of protest, "revelation," or by a conversion experience, and work to spread this experience throughout the society, often by military measures, even to the civilizational and intercivilizational levels.

In short, the civilizational model argues that collisions among great civilizations work downward, shaping political structures. Likewise, we will explore how war at the supermacro, macro, and micro levels works upward to the intercivilizational level and affects the fates of civilizations. This is the core idea of this civilizational structure theory.

## A Preview of the Civilization Struggle Thesis in Action: The Existence of Competing Civilizations

### *The rise and fall of the Carolingian state system and the origins of feudalism*

The struggles among the European, ancient Roman, Islamic, Viking, Byzantine, various Steppe warrior, Ottoman, Native

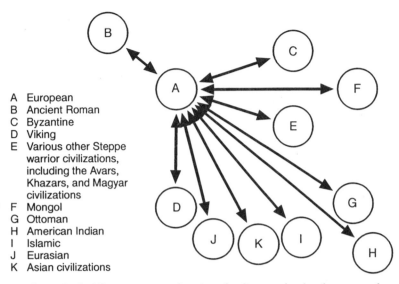

A European
B Ancient Roman
C Byzantine
D Viking
E Various other Steppe
  warrior civilizations,
  including the Avars,
  Khazars, and Magyar
  civilizations
F Mongol
G Ottoman
H American Indian
I Islamic
J Eurasian
K Asian civilizations

**Figure 2** *Conflict among civilizations leading to the development of the Western European state system*

American, Eurasian, and Mongol civilizations led to European state-building and state transformation (see figure 2). Political structures established by the Germanic bands that overran the Roman empire formed the structure of the modern European state system. By the sixth century, Roman efforts to restrain Germanic tribal civilization had failed, and the western Roman empire collapsed with the invasions of these warring bands. After a period of struggle among the Germanic tribes, the Franks established the Carolingian empire, a centralized state system in Western Europe. This centralization was short-lived and crumbled under the pressure of internal dynamics and the Vikings, creating feudalism.

Between the ninth and the sixteenth centuries, struggles against the Islamic, Viking, Steppe warrior, and Byzantine civilizations slowly created a pulsar-like centralizing dynamic that led from feudalism to state-building and the development of capitalism: the modern binary system (see figure 3). Prior to the Reformation, the ecclesiastical structures emanating from Rome were useful to the feudal elites in Western Europe in order to give some coordination to their efforts to keep the Mongol, Byzantine, Viking, and Islamic empires from

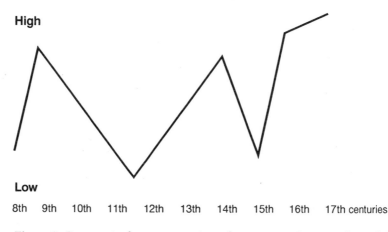

**Figure 3** *Patterns in the concentration of state power between the eighth and the seventeenth centuries*

conquering Europe. The papacy also helped coordinate European efforts against these civilizations.

In their earliest forms, there was not much of a distinction between ecclesiastical and manorial entities; they were populated by the same class, the landed aristocracy. As time went on, however, the divisions between these groups, the ecclesiastics and the manorial elites, were real, and they became more pointed as the local geographical power of the manor eventually ran up against the ecclesiastical structures, and both of these conflicted with the rising urban power-wielders and the crown.

Islamic, Viking, Mongol, and Byzantine civilizations created a social structural forge, and the pressure from this forge formed the modern Western state system. Competition among civilizations produced the high medieval age and the modern Western state system was born, making early European civilization one of the most militarily oriented societies known to humanity.

The shaping of the Western state system at the universal level occurred because of its collision with other structural entities. Initially the wars with these other civilizations created a centralizing dynamic, followed by a decentralized structure in order to fend off and attack these competing structures. This fluid military structure could both raid and defend in a manner that would be necessary against the pressure of these military adversaries. This system, known as feudalism, replaced the more centralized Carolingian system, and the feudal ecclesiastical structure helped orchestrate, with much tension and conflict, the dealings with these enemies by providing a unified structure, culture, and ideology for the manors.

During the high European Middle Ages, the feudal structure of Europe was a geographically smaller civilization when compared to the incredible span not only of Islamic civilization but of Mongol civilization as well. Mongol civilization, stemming from Karakorum, dominated all of the area that was to become the Soviet Union and China, and about half of India. Islamic civilization stretched throughout the entire borderland of the southern Mediterranean seaboard. Mongol civilization was three times as large and Islamic civilization was about twice as large as the early foundations of modern Western European civilization.

The rationalizing effects of ecclesiastical power eventually confronted the atomic political unit of the Middle Ages, the manor: the church threatened to absorb the manor. The monastic movement posed another similar threat to the manorial structure with the growth of monasteries, which were competing farms; Cluny and other monasteries were centers of political and economic power.

With the structural support, legitimation, and ideological power centered in Rome, the expansion of Western Christendom against the "heretics" was, according to the papacy, the will of Yahweh. This call to arms against the "infidel" helped cultivate the general drive for power that already existed in the landed elite, led to the Crusades, victories, stalemates, terrible defeats, and the eventual collapse of the various frontiers that made the early growth of the West possible.

The eastern reaches of Europe were also under assault from the Mongol warriors, whose invasions reached their peak in the thirteenth century with the rise of Genghis Khan and Steppe warriors. These invasions affected all the known world. To be sure, early Western European civilization, Japan and part of Asia were successful in warding off these invaders, or in being far too removed to be of use to these invading civilizations. This conflict, particularly the ascent of Mongol civilization with the invasion of the Steppe warriors, had an impact on almost all the rest of the Asian-European continent.

Not only the attack of Mongol civilization but the Crusades and their aftermath fueled state transformation during the period of the Middle Ages. After an initial capitalist boom, the failure of the Crusades led to the collapse of the European economy, and the culture of cynicism and antagonism towards the papacy for this decimation created a prevailing spirit which prepared the way for the Renaissance and the Reformation. The fall of the Crusader kingdoms accelerated the implosion and centralization of European states. As the papacy lost power, the crowns of Europe became the secular powers.

## The struggle for control of the world arena

As late as the fifteenth century, in contradiction to the Eurocentric perspective on this, Islamic civilization was larger than the more decentralized, fragmented civilization of the West. The attack by Islamic civilization in the form of the Ottoman empire continued to aid the centralization of European states and finished off the last remnants of Western Christendom. International coordination was necessary for the Habsburgs to meet the Ottoman threat to Europe, as Europeans formed an international army to meet the Ottomans in battle. This military mobilization allowed the Reformation to take hold. The formidable army of the Ottomans created the need for Lutheran soldiers in the European army. The papacy made a strategical miscalculation by opposing the Habsburg power during this period, and the papacy paid for its opposition with the near destruction of the papal states, the seat of papal secular power.

In the long run the Habsburgs were unable to prevail in conquering the Ottomans; with the collapse of Byzantium and states in Eastern Europe to the Ottomans, an iron wall turned the means of destruction of the European crowns inward. The Ottomans also aided this process by providing economic support to France and the Reformation states of England and the Netherlands against the Habsburgs, who attempted to restore a

new Catholic Western Christendom. With this Ottoman economic support, the monarchs warred against each other.

Eastern Europe and much of Asia and Eurasia were now
beyond the reach of Europe. Ottoman pressure on Europe created a centralizing dynamic at the macro level and a continental imploding of the European state system. An emphasis on its
maritime military colonial expansion overseas to the west was
the line of least resistance.

This book will explore the contours of the rise of the
European state system. In chapter 2 I will examine the decline
of the Roman empire and the rise of the Carolingian centralized state. In chapter 3 the collapse of the Carolingian state
system and the origins of feudalism will be explored. In chapter
4 I will examine the gradual development of powerful monarchies, as well as the rise and fall of the European Crusader
empire and the impact of Islam and the Mongols on this trajectory. In chapter 5 I will investigate how the forces of the
Renaissance and the Reformation, and the attacks of the
Ottomans, destroyed Western Christendom and completed the
transformation to the foundation of the modern European
state system. In chapter 6 I explore the central points of the
civilization struggle thesis and their implications for the
Americas.[3]

# 2

# Early Foundations of Western European Civilization

## Overview

Although historians have long argued about the complex events that led to the collapse of Roman civilization, they agree that the Germanic tribal political structure that replaced it developed the most militarily powerful form of political organization in Western Europe. This chapter explores the origins of early European civilization, from the spreading of decentralized networks of Germanic tribal society to the rise of the centralized Carolingian system.

The civilization struggle model's central thesis is that the origin of the Western state system was the product of the clash among great civilizations. Here, the wars between the Germanic tribes and Rome, the clash and fusion of Germanic and Roman upper classes, followed by the imposition of the Carolingian class structure on all of the surrounding Germanic tribes (as well as the Avars) demonstrate the model's design: the dynamics and statics created by both the success and limitations of dealing with other civilizations led directly to centralization, resulting in the Carolingian empire.

The struggle between Rome and the Germanic tribes is at the universal level of magnitude, the level of civilization conflicts. Supermacro struggles are lower down the ladder of geopolitical magnitude in the civilization struggle model. The supermacro conflict between the Lombards and the Franks, for example, or the macro conflict between the Merovingians and the Carolingians, refashioned the Frankish political system. At the same time, this macro conflict also influenced the nature of the larger struggle, the Frankish warfare against Islamic civilization at the universal level. The upper classes of the Carolingians won over the Merovingians and expanded their power into other arenas; the Franks were successful in dominating all of the other Germanic tribes. Through this gradual process, each struggle helped form a centralized state system and a world historical civilization.

We can look more closely at the successes and failures of the Franks during this period to see the model at work. In the civilization struggle, classes attempt to extend their national domination into international domination. Thus the Franks were successful in dominating the Avars, but not in dominating the class structure of the Byzantines, Khazars, Vikings, or the Umayyad Caliphate in Spain. The civilization struggle model alerts us that states develop through their relations and war with other civilizations. The limited territorial successes of the Franks established a small empire of considerable power, but one bordered by formidable military enemies: the Islamic powers to the southwest in Andalus (Spain) and southeast across the Mediterranean; the Byzantines to the east; the Norse warriors to the north. In addition, the Franks needed to pay attention to the infusion of Steppe warriors, less powerful but still potential aggressors from the northeast and eastern Europe, the Khazars and the Avars.

On the other side of the battlefield, however, each enemy, whether a relatively small group such as the Khazars or a great civilization such as Byzantium, had its own sometimes complicated struggles to resolve. The way that the Franks' competitors dealt with each other also fashioned the fates of state systems forming in the West. Byzantium's conflicts on the universal level, with the aggressive Lombards, Ostrogoths, and Khazars, as well as with the mighty Islamic civilization itself, diverted the Byzantine empire from protracted warfare with the Franks. For a time these groups posed greater short-term threats to Byzantium than did Francia, the civilization of the

Franks, but this situation changed during the Crusades, when the Franks became a central threat.

The papacy, an institution that was both a secular and a religious power, broke ties with the Byzantine empire and formed a coalition with the Franks, who in return defeated the Lombards. The papal/Frankish coalition quickly became a new factor in the power balance. The coalition not only represented a latent threat to Byzantine power, but also generated a prototypical cultural model for throne/papal relations. Throne/papacy coalitions would serve as unifying structures in Europe for several centuries, well into the high Middle Ages.

The Frankish state system gradually taking shape owed some of its features to the (only partially successful) warfare with the Islamic civilization in Andalus to the west, because it vaulted the Carolingian dynasty into power over the former Merovingian dynasty of Franks. The Carolingian empire, which reached its apex with the arrival of Charlemagne, took full advantage of its alliance with the powers of the Catholic Church, both as a unifying force among the Franks and as an organizational weapon that the Franks used against the Lombards.

The massive implosion and destruction of the centralized Carolingian empire, while caused in part by internal dynamics, can be traced more directly to the civilizational warfare that transformed the structure of Frankish society towards the end of Charlemagne's reign: the struggles with the Islamic, Byzantine, and (most importantly) Viking civilizations, and the war-making that occurred among these civilizations. What follows is a more detailed analysis of these events, applying this civilization struggle model.

## The Fall of Rome and the Ascension of Germanic Civilization

The fall of the Roman empire was a gradual process that worked itself out in the tension between the Germanic and Roman civilizations, especially over the problem of the Roman military and its relationship to the incoming Germanic migration/invasion.

The centuries-long fall of the Roman empire occurred between AD 400 and 700; Rome had always been at war, but there were specific reasons why this war with the Germanic tribes was decisive. Although many of the Germanic tribes were already a part of Roman civilization, the Romans thought that the Germans were barbarians, and subjected them to oppression and violence. However, this violence and discrimination did not detract from a healthy respect for, and a high assessment of, the Germans' military prowess. Germanic tribal members often became soldiers, and sometimes even generals, inside the Roman military structure. Without dismissing the many other causal variables, it can be argued that the fall of Rome occurred in very large part because the centralized Roman state was unable to deal effectively with these internal and external Germanic warriors.

To understand how this failed assimilation actually damaged the Roman empire, we must look at certain Germanic cultural and structural features. The Germanic tribes all shared a tightly knit kinship structure. In the sedentary Germanic groups, the upper class consisted of monarchs and a landed aristocracy. For the migrating groups, there were a king and warriors. So complete was the infusion of the Germanic tribes into Rome that marriage occurred between the nobilities of both groups. We would expect a gradual fusion of the two cultures, but despite these marriages and the incorporation of Germanic warriors into the Roman military, Roman society was always subject to attacks from new Germanic groups who were *not* part of Roman civilization.

Emperor Justinian, on coming to power, was able at first to thwart the Germanic invasion of the eastern empire by controlling the Mediterranean area through a series of forts and defensive constructs in Italy. Although they were temporarily successful, there is no strong archeological evidence that these fortifications, which created a terrible financial drain on the eastern empire, were ultimately a match for the rapid deployment of Germanic invaders. This was in large part because these invaders had previously established beachheads within the Roman population, making these forts ineffectual.[1]

*The decisive attack of the Lombards*

The collapse of the eastern sector of the Roman empire began after Justinian's death in 565. The Visigoths, Ostrogoths, and Vandals overran Italy before this, but the end game occurred in 568 when the Lombards, led by King Alboin, flowed into the upper Italian peninsula, attacking from the area that was to become Hungary and eastern Austria.

Unlike previous invaders, the Lombards did not want to make accommodations with the now demoralized and disorganized Romans – they quite simply wanted to plunder Italy. Even when facing such a ruthless invading force, the Romans were still able to strike a land deal. As late as 593, Rome was able to hold out against the Lombard onslaught, although most of the Italian peninsula was in Lombard hands. The Lombards, setting up something resembling a tribute system, forced the Romans to give up about one-third of the Roman crops.

The Lombards also proved more powerful than Tiberius II, who tried sending the forces of the imperial army of the eastern Roman empire from Constantinople to recapture Italy. Frankish mercenaries fared little better, happy to take the Roman emperor's money but making rapid peace with the Lombards. The bulk of Italy remained in Lombard hands.[2]

## Conflict at the Universal Level between the Islamic and Frankish Civilizations, and the Centralization of the Frankish State System

Although the origins of the Franks are lost in history, the Franks themselves may have encouraged mythic connections as the descendants of Troy as a way of legitimizing themselves in the eyes of the cultured Romans. The evidence supporting the link between the Franks and the Trojans is, however, problematic.

As Chirot has explained, the fertile soil of Europe was the home of the Franks and other Germanic tribes, who used the forests to build sturdy buildings and feed their fires. The presence of natural resources – metals, timber, navigable rivers –

invited long-term capital accumulation. For the time being, Europe was fairly well isolated, and relatively immune to attack from outside, an agrarian, decentralized society radically different from the Carolingian society that was to follow.

Despite the rich soil, the rugged terrain made farming difficult, and explains in part the nomadic tendencies of the Germanic tribes. The Frankish landed aristocracy, while a formidable military power, was not agriculturally very productive. It was not an easy or luxurious life; most people outside the nobility had just the bare means of survival, and hunger was common.

The Carolingian empire grew out of this first loose arrangement of Germanic bands. Clovis, the son of Childeric and founder of the Merovingian dynasty, united the Franks and institutionalized Frankish power in Gaul, the area that overlaps with today's France. A Roman Catholic convert, Clovis used his conversion as a rationale to battle those outside what he considered the true faith. When the Franks followed Clovis in his conversion, the establishment of a diplomatic relationship with the Church of Rome allowed the Pope to intervene in Frankish politics and to use the Franks as allies against Byzantine civilization.

In the decentralized structure that emerged, power remained among nobles known as mayors of the palace. The mayors of Neustria and Austrasia were ultimately successful in dominating the Merovingian dynasty. Pepin of Heristal, the Duke of the Austrasians, defeated the mayor of the Neustrian palace in war and became the sole mayor of the palace, even though a Neustrian king, Theodoric III, was the figurehead. By uniting both kingdoms, Pepin united the Frankish state itself; with this newly found power, he attacked the local nobility and became the head over the entire Frankish political organization. Pepin became the de facto ruler of the Merovingians by the end of the 600s and expanded his power into the once-Roman province of Gaul, forming the early Carolingian empire.[3]

## *The Franks and their struggle with the Islamic empire*

Mayor Charles Martel, the son of Pepin of Heristal, was an outstanding general who was able, through the development of an elite cavalry corp, to ward off repeated attempts by the Islamic warriors of Andalus to conquer the Frankish empire.

To understand Charles Martel's contribution to the centralization of Frankish civilization, it is important to understand the circumstances that brought Islam to Western Europe, and something, too, about this civilization's internal structure and the social dynamics that brought Islam and the Carolingian empire into conflict. Islamic civilization, successful in establishing a foothold in Western Europe with the conquering of Spain and a portion of Narbonese Gaul before 770, had inadvertently helped the Franks by conquering the Visigoths and attacking Byzantium. During the eighth century, the Byzantines fought the caliphs of the Umayyad regime for control of Byzantium. The term "caliph" stems from the word *khalifa* to designate Muhammad's successor, originally one of Muhammad's early companions; however, by the time of the rise of Mu'awiya, the fifth caliph, the caliphate was a hereditary institution. The Umayyad caliphate, which drew its name from one of Mu'awiya's ancestors, Umayya, moved the capital of Islam from Medina to Damascus.

A force of about 7,000 Arabs, under their leader Tariq, first attacked Spain (known as Andalus in Arabic) in the year 710, crossing the strait of Gibraltar into Andalus and defeating the Visigoths under King Roderick. The strait and the rock take their name from him – "Jabal Tariq" is Arabic for the Mount of Tariq. The conquered territory became a province in the Umayyad caliphate, and served as a sanctuary for the Umayyad family after the Abbasid overthrow of the Umayyad caliphate.

The Umayyad dynasty ruled in Andalus for close to three centuries, but it was not until the tenth century that the ruler claimed the formal title of Caliph. Islamic conquerors named their new capital Cordoba, and the gradual "conversion" to Islam of much of the resident population began, although there still remained a significant number of Christians and Jews in Andalus.

With the setbacks of Islamic civilization against the Byzantines in the Mediterranean, there was a movement away from control of the sea to a land-based empire. The Abbasids overthrew the Umayyad caliphate and created a new capital, Baghdad, the place where the important trade routes to the Far East met.

The Abbasids' claim to power was from Abdu'l-Abbas and his successors, as relatives of the Prophet, descending from Muhammad's uncle Abbas. The theology of this rule received cultural legitimation through the claim that the caliphs ruled in terms of the Qur'an, and the rules of right conduct based upon the Prophet's habitual behavior, known as *sunna*. This group and their theology eventually created Sunnism.

After a period of military consolidation into Andalus, the Muslims attacked France, and were able to penetrate into French territory and establish bases there. There were also Islamic naval attacks in the western Mediterranean area. This invasive military activity, however, should not suggest that the Islamic conquest of Andalus was complete or permanent. Pelayo, a legendary Christian warrior, stopped the advance of the Islamic forces in about 718. Except in the southern area of Andalus, the Islamic powers were dealing with a volatile internal military situation because of internal dissension in the Islamic forces and uprisings by the native Iberians.[4]

### Martel's containment of Islamic expansion and the rise of the Carolingian state system

The Islamic forces to the West would meet Charles Martel in battle. The Carolingian dynasty named after Charles Martel (others argue that it was a result of the fact that Charles was the name of so many of the early leaders in this dynasty) formally began with him, although the earlier victories of Martel's ancestors made his accession possible. The power transformation to the Carolingians geographically shifted eastward, from the Seine to the Rhine.

Martel's efforts to infiltrate pro-Merovingian monasteries were successful. He replaced the leadership in the monasteries with those loyal to what was to become the Carolingians, gradually wresting control and establishing beachheads in Merovingian-dominated areas. Nonetheless, Martel did not gain control until 723, and then only after a protracted struggle.

Islamic forces launched an expedition over the Pyrenees in 99/717 (Islamic/Christian dates). This invasion had the rather visionary objective of conquering all the lands in Francia, ending with the invasion and defeat of the Byzantine army in Constantinople. The warriors had very limited knowledge of the geography, part of the problem with their long-term objective. The short-term objective was to pillage monasteries and churches. In 101/719–20, these forces captured Narbonne, which became a military center of operations. Eudo, Duke of Aquitaine, deflected the Islamic attack toward the Rhone Valley.

In 114/732, the Islamic forces again crossed the Pyrenees and evened the score with Eudo, driving him almost to Tours. In desperation, Eudo asked Charles Martel for assistance. Unexpectedly, given the military imbalance, Martel's forces defeated the Muslims at the Battle of Poitiers (also called the Battle of Tours, because the battle actually took place between these two towns) in October of 114/732, ousting the Islamic forces in what may rank as one of the most important victories in European history.

Some historians argue that Martel's success at the Battle of Poitiers was of only secondary military importance, stopping what was nothing more than an Islamic raid, but it resulted in fame and internal power for him in Francia. Martel's forces drove the Islamic army from the Frankish kingdom and contained the Islamic forces, for the time being, in Andalus. At the same time, the Martel faction assumed de facto leadership of the Franks over the Merovingians.

A coalition of powerful pro-Martel abbots, bishops, and nobles supported Martel in his efforts to wrest control from the Merovingians. Martel spent the rest of his life expanding state power into the principalities that encircled the Frankish kingdom, warring against the Alemans, Bavarians, Frisians, and Saxons. His power was so great that Martel did not even appoint another figurehead after the death of the figurehead Merovingian king, Theuderic IV, in 737. Instead he ruled himself, although he did not have a formal coronation. Perhaps Martel remembered the sad end of his great-uncle Grimoald, who temporarily made his son the first Carolingian king, only to fail to secure power permanently.

Pepin the Short, the younger son of Martel's first wife, formally transferred the power from the Merovingian house to the

Carolingian house. He became King Pepin I, and aligned himself with the ambitious Pope Zacharias I. The ensuing intrigue demonstrates the political power of the papacy and the importance of Catholic support for any ambitious monarch. Pepin planned a coup, but overthrowing even a figurehead Merovingian prince was no easy feat. Pepin took Abbot Fulrad of St Denis and Burchard, Bishop of Würzburg, into his confidence. He sent them to discuss his plan with the pragmatic Pope Zacharias I. They asked for and received Zacharias I's support; indeed, he assured the emissaries that, should Pepin prevail, he would not risk alienating the Catholic Church. Perhaps Zacharias I was ensuring a friendly regime regardless of who won in this struggle.

The future King Pepin I used his army to obtain both royal lands and royal monasteries from nearby abbots and nobles. With force, Pepin took the lands of the Merovingians, as well as territories in the southwest, overcoming the opposition to Carolingian rule in Aquitaine. Pepin also deposed the reigning ruler of the Merovingians, Childeric III. However, it is a matter of debate whether the previous ascension of Childeric III was a sign of Pepin's weakness, or a ploy by Pepin to appoint someone who would pacify the Merovingian loyalists.

Once Pepin had become the new ruler of the Franks, he was reanointed king by Pope Stephen II; sending a clear signal to all that his new powers would cover his family, he also had his two sons, Carloman II and Charles, anointed by the Pope.[5]

### The Franks, Lombards, and Byzantium

Through its complicity with and support of Pepin I, the papacy established the role that it would play throughout the Middle Ages: it would continue to legitimize secular rulers through traditional religious authority; in return, the Franks would serve as a papal attack dog against the other Germanic tribes.

To show how the new arrangement worked in practice, we can look at the Lombards, who had overrun Ravenna, the symbol of Byzantine power in Italy. The Byzantines were the protector of the papacy, but, with the increasing power of the Lombards (who, with the Islamic civilization, were not friendly toward the papacy), the papacy could no longer be assured of Byzantine protection.

The growing alliance between the Franks' power and Rome was at the expense of the Byzantines. The differences between Rome and the Byzantines widened when Pope Stephen II relied on military aid from Pepin I, acknowledging Pepin I as the King of the Franks, to vanquish the Lombards.[6]

### Charlemagne, War-Making, and State-Building

After Pepin I's death in 768, his sons Charles and Carloman divided Gaul into two large territories. When Carloman died, Charles (Charlemagne) assumed power over all of Gaul.

Charlemagne was a complex individual who brought to his emperorship a love of battle, along with excellent military and political skills. But he also supported the arts and learning; he was literate in Latin (but never learned to write) and collected manuscripts. Excellent horse-rearing, use of geographers, stirrups, and superior metalworking techniques all contributed to Charlemagne's success at realizing his ultimate intention: to expand the Carolingian empire into a force which would dominate the (known) world. Charlemagne's military advantages – strong fast horses, sharp durable broadswords, and a superior understanding of the terrain when compared to most of the Carolingian enemies – can be seen in the Germanic military culture that continued to flourish even when Christianity became the religion of all the Franks and the people they conquered.

The Carolingian forces of Charlemagne and his brother Carloman dominated the Germanic tribes west of Scandinavia, Charlemagne supervising much of the land from his palace at Aachen and other bases. To some nobles Charlemagne gave the title of "count", with control over extensive landholdings (thus the term "counties"). Dukes were the intermediaries between the counts and the palace.

The ideological basis of Christianity was an umbrella for the Germanic tribes, as well as for the more Latinized tribes within Italy. Some problems presented themselves with this arrangement, however. For example, the ideal of the Christian crown necessarily eroded tribal authority. On the other side of the new alliance, conflicts between the church and nobles were unavoidable over such issues as granting upward mobility to subjects through the establishment of monastic estates, and the granting of titles such as "bishop" in competition with Rome.

While Charlemagne dealt with these problems and maintained the papal alliance, he also strengthened his own rule, and managed to wield greater internal power than his predecessors by means of a new relationship with his nobles. He made the counts public servants of the emperor, with the duties and privileges of diplomats but with far more power. The essence of Charlemagne's plan was to keep the counts circulating, moving from place to place on imperial errands, to prevent them from establishing a hereditary power base. As a safeguard against their personal agendas, Charlemagne created an office called the "messengers of the lord king," palace overseers of the counts, in reality spies who would report to the emperor to ensure that the counts were doing the crown's bidding. Messengers of the lord king were appointed in pairs: one was a cleric, the other a lay member of the nobility. The divide-and-conquer nature of this system of envoys allowed Charlemagne to prevent the buildup of any substantial power base by any of the counts.

Between 750 and 871 the Byzantine and the Frankish power networks became more centralized. Interestingly, although both activities played a role, Byzantium expanded primarily through trade, while the Franks expanded mainly through military force. Byzantium had also worked out a far more efficient internal structure of taxation than had the Frankish state, which relied more on coercing its nobles.

Charlemagne's military genius was at least partially responsible for the success – the greatest in the West since the fall of the Roman empire – of his relatively small army (under 10,000 troops), which consisted of an infantry supported by cavalry armed with spears and lances. Spring was hunting season for the Franks, and their prey was other societies. Continuing the expansion that his father, Pepin I, had started, Charlemagne slaughtered the Lombards, destroyed their political organization, and became the de facto ruler of Italy. As a gift he made his son the king of Italy. Internal opposition to Charlemagne's great power was met with crushing military action, such as the decisive defeat of the revolutionary attack emanating from Thuringia, led by Count Hardrad.

When facing external forces, however, the military adventures of Charlemagne were not always successful. He was unable to make inroads into the Islamic Umayyad kingdom of Spain, as shown by his military failure against Islamic Andalus, where his forces retreated with heavy losses. He learned well from this defeat, however, and set up the territory called the Spanish March, which served as a buffer against Islamic civilization in Spain and established a relative balance of power between Carolingian and Islamic forces in northern Spain.

Charlemagne was far more successful in his efforts against the Saxons, the name given by Roman historians to the groups of north German descent who settled in England. He forced Christianity on the conquered Saxons, with death as the alternative. Shortly after Charlemagne's rule, the Frankish kingdom included all of France, Bavaria, Saxony, most of Italy, and eastern fragments of Spain.

The Carolingians also expanded the Frankish state into northwest Germany, into the domain of the Slavs. They scored some success against the Avars in Hungary. The Avars were originally nomads of Turkish descent from the central part of Asia, whose attacks in the Balkans led, with the obvious exception of Constantinople, to the decline of urban society. They had destroyed the Germanic tribe known as the Gepids. The Lombards invaded Italy in 568 largely in response to this pressure from the Avars.

The Avars used a structural arrangement usually effective in war for their command station and capital; it was known as the Avars' Ring, a circular array of tents. The Mongolians launched attacks from a similar strategical setup. Charlemagne was able to destroy the ring in 796 by a strategically brilliant attack in which three Frankish armies converged on the Avars. The central leader of the Avars, Tudun, "converted" to Christianity, with Charlemagne serving as his godfather. To rule the Avars, Charlemagne extracted resources from the nobility in the form of goods and food. In return for their cooperation, he spared their lives and even shared royal lands with the nobles.

Politically, Charlemagne (following the practices of Pepin I) extended his influence by appointing bishops and creating bishoprics that rivaled the Pope's own power. Given the need for Charlemagne's protection, the papacy did not dispute his rights. In exchange, the Franks offered the Pope military protection against the Byzantines, Muslims, and Lombards.

The significant events of the year 800 mark the pinnacle of Charlemagne's alliance with the papacy. Pope Leo III, who was in exile, was successful in returning to Italy with the aid of Charlemagne. After regaining his power, the Pope invited Charlemagne to court and after Mass on Christmas day crowned Charlemagne the new Emperor of the Romans.

There is much debate over the significance of this event. On the surface it would seem to be a payback for saving the power of Leo III through military intervention. But the Pope was also under investigation for immorality, and Charlemagne cleared him of the charge through an imperial investigation. Whatever the impetus for this coronation, it signified the fusion of three cultural strains: the Roman empire, the Germanic heritage of the Franks, and the Christian-Judaic culture.

The period following the coronation – before inevitable disagreements began to tear at the alliance – has been called the Carolingian Renaissance. A patron of learning, Charlemagne established a palace school that educated children and adults; important monks, often from the monastery at Fulda, taught at this school. Charlemagne also took it upon himself to educate the officials in his government, and he understood the necessity of having a stratum of literate priests.

The court of Charlemagne became the center of learning for all Europe. So famous was Charlemagne's court that scholars from all over Francia, as well as Italy, England, and Ireland, came to study, work, and do research there. The person in charge of the palace school, the most famous scholar of his day and also an advisor to Charlemagne, was Alcuin, originally from Northumbria in England. His impact on Christian theology and spirituality is lasting but underrated, because his ideas became the working postulates, often uncited and unacknowledged, of the theologians and spiritual masters of the Middle

Ages and Spanish Renaissance. It is to Alcuin, drawing on Cassiodorus' ideas on the sevenfold nature of knowledge, that we can attribute the notion of a modern liberal arts education.

Besides the increasingly educated courts, the quiet religious monastic communities also provided a haven for learning. The monasteries, under the protection of the papal/imperial alliance, housed the central libraries and archives of early European Western Christendom. It was the monks who instituted the revival in classical studies, and who copied and preserved works of the church fathers, along with Latin translations of the Greek classics. Irish and English monks trained the Carolingian monks, who took advantage of technological advances and produced books using parchment and sheepskin instead of papyrus. The Carolingian monks also made advances in writing, developing a script called the Carolingian miniscule, which was easier to read than the Merovingian script.

The Carolingian Renaissance could not last forever. Among Alcuin's priceless chronicles of Western civilization is his account of the first attack of the Vikings, primarily Danish in origin, on Aquitaine in 799. Without realizing it, Alcuin, sitting quietly in his study somewhere in the great court of Charlemagne, was chronicling the beginning of the end of Carolingian civilization.[7]

## Civilization Conflict and the Coming Implosion of the Carolingian Empire

The institution of the church and the institution of the crown began to tear at each other even during the reign of Charlemagne. The early structure of Western Europe had emerged by the final years of the eighth century, in a cultural fusion of the Germanic warrior tradition with two major syntheses that the great tribes absorbed from the Roman world – Christianity, and the aesthetics, art, and philosophy of Greece. Culturally, then, we see multiple forces at work: the Christian, the Germanic warrior, and the Greco-Roman philosophical strains.

In spite of Charlemagne's success, the Carolingian empire was under constant threat from competing civilizations. One such threat was from the Turkish confederacy. Internal struggles had destroyed the large Turkish confederacy by the mid-seventh century. Turkish tribes also dominated two other confederacies: the Bulgar and Khazar power structures. The Khazars, a confederation of Turkish tribes from the Asian Steppes, launched raids on Francia and Byzantium, and with their guerrilla-like tactics were successful against both the Byzantine and Frankish powers, who were ill-prepared to meet these raids. The Byzantines during this period attempted to control the area of the Danube and the Islamic powers to the south by establishing a diplomatic network with the Khazar confederation. The Byzantines tried to use this relationship to force the Khazar empire to be their military buffer in their conflict with Islamic civilization and the Bulgars. This failed, and the Byzantines had to deal with the powerful Bulgars. The Bulgars filled the power void after the collapse of the Avar forces that transpired in the part of Eastern Europe west of the Byzantine empire.

The threat of the Khazars to the Carolingian empire was ended finally by the very Vikings mentioned in Alcuin's chronicles. The Vikings were fierce warriors and formidable river pirates, and the first western invaders of the Americas. They attacked and ransacked the Khazar capital in the Volga region in the 960s. They had a devastating impact upon the Carolingian empire.[8]

## Recapitulation and Causal Reflections

The collapse of Roman civilization and the rise of Germanic tribal civilization as the dominant form of social organization transformed Western Europe. Early European civilization vaulted into being with the ascent of the centralized Carolingian empire out of the decentralized Frankish society.

The civilization struggle thesis is borne out by this analysis of the interactions among the civilizations. The Franks, Islam, and Rome transformed Europe during this period. The trajectory of European state-building was heavily influenced by the collision between Rome and the Germanic civilization on the universal level, as external war-making between these two civilizations and the flawed incorporation of the Germanic bands into Roman society (particularly into the military) caused state-building in Francia. From the competition among these Germanic tribes and Rome, three contenders emerged as the potential superpowers of Western Europe: the Visigoths, the Lombards, and the Franks. In addition, the papacy with its secular power was also a contender. The Islamic civilization's Umayyad caliphate in the early eighth century dealt a death-blow to the Visigoths during their warfare. Byzantium, the successor to Rome in the east, and Islamic civilization, dominant to the west and in the Middle East, were both threats to Western Europe. The Lombards conquered the remains of the western Roman empire, by this time only a small geographical remnant of its former greatness; they were in the process of consolidating their power when the Franks, in conjunction with the papacy, defeated them.

Throughout this chapter we see in action the Tilly–Giddens principle regarding the primacy of warlike behavior as a central engine in the rise of the West. As maintained by the civilization struggle model's thesis, the exogenous classes imposed their structures on other civilizations, at first through marriage between the Germanic and Roman nobility, and later by the Lombard attack on Rome, where the new conquerors dominated the Roman upper classes. Through the crucible of war, the Franks absorbed other Germanic tribes or eliminated them from the European stage.

The civilization struggle's thesis is that the rise of Frankish society was the result of its warfare and the containment of the great civilizations on its borders; in particular, Frankish success required the containment of Islamic civilization in Andalus to the west. The Franks under Pepin I, and in turn, Charlemagne in conjunction with the papacy, defeated the Lombards, who had conquered the remains of the western Roman empire.

The civilization conflict model, drawing on Toynbee, Tilly, and Giddens, provides a framework for analyzing the way that societies develop through their wars and relations with other civilizations. The Franks established their empire but were, nonetheless, in a constant state of siege from enemies and raiders on all their borders: the Islamic powers in Andalus and the Mediterranean, and the Norse warriors to the northeast, who began effective raids on the Carolingian territory even during the rule of Charlemagne. The Carolingians conquered the Avars, but the Khazars harassed the Carolingians, who found no sure way to prevent these raids.

The dealings of a civilization's competitors with other civilizations provide a useful analytical tool. The Byzantine empire did not engage in total war with the Franks – the Franks' small austere Western European empire, even at its apex, was not much of a prize. Besides, wars with the Ostrogoths, Lombards, Khazars, and Islamic civilization also kept Byzantium occupied. Byzantine power was threatened when the papacy broke ties with the Byzantine empire and formed a coalition with the Franks, who in return, defeated the Lombards. The papal/Frankish coalition formed a cultural model for throne/papal relations that continued well into the high Middle Ages and Renaissance.

While the universal-level events fashioned the structure of Frankish society, supermacro and macro struggles occurred where nations, kinship groups, clans, and tribal organizations struggled with each other either to maintain their societies or to advance within their theaters. By uniting or conquering all other Germanic bands, the Carolingians formed their empire and engaged in both state-building and empire expansion.

Finally, towards the end of Charlemagne's reign, universal-level struggles once again interacted with supermacro warfare to fix the trajectory and transform the structure of Frankish society. The early rumblings of the collapse of Carolingian society shook this centralized regime. Small groups of Norse seagoing raiders started attacking Francia. The Vikings challenged the state-building efforts of the armies of Martel, Pepin I, and Charlemagne, with a massive implosion and destruction of the Charlemagne empire impending. These developments, which emerged from the war and ashes of the centralized Carolingian empire, formed the decentralized civilization of the high Middle Ages.[9]

# 3

# Early Feudalism and Competing Civilizations

## Overview

The civilization struggle model's central causal argument is that the medieval political system originated when conflicts with other civilizations interacted with the internal dynamics of the Carolingian state system. Civilizational attacks on all sides of its borders, and supermacro and macro conflicts within the empire erupted, leaving the Carolingian social system in disarray and tearing asunder the centralized empire established by Charlemagne and his ancestors. After the death of Charlemagne, external and internal warfare hastened the empire's disintegration and reversed Carolingian centralization.

While conflicts with Islamic, Byzantine, and Steppe warrior civilizations devastated the peace, resulting in the collapse of the Carolingian empire and the rise of the civilization of medieval Western Christendom, the worst of these external attacks was the Carolingians' battle with the Vikings. Through this conflict, the mighty Carolingian state system, a centralized power structure, imploded into the decentralized form of political organization most commonly associated with the Middle Ages. This system of relatively isolated and independent fortresses, when compared to the centralized Carolingian empire, is known as feudalism.

An analysis of the dynamics among the constellation of competing civilizations is crucial to understanding the trajectory of the Carolingian state system during the rule of Louis the Pious, and the subsequent period of his sons' rule. Military enemies harassed the Carolingian borders: the Islamic powers in Andalus and across the Mediterranean, who continued to launch attacks on Francia; the Magyars, Steppe warriors from northeastern and eastern Europe; the Norse warriors to the north, pillaging continental Europe, Russia, and England, and devastating these societies.

Drawing on the civilizations struggle thesis, we observe that below the level of civilizational conflict are the supermacro and macro struggles during this period. Carolingian domination in these smaller arenas during this era was problematic; far from expanding its world historical empire, the Carolingian system actually lost ground during these years, largely because internal dissensions drained its energy and distorted its military focus. Chief among these dissensions were the intranational and quasi-international battles among the sons of Louis the Pious.

The sons first battled with Louis himself, and then with each other, for supremacy within the Carolingian state system. Louis attempted to appease them by dividing the Carolingian empire into three superstates, with each son governing a separate state. These superstates, still quite centralized when compared to the civilization that was to emerge, were ravaged by warfare among themselves, with no clear winner. Not unexpectedly, Islamic civilization, the Magyars, and most importantly the Vikings attacked weakened defenses more effectively as a result.

As indicated by the civilization struggle model, collisions at both the universal and supermacro levels work downward and shape military, economic, and political structures and networks at the macro level; in turn, class conflicts at the macro level interact with the international dynamics of classes at the supermacro and universal levels. As these ideas apply to the demise of Carolingian civilization, empirically, these superstate collisions led to the collapsing geographical power of the Carolingian empire, and the landed nobles had to fend for themselves against the Vikings, as centralized royal defenses broke down.

Local control of military defenses against the Vikings

weakened the centralized authority of the Carolingian system. A decentralized construction boom began, with local nobles directing the fortification of towns, bridges, monasteries, and castles. These fortifications dotted the landscape and became the political, economic, and military infrastructure of feudalism, creating a loosely linked decentralized political confederation throughout Europe. Under this new system, far different from the situation where Charlemagne integrated the nobles directly into the Carolingian state, nobles built up competing fiefdoms, and chose their crowns for their *inability* to centralize power.

The relationships of competitor civilizations with each other (according to the civilization struggle framework) are important independent variables when forecasting the outcomes of internal struggles. The warfare among the Islamic empire, the Bulgars, the Magyars, and Byzantium protected the disintegrating Carolingian society from protracted warfare, at least temporarily. Internal dissension within the Byzantine civilization also helped distract it from any aggressive designs on Western Europe, and acted as a buffer from the Islamic civilization to the south. The Byzantines were not unduly concerned about the attacks on the Carolingian state system by the Magyars in the east or the Islamic forces to the west. The Byzantine ruling classes had their own problems with Islamic and Viking civilizations, and considered the Carolingian system to be a relatively minor, if potentially threatening, civilization.

As for the Vikings, they launched their assaults not only on the Carolingian state system but on England, Russia, and Byzantium. In England, as in Francia, an implosion occurred that led to a decentralized defense system against these aggressors. The Swedish Vikings conquered Russia and established permanent settlements. Byzantium used war, diplomacy, and intermarriage between the Vikings and the Byzantine ruling class to deal with the Vikings.

Throughout these conflicts, universal level dynamics interacted with macro dynamics. Although unsuccessful in warding off the Vikings, nobles within the collapsing state structures of Western Europe eventually succeeded in incorporating the Viking warrior class into early feudal society by giving the Vikings titles, land, and bribes. After this decentraliazation, Otto I, who tried unsuccessfully to restore centralized

Carolingian rule to Europe, successfully contained the Magyars.

This civilization conflict led to the decentralized feudal system of Latin Christendom, which would have a most profound bearing on the rise of the subsequent European nation-state system. The forces that held feudalism together were the culture of Roman Catholicism (which would serve as a unifying structure in Europe well into the high Middle Ages), the military and economic institution of the manor, and the papacy, a secular and religious power capable of maintaining a coalition with the crowns of Europe during and after the Carolingian implosion. Positive throne/papal relations, good for the throne and good for the papacy, gave religious legitimacy to the institution of the monarchy, while acting as a brake for aspiring nobles who wished to overthrow the monarchs. For the papacy, this coalition guaranteed military aid to the papal territories in Italy, and provided resources and influence in the parishes and courts throughout Europe.

The civilization conflict perspective also provides a framework for analyzing how civilizational conflict at the universal level creates changes in economies. The feudal West, after the massive decentralization of Carolingian civilization, established capitalist trade with Byzantium and the Middle Eastern Islamic civilization, an early capitalism (not of the pure market type) in which soldiers, pirates, and bandits were as common as merchants.

What follows is the empirical analysis of this conceptual survey.[1]

## The Carolingian State System and Universal War among Eastern European, Islamic, and Byzantine Civilizations

*The Carolingian state system under siege from Islamic civilization*

From the eighth through the ninth century, Islamic civilization went into a period of consolidation. Islamic forces had not been idle. From outposts in the areas of Africa, southern Gaul, and Spain, Islamic Saracens launched successive waves of attacks against the Europeans. They invaded Septimania in 793, setting fire to the outskirts of Narbonne, and launching an attack on Carcassonne. By 827, Islamic states located in North Africa were subjecting Francia to a new round of attacks, wresting control of Crete, even in the face of a substantial Byzantine military presence.

Southern Italy became the target of new attacks from the Islamic civilization. A major campaign against Sicily started with successful attacks in 827 and culminated in the conquest of Sicily by the Aghlabids from Tunisia in 902. The Aghlabids, ostensibly a part of the Abbasid caliphate, exercised, like many other powerful families on the frontiers of the Abbasid caliphate, great autonomy in their political behavior. Meanwhile, the Franks were engaged in their own military mobilizations, conducted by Louis the Pious and his sons. The Franks laid siege to Barcelona in 800. In 846 Lothar, a son of Louis the Pious, requested aid from the Franks to oust the Islamic forces in Italy. The Franks drove out the Muslims from the city of Benevento, and in 871 they were successful in ousting the Muslims from Bari and Campania, but Sicily remained in Islamic hands until the eleventh century.[2]

### *The partial protection of the Carolingian state system through wars among civilizations*

During the seventh and eighth centuries the Byzantine empire declined in power, diverted from total war with the Carolingian empire by threats from former Asian Steppe warriors, Vikings, the growing sedentary kingdoms in Eastern Europe, and the Islamic civilization, losing some of their border territory to the Bulgars, Muslims, and Slavs. The Bulgars were descendants of the nomads from Bosnia who eventually adopted many of the customs of nearby Byzantium. By the ninth century, there existed a Bulgarian-Slavic state where the Eastern Orthodox Church eventually pulled the Bulgarians into its cultural orbit. Eastern Slavic society was a result of migration to the area that is now Russia and the Ukraine.

These Eastern European kingdoms, brutally attacked from both sides, acted as buffers between the Carolingian and Byzantine civilizations. Byzantine civilization determined the southern, eastern, and western population's fate. Hungary, not originally a Slavic kingdom, was formed as a result of the defeat of the Magyars in Lechfeld. The Hungarians and the Poles became integrated into the Catholic Church.

The Carolingian empire also had Byzantium to thank for acting as a buffer from the Islamic civilization centered in the Middle East and North Africa. At the time of the rise of Charlemagne, the Byzantine empire occupied the areas of Asia Minor, part of the Balkans, and the bottom of the southernmost coast of Italy. In 358–969, the Islamic Hamdanid dynasty of Syria provoked the Byzantine army, launching an ill-fated holy war against the Byzantine empire. In retaliation, the Byzantines headed southwest and fought a campaign of expansion against the Hamdanid dynasty, aimed at reconquering Syria. They battled into Beirut and came close to Jerusalem.

Despite these victories, however, Byzantine civilization was unable to isolate the Islamic states, which maintained a lucrative and powerful trade network that included the entire North African coastal area, and resulted in the rise of the powerful sub-Saharan African states during this period. Even the formidable Sahara desert was a highway over which capital flowed, particularly gold and slaves.

The energetic and violent Macedonian dynasty that began in 867 with Basil I eventually transformed the Byzantine empire. The period around the tenth century, the Golden Age of Byzantine civilization, saw the growing might of the Byzantine forces, which followed a relative power decline during the seventh and the first half of the eighth century.

The Golden Age of Byzantium was not without its own internal struggles. During the period of the rise of the Macedonians, the bulk of the Byzantine population were free farmers under constant threat from the land-hungry Byzantine landed aristocracy. To checkmate the growing power and appetite of the landed elites who threatened the emperors of the Macedonian period, the royal administration drafted these well-trained free military-farmers into the cavalry whenever threats arose. This draft served the emperor's dual purpose: it kept the landed elite at bay and supplied the emperor with an army against outward threats – particularly from Charlemagne and Otto I, whom the Byzantine rulers viewed as no more than barbarians.[3]

## Internal Conflict, External Civilizational Warfare, and the Implosion of the Carolingian State System

During the ninth century the invasions from civilizations caused the collapse of Carolingia. The Magyars, Muslims, and Vikings, taking advantage of the internal strife within Francia during the reign of Louis the Pious, destroyed the remaining Carolingian system. Their relentless attacks led to an implosion of the Carolingian centralized structure, and devastated Western Europe.

Louis the Pious, the third of Charlemagne's sons by his wife Hildegard, inherited Charlemagne's empire because of the untimely death of Charlemagne's elder sons. He became the king of Aquitaine in 781 at the age of two; yes two! In 814 he became emperor, successfully putting down a revolt from a coalition of the landed nobility and his own sons. Perhaps partly as a reaction to these threats, and in part because of the Frankish custom of giving land to male offspring, Louis partitioned the Carolingian empire into three superstates and gave one to each of his sons. The three brothers, rather than feeling this division was just, turned on each other and continued to fight a territorial war for years, wastefully consuming the limited resources of the Carolingian empire, devastating the economy and society at large.

The brothers eventually obtained a truce through the Treaty of Verdun (843), which, marking the formal end of the Carolingian dynasty, divided the empire into three parts. Charles the Bald obtained the westernmost Frankish lands that would later become France. Louis the German took over the eastern Carolingian empire, which, of course, would later become Germany. Lothar took the Middle Kingdom, a geographically diverse strip of land that reached to the North Sea and south to Italy. The Middle Kingdom became a target of acquisition for the brothers Charles and Louis, who did not stop their hostilities even after the Treaty of Verdun.

Louis the Pious cannot simply be dismissed as a weak and ineffectual leader because he made decisions that led to civil war – he was responsible for many successful administrative reforms. His behavior was a product of the culture of his time; seeking to relieve the incessant military pressure from his own offspring and end internal bloodshed, he drew on a Frankish custom to divide kingdoms among sons. Clovis, who in 511 divided his kingdom among his four sons, also illustrates the precedent Louis observed.[4]

### *War with Viking civilization and the decentralization of the Carolingian state system*

The adventure-loving and violent Vikings, the greatest threat to the Frankish civilization, used Frankish strategy to defeat the Franks. That strategy, from Charles Martel to Charlemagne, was to conquer by offensive; the Franks were not well suited to defense, in spite of some success in containing the Islamic attacks from Andalus. The Franks were vulnerable to surprise attacks, and the Vikings conducted lightning waves of military strikes, sometimes repeated for years. The attacks were so powerful, and the Carolingians so ineffective in defending against them, that they ultimately transformed the Frankish state system, leading to a decentralized fortification construction "boom." This defensive system in turn led to a new form of social organization, which we know as feudalism.

During Charlemagne's northward expansion of the Frankish kingdom, the Franks fought the Vikings. However, the Viking offensive began with raids in 799 against Aquitaine. The Danish King Godfred, with a league of Danish chiefs, led raids in 808 that reached all the way into the coastal area around present-day Hamburg, followed by attacks on Frisia in 810, and Flanders and the Seine area in 820. King Godfred's offensive during this period we can see as primarily a "demonstration" against the forces of Charlemagne. Ruthless and vicious as these lightning strikes must have been, they were just preliminary skirmishes in the protracted war between the Franks and the Vikings.

The Vikings' military activities outraged Charlemagne, who saw them as a violation of a peace treaty he had earlier established with them. In what must have been one of the more bizarre examples of psychological warfare in early medieval history, Charlemagne launched a counterattack, using an elephant. Charlemagne's plan was to frighten the Vikings with this elephant's strangeness and formidable size, but it apparently died at Luppenheim before the battle.

As a demonstration of the complexity of relationships among civilizations during this time, however, the elephant serves us well: it was a gift to Charlemagne from Abbasid Caliph Harun al-Rashid for establishing diplomatic contact with the Abbasids. The Caliph also granted certain rights to Christian clergy in Jerusalem. The two sovereigns established embassies in part because they were both hostile to the Islamic rulers in Andalus.

It was clear to the Franks after Charlemagne's death that defensive tactics as well as innovative offense needed to be a part of the general military strategy against the marauding Vikings. Louis the Pious made efforts to strengthen Frankish defensive capacities against Viking assaults along the coastal areas. From about 834 to 850, the Vikings staged their attacks during the warmer weather, between spring and autumn. Vikings raided northern Francia and attacked along the Loire and Seine rivers, as well as the coast of Aquitaine. From around 850 to about 875, however, the Vikings established outposts and remained a threat even during winter.

During a 60-year period Vikings succeeded in penetrating Frankish society. Between 841 and 892, Francia was barraged by Viking assaults. In the mid-800s Vikings were attacking parts of Amiens, Angers, Blois, Bordeaux, Chartres, Paris, Toulouse, and Tours, among other towns. They captured horses and launched land campaigns. From 856 they were on the Island of Oscelle in the Seine. In the first great invasion of Europe, between 856 and 862, the Vikings made inroads not only in Francia but also in Islamically held Andalus. The "great attacks" between 879–892 had a permanent impact on the structure of Europe. Between 911 and 918, the Vikings forced Charles the Simple into giving them the area that was to become the ducal state of Normandy, and the Vikings established permanent settlements there.

The Viking ships were great maritime engineering achievements, and the Vikings' sailing skills were remarkable even by today's standards. They had different types of vessels, some designed for fishing, others for local boating, others for trade; a few were made for North Atlantic voyages. All Viking ships had oars; many had both sails and oars. The ocean-going ships, rugged enough to sail across the Atlantic, were nevertheless so high out of the water that they could sail up shallow rivers, raiding river towns and villages.

Their military organization, too, was fast and flexible. Vikings were usually organized into small bands. They would engage in blitzkriegs and their fierce attacks were very difficult to parry: they retreated quickly back to their ships in the face of strong resistance, and once safely back on board, there was no European boat in existence that could catch them.

Viking civilization was composed of three castes: the ruling caste, the free caste, and the slave caste (the thralls). The ruling caste, who believed that they were descendants of the gods, staged military operations, including raiding and pillaging expeditions. They also "traded," often a form of blackmail involving military threats to other civilizations: in return for precious metals, the Vikings would promise not to attack the civilization under threat.

The Danish Vikings launched successful raids against the coasts of England, Scotland, Ireland, Frisia (the lowlands), the Rhineland, and the Frankish lands in the west and east. It was also the Danish Vikings along the Seine area in 853 who sacked Nantes. The Norwegian Vikings established outposts in Ireland and Western Europe. The Swedish Vikings eventually controlled the Baltic Sea and adjacent lands in the Slavic societies in the east, attacking Russia and setting up settlements there.

Because of Byzantium's military strength and political astuteness, the Vikings rarely fought the Byzantine empire, but engaged in sporadic piracy, pillaging, and even peaceful trade with Byzantium. They concentrated their military attacks against the European kingdoms in the west, whose resistance was so weak that often the most successful defense against the Vikings was simply running away. They successfully attacked towns and monasteries, stealing treasures and relics. The

Vikings murdered many Franks and forced others, including members of the landed nobility, bishops, and clergy, into slavery. The earliest histories suggested that the Vikings were akin to "long-haired tourists who roughed up the natives," but this idea is a myth. They had relatively large forces which established beachheads in Frankish held territories.

From their base at Oscelle the Vikings attacked the surrounding communities almost at will. So feared were their warriors that Charles the Bald, the western king of the Franks after 843, had difficulty in motivating his army; when he eventually put troops together, they were no match for the Viking warriors. Charles the Bald did not make serious defensive efforts until 862, when he started to build fortified bridges, hoping to obstruct Viking ships from moving upriver. Hypothetically this strategy would drive the Vikings ashore, where the Franks could defeat them. Charles the Bald once again, however, had great difficulty in finding a willing and capable workforce. The builders of fortified bridges were well aware that they were easy prey for the Vikings who controlled the rivers. Eventually the Franks built some bridges by drafting in a workforce, but these bridges were not very effective in stopping the Vikings.

The Franks next attempted a divide-and-conquer strategy. For example, Charles the Bald saw that one group that could oppose the Seine Vikings, the most violent threat to his kingdom, were the Somme Vikings, named after their operating base on the Somme and Scheldt rivers. The unification of the Seine and Somme Vikings would have spelled disaster for the disorganized Frankish forces, so in 861 Charles bribed Weland, the head of the Somme Vikings, to attack and drive the Seine Vikings from the area. Temporarily successful, this containment of the Vikings, however, was simply a lull in the storm.

In 856, the Vikings, in their first siege of the city, had been able to sack Paris. They burned most of the churches, but spared a few buildings in exchange for French silver. However, the second siege of Paris, between 885 and 886, was politically more complicated. Emperor Charles the Fat, ignoring the pleas of Count Odo of Paris for reinforcements, instead bargained with the Vikings, agreeing to let the Vikings have access to Burgundy if only they would lift the siege of Paris. The Parisians rebelled against the terms of Charles the Fat, and refused to let the Vikings use the Seine to pass Paris, forcing them to carry their ships on the land to bypass the city. Charles the Fat eventually paid the Vikings to leave, and from the point of view of the Parisians, justice prevailed when German magnates, through both political and military means, pressured Charles the Fat, who was suffering from debilitating headaches, to abdicate his throne. Count Odo became king of the Western Franks and Arnulf became king of Germany, both through elections by the nobility.

Of all the defensive strategies the Franks attempted, however, the most lasting in terms of the development of Western Europe was an unparalleled period of construction work in building fortifications and castles that began in 862. In 864, Charles the Bald convened an assembly of nobles and gave his selective permission for the nobles to build fortresses throughout his kingdom. It was a dangerous precedent, because those very castles could be (and were) used to undermine Charles's sovereignty.

The Franks built castles with and without authorization, since it was clear to the Frankish nobles that, because of Charles the Bald's limited ability to solve the problem of the Vikings, to survive they would have to fend for themselves. The long-term construction boom continued throughout the 870s and 880s, between Viking attacks. Castles with large walls were scattered over the landscape, visible evidence of the radical decentralization of power throughout Charles the Bald's kingdom. Bishops, such as Bishop Geilo of Langres, started the same fortification building process in the cities. Monasteries, too, began to fortify themselves with walls. There is some archeological evidence that at the same time that the Franks were building fortifications, they were also tearing down other walls that guarded the towns, in the belief that relics and patron saints would protect town dwellers from Viking attacks. Town populations believed that they were being punished for their sins, and that if they reformed, the Vikings would go away.

Pained, the Franks bartered with the Vikings for peace, giving them concessions of land and precious metals. In return, the Vikings would establish a temporary peace. Eventually the Franks tried to co-opt the Vikings by offering them titles. One of the first of these new nobles was the ruler Rollo, probably of Danish descent, who led a predominately Danish army in an attack on Chartres. In 911, Charles the Simple raised Rollo the Viking warrior leader in Normandy to at least the status of count. An unsupported legend says that Rollo intentionally tripped up Charles the Simple in defiance when they met in the late fall of 911. Charles the Simple gave Rouen and its adjacent area to the Viking leader Rollo. In return, Rollo promised to abstain from attacking other areas of France. His royal family maintained this area and extended their power, until by the late tenth century it had become the French duchy of Normandy. Ironically, with time, the Normandy Vikings would be forced to fight off newer waves of Vikings attacking this area. The Franks' efforts of co-optation seemed to be relatively successful; there was a reduction of raids by the Norman Vikings on the river valley of the Seine.[5]


## *Viking civilization, Byzantine civilization, and Russia*


In spite of European fort-building, the Vikings still successfully navigated the rivers of Europe. The Byzantine empire showed the ability to form shifting coalitions in this precarious situation, and was able to survive Viking attacks by the finesse of Byzantine diplomacy. Combined with great financial resources and military power, their diplomatic skills were eventually successful enough to ward off the Viking forces that ultimately destroyed the Carolingian superstate system.

Swedish Viking warriors also followed the river networks into Russia and adjusted to the cultures of the conquered people. The name *Russia* comes from the tribe of a legendary and partly historical Viking figure named Rurik. His followers and warriors were the *Rus* – hence the term *Russian*. Like the other Vikings, the Rus believed in slavery and carried slaves around with them for service, also selling them or exchanging them for goods. After a period of intense conflict and raids from the Rus, the first Russian state, Kiev, was successful in forging a solid link to the Byzantine empire through the marriage of the Rus leader Vladimir to the sister of the Byzantine emperor.[6]

*Civilizational conflict: the Vikings and the
decentralization of England*

During the ninth and tenth centuries, a decentralized English
kingdom developed in a manner similar to the Eastern and
Western European kingdoms. As in the east, the decentralization of England occurred as a result of the wars against the
Danish Vikings. The Vikings' first wave in the invasion of
England occurred between 835 and 954. The first major
attacks, however, began in 865. These raiders did not follow
the same sporadic raiding pattern of the spring-through-fall
raids of the preceding years; instead, this attack had the coherence of an actual campaign. It was the intent of the Vikings to
capture and control land.

The Vikings conquered most of north and central England.
They ruled over these areas, along with Dublin, making York
their capital and their base of operations. The Vikings sporadi-
cally ruled these lands from 919 to the middle of the tenth century, and under their control, York developed several textile
and metal manufacturing industries, also producing wood and
leather products.

The early chroniclers of these events gave Alfred the Great,
King of Wessex, the credit for defeating the Vikings and
obtaining peace. To defeat the Danes it was necessary for the
English to forge a unified front, an achievement during the last
30 years of the ninth century that resulted in a peace treaty
with the Vikings in 886. When Alfred of Wessex first became
king, the Vikings had only a small part of England in
Northumbria, in and around York. By 899, the year of Alfred's
death, they had expanded their geographical holdings in eastern, northern, and central England and continued to threaten
Wessex. The English and the Vikings' peace established
between 878 and 886 was the peace of a balance of power, not
the peace of a defeated Viking force. The Vikings still, even
after the settlement, owned large plots of land and continued
skirmishes with the English.

The extent of Alfred's victory in obtaining this peace is no
doubt overestimated by the chroniclers of these events, and the
general histories that tout Alfred as the savior of England are

now being revised. The early historians were clearly kind to their patron. Like the Franks, he realized that the way to resist the Vikings was through a war of decentralized attrition, so that, during the period of relative peace before 892, Alfred the Great built new fortifications.

The image of the Vikings attacking England on ships is incomplete. To be sure, Alfred the Great built his fortifications with burhs (fortified places) facing the rivers, but, unfortunately for the English, the actual campaigns of the Vikings were on horseback, not on the rivers. The Vikings made their most telling victories by capturing horses and riding inland down the Roman-constructed roads of England. They then dismounted and fought on foot. There seems to be substantial evidence that the English stopped the Vikings in spite of the plans of Alfred the Great, not because of them.

A second wave of Viking attacks occurred between 980 and 1035. An army led by Thorkell the Tall was so successful that the English had to ward off the Vikings with money. Alfred the Great's successors eventually liberated the areas controlled by the Danish Vikings, who, through their attacks, changed the entire social structure of England.[7]

## The Attack of the Magyars and Failed Frankish Attempts at Centralization

The Magyars were originally from Asia, but by the ninth century, attacking from the Volga region, they had conquered the forest-dwelling Slavs in the area that is now Hungary. From this base, the Magyars attacked Germany, France, and Italy, developing into the kingdom of Hungary.

Magyar expansion to the west was thwarted in large part by Otto I, one of the most successful military leaders of the Frankish dynasty that followed the collapse of the Carolingian empire. He defeated the Magyars at the Battle of Lechfeld in 955 in the territory that is now Germany, and was responsible for the "Christianization" of the Slavic areas in the east and some of the Scandinavian areas in the northwest.

Although Magyar raids continued, their threat was diminished, allowing Otto I to pursue his lofty vision of becoming the new Charlemagne. As a repayment for helping the church in Italy, Otto I was crowned the Emperor of the Romans by the Pope; one can see that Charlemagne served as a role model for Otto's ambitions. His capabilities, however, were no match and the situations Otto I faced were far different than Charlemagne's. Charlemagne had been an excellent judge of his military and administrative capabilities. Otto I's ambitions, on the other hand, were greater than his state's administrative capacity. Otto I, attempting to centralize Europe once again, believed it was his prerogative to intervene in the politics of any locale in Europe, especially Italian politics. Although his attempt to reverse the decentralization failed, Otto I was still the most powerful monarch in Europe during his lifetime.[8]

## Civilizational Warfare and the Structure of Feudalism

As we survey the turbulent years after Charlemagne, we can see how feudalism in Western Europe developed in response to these military attacks and threats from the Viking, Islamic, and Magyar civilizations. The social structure that emerged in Europe was a decentralized one composed of vassals, similar to a structure Carolingian mayors established in the eighth century. Lords gave vassals benefices of land in return for the vassal's loyal military service. In the face of warfare among these civilizations, the Franks revived vassalage as a defensive structure to deal with the Viking and Magyar attacks that assaulted Germany and France throughout the ninth and tenth centuries.

The decentralized *fief*, as the landholding of the vassals was called, was not universal throughout Europe. Fief-holding became widespread in Germanic, French, and English societies – the result of developments in the remains of the Carolingian empire, Eastern Europe, and England – but not in Spanish, Scandinavian, and Byzantine societies. Western Spanish society was under the domination of the Umayyad dynasty;

Scandinavian society was the home of Viking civilization; Byzantine civilization remained highly centralized.

The major repayment for the vassal's grant of land was military service in the crown's or overlord's armies. Their other responsibilities included providing a free dwelling for the sojourning lord or lady, engaging in court duties when asked by the lord or lady, and paying a tax to the lord or lady on the occasion of the marriage of the oldest daughter. Should the lord or lady have a son, the vassal paid a tax for the elder son upon entering knighthood. If the vassal fulfilled these duties satisfactorily, the fief became hereditary, although land disputes were not uncommon if there was no son to claim the land.

Other than the granting of a fiefdom, it is less clear what the lord's or lady's responsibility was to the vassal. In principle, of course, the major responsibility was to defend the vassal from invasion by enemies. In large part, this defense was simply a matter of self-interest for the lord or lady anyway, so it is questionable whether this was a responsibility owed to the vassal. Another responsibility of the lord and lady was to defend the vassal in court, where the crown and overlords dealt with legal issues rather capriciously. The side the lord and lady took, of course, depended on the noble's interest and not necessarily on the welfare of the vassal. As an added token of a noble's power at court, the noble could pronounce negative sanctions against an unfaithful vassal.

However the noble–vassal relation was defined, it clearly limited the vassal's power to make war, and guaranteed an army with which the crown could negotiate arrangements with other parties. For example, there was a political logic to the working coalition between the Catholic Church and the crowns of Europe during the period of the early Middle Ages, and the throne discouraged nobles from attacking the secular territories of the papal state. The church/crown coalition also granted the crown symbolic legitimation and hence discouraged direct military challenges to the throne from the powerful landed aristocracy. The pope could excommunicate the nobles who tried to overthrow the throne; the church and the crown would then seize the noble's land.

Yet the system of vassalage was not without its risks to the noble or the throne. The crown or noble granted a fief to the vassal in exchange for military and civil service, resulting in a system that gave the local nobility power at the same time as it drained the crown of its royal landholdings.

In societies where nobles elected their monarchs, they tended to elect the weakest noble among them, thereby ensuring their own autonomy. Sometimes, however, this strategy backfired. After the death of the Otto I, the Western Franks elected Hugh Capet king of France, elevating him with the knowledge that he was not the wealthiest noble of the group, and therefore assuming that he would be easier to control than some of the other more powerful and richer nobles. But they underestimated Hugh Capet's shrewd intelligence: he ushered in the Capetian dynasty that would threaten these nobles and their descendants for centuries.[9]

## The Conflict among Civilizations and the Rise of Early Capitalism

Military aggression and the decentralizing defenses shaped and interacted with the forces of economy and world trade. The Middle Ages had a far more extensive "capitalist" economy than was recognized by Karl Marx, who did not have later excellent secondary historical work on the Middle Ages to inform him. The European crowned heads and their nobles needed luxury goods as a sign and privilege of their office. Their desire for luxuries led to commerce or war, whichever was more effective, with adjacent civilizations when the opportunity arose.

Traders brought goods to Western Europe from the city of Baghdad in the Middle East and from Constantinople within the Byzantine empire, not always without incident. Mercenaries, who were often European nobles, would attack caravans and take the luxury items for themselves; if trade was good, raiding was more profitable. As they began to see the East as a source of easy plundering, the pecuniary drive was a strong motivation for many of the soldiers in the Crusades that were to follow.[10]

## Conclusions

The civilization struggle thesis provides a lens through which to observe the implosion of the Carolingian state system. Starting in the ninth century and continuing into the tenth century, external attacks refashioned the social structure and the lives of the inhabitants of Eastern and Western Europe. The external threats came from the Viking, Magyar, and Islamic civilizations, interacting with the internal developments of the Carolingian superstate system, and together destroying the Carolingian empire.

The Carolingian empire emerged from decentralized competing German tribes and reached its pinnacle with Charlemagne, who controlled most of Western Europe south of Scandinavia. Starting as early as the eighth century, Vikings and other invaders launched attacks in the Baltic area, in the Italian peninsula, Bavaria, and Swabia, assaulting the area once occupied by the Avars before they were slaughtered by Charlemagne's armies.

For Europe, the most important factor of these attacks was the inability of the centralized bureaucracies in France, England, the Middle Kingdom, and Germany to react quickly enough or to develop adequate defenses against these warriors. By the time the news of a Viking lightning attack reached the palace, the raid was over. The local elites, who could react and defend more effectively, were able to gain power by developing a decentralized and fortified defense network. The network evolved into feudalism, which led to lifestyles, defense systems, and institutions that worked against centralization. Indeed, the onslaughts of the Vikings made it difficult for urban life to develop.

The papacy also played an important role in legitimizing the monarchy, even in this age of the crown's relative weakness. Roman Catholicism acted as a cultural umbrella throughout Western Europe, preventing the cultural splintering of Europe after its political splintering. Intercivilizational relations are also important in understanding how the European state system became decentralized during this period, as when the Byzantine empire acted as a buffer for Western Europe against the Islamic civilization to the southeast.

The history of the Crusades, however, shows us that Europe, despite the decentralization described above, would very soon unite under the Holy See to face the East. Let us examine the evidence that demonstrates that this lull in centralization was only a temporary interstice in the growing power of throne and papacy, two forces that would unite to mobilize all of Europe in an assault on the Islamic empire.[11]

# 4

# The Manor and Church: Internal and External Conflict

The civilization struggle thesis views the primacy of warring behavior, particularly among civilizations, as an important independent variable in the rise and transformations of states. This process is discernible throughout this period of the Middle Ages and the rise of the nation state.

After the Vikings pulverized the centralized Carolingian state, the Franks replaced it with the decentralized manorial system. The nobles of the atomic unit of the Middle Ages, the manor, began launching wars on other weaker manors. Through this process of acquisition and expansion, the victorious warrior nobles were able to reverse the decentralization wrought by the Vikings. When the centralized units reached critical mass, the noble's growing appetite for land and wealth could only be satisfied by expanding into other civilizations. In particular, the conflict between the Islamic and European civilizations led to a new centralizing dynamic within Western Christendom, resulting in warfare and competition for territory in Eastern Europe. Here, the Teutonic Knights were particularly successful, conquering areas in Eastern Europe and establishing a Prussian empire.

Using the civilization struggle thesis, we see that the society based on the manor and the church rose and fell, shaped internally by its external, universal-level wars. War-making transformed that European decentralized structure arising out of the collapse of the Carolingian empire. The international theocracy of Latin Christendom, too, reached its apex and suffered its decline during this era of the Crusades. During this period three general trends can be observed.

(1)   Internal wars took place within Western Christendom and there was a slow growth of the monarchy at the expense of the decentralized feudal structures. This led to counterinsurgency by the landed elites and the city dwellers against the growing power of the crown. Landed elites demanded concessions from the crown by forming parliaments to give them input into royal policy decrees. While the landed aristocracy used parliamentary and democratic movements to gain rights, the thrones displaced these social movement goals: in other words, the thrones used these very democratic institutions that were designed to give more say to the landed elites, to raise taxes from this very elite. This democratic movement had little impact on Eastern Europe, Italy, and Germany.

(2)   This internal conflict among the crowns, landed aristocracy and urban dwellers (who might or might not be members of the landed elites) interacted with a period of centralization, expansion, and warfare at supermacro level, via the Crusades. The papacy–crown coalition led to the enhanced power of both and the further erosion of the decentralized feudal system. The Italian city-state system profited from the Crusades. Capitalism grew rapidly in urban areas during this period. Moreover, shifting coalitions of capitalists with nearby landed elites and the crowns occurred, as capitalists plotted to obtain military support and maintain their trade, wealth, and independence from both the landed elites and the throne. This also led to the decline of those landed elites who could not or would not participate in the capitalist revolution. The papacy reached the apex of its power during this period, even for a brief period eclipsing the monarchy as a powerful institution.

(3)   A period of centralizing implosion occurred with the loss of Crusader states, the encroachment on European society by the Mongols, the battering of Western Christendom by the Ottomans, and the early splintering of the papacy–crown coalition. These intercivilizational wars led to the decline of the

power of the papacy, a recession and collapse of the European economy, a tightening of the control of the monarch over European society, and ultimately the Reformation. What follows is an exploration of these dynamics.[1]

## The Decentralized and Fortified Structure of Post-Carolingian Society at the Macro and Supermacro Levels of Europe

The period between the eleventh and thirteenth centuries was the high point of the European Middle Ages. After the collapse of Carolingian civilization, a mobilization of the German kings established the Holy Roman Empire. In the end, this empire failed, and with this failure the barons of the Frankish system grew in power. Scholars, artists, and writers during the high European Middle Ages reversed the cultural collapse and superseded the achievements of the Carolingian Renaissance.

On the other hand, Western Europe during the high Middle Ages was still a relatively minor, decentralized civilization bordered by titans. The feudal structure of Europe was smaller than both the Islamic and Mongolian civilizations. Geographically, Mongolian civilization was three times as large, and Islamic civilization was about twice as large as Western European civilization. Culturally, compared to the high civilizations of the cosmopolitan Islamic and Byzantine civilizations, Europe remained an underdeveloped provincial area well past the eleventh century.

Western European survival still depended on the network of decentralized manorial castles built by the nobles during the earlier Viking attacks and to prevent raids from Islamic marauders. These latter were the most pronounced in the kingdom of Castile, where the Castileans built ramparts that actually surrounded whole groups of villages. The feudal system, just before the development of nation states, was the product of this decentralized system. The strategical setup of feudalism continued to be advantageous to Western European civilization, which presented the Steppe, Byzantine, Islamic,

Scandinavian, and Ottoman civilizations with a costly war of attrition, difficult to win. Even with the growth of towns in Italy and throughout Western Europe, the castle was still the model for the defense of urban areas.

In the eleventh century, the state system in the west of Europe reversed its implosion and became an expanding empire, a growing, centralized network of states at the supermacro level. The larger Byzantine civilization and the Middle Eastern civilization to the south kept the European expansionary dynamic controlled through military threats. Byzantium did not subject the European west to wars of conquest, partly because it viewed the scattered landholdings in that area as only a minor jewel compared to the wealth of other civilizations.[2]

## Internal Macro Struggles and Centralization in Latin Christendom

In the midst of political turmoil and constant warring, Europe began to grow and expand during the period between the eleventh and thirteenth centuries. The manor, crown, and ecclesiastical powers competed or cooperated, depending on the specific circumstances. The landed elites and crowns moved aggressively in every direction until they ran up against a force that was able to ward off their predatory invasions, then backed off and consolidated their forces. The result of this process was the slow centralizing dynamic that would culminate in the creation of various nation states.

One clear advantage from the effective development of knights and manors was that, during this period, the attacks of the Vikings, Slavs, and the Magyars had come under control; by the year 1000 all of Western Europe was under the cultural umbrella of Christianity, and both Vikings and Magyars had been assimilated within European society.[3]

### *Supermacro and macro war and the evolution of manors*

As the Middle Ages progressed and the institution and culture of the warring knights evolved, the means of destruction would

become more potent. The wealthier landed aristocracy continued the construction of more impenetrable castles, as a defense
not only against invaders but against other ambitious nobles.
Wooden castles were laboriously replaced by thick-walled
stone castles, mostly for protection but also as the product of
Veblen's conspicuous consumption: symbols of wealth and military might. The castle was a training camp and a military
storehouse containing armor, lances, swords and the like for
offensive operations launched by European nobles against
other nobles and other civilizations, and a dwelling place for
the landed elites and their servants.

Very difficult to breach, the castle in its later stage of development fits the maxim that the best offense is a good defense.
In case of an attack, nobles allowed the serfs farming land surrounding the manor to seek shelter inside the protective walls.
Attackers, to be sure, used weapons such as battering rams,
catapults, ladders, and undermining techniques to breach the
walls, but among the difficulties they faced from the defenders
above were scalding water, arrow showers, and stones from
catapults. Trying to wait out the inhabitants of the castle until
the defenders' water and food supplies were gone was not a
wise strategical choice, given the large capacity of the store-
houses in the castle. It was usually the attackers who would
end up hungry and thirsty, not the castle dwellers. The best
strategy for a noble who relished his or her neighbor's land
was to have the castle infiltrated before launching a siege, by
whatever means possible; the confederates could then undermine the defenses from within and thus give the offense the
advantage.

The serfs normally lived in the villages that surrounded the
castle, providing farm crops, rent, taxes, and labor for the ruling family. Peasants often ran markets, which during times of
peace were frequented by other serfs and landed elites.[4]

## *War and the growth of urban areas in Latin Christendom*

Cities contributed to the explosion of capitalism during the
Middle Ages. The cities that grew during the Middle Ages were

*burgus*, meaning walled enclosures. Like the castle walls, the long, running walls of fortified towns and cities were fairly successful at warding off attacks from armies of foreign civilizations or from nearby predatory nobles or crowns. Feudal lords sometimes lived in these towns.

Part of the new urban activity was in the old Roman cities. These cities had lost most of their magnificence from earlier Roman times, but they had become the seats of bishops and acted as social magnets, attracting merchants and skilled craftspeople. Different in their evolution, there were also new towns in which the inhabitants enclosed themselves within walls. These newly walled towns were often built next to castles. In addition, with the help of the nearby nobility, those villagers who could not afford to build their own walls helped to fortify the lord and lady's castle to include the village.

There were considerable variations in the structure and environment of cities across the European landscape. Many of these new cities may have started out as temporary bazaars or fairs: eventually merchants realized that they could maintain a permanent business at that site, and no longer took their wares down after each fair. As the markets grew, the aristocracy offered protection in return for tax revenues. The defensive wall incorporated the merchants into the manor, or (as in Italy) the nobility into the city.

Capitalists prospered during these post-Carolingian Middle Ages in these urban areas, gaining some limited political freedom, intersocietal and intercivilizational trade, and the establishment of cities as corporate entities. In contrast to the Italian urban capitalists, French and English burghers were willing to submit to some systematic control over their territories, given other less desirable alternatives, but even here the crown and the urban dwellers determined taxes through a conflictual process in which cities would often protest. The unpleasant alternatives available to those cities that refused any form of affiliation with landed elites or crowns were royal raids, conquest, and probable confiscation of all the wealth accumulated by the city. As a consequence of these threats, the development of capitalism eventually came under the jurisdiction and protection of a king or queen.

The decentralized nature of Germany and Italy, however,

allowed the development of capitalists within their cities who were free from the influence of monarchs. Italian capitalists often challenged the leadership of the bishops who were originally in control of these urban areas. Town dwellers were able to wrest political control of their areas from the power of the prelates and local nobles. In the cases of Rome and Milan, townspeople led uprisings against the prelates, but these transitions were often relatively peaceful, with only occasional conflict among the nobles, bishops, and townspeople.

Eventually these communes became wealthy enough to buy warlords, or buy them off so they would not attack, and they established independent city-state status. Some communes in England, Flanders, and France were independent from both the manor and the church, but the crown was often too powerful for a city to gain total independence from royal power. In these cases, autonomy from the state was only relative, with the crowns demanding and receiving tax revenues.

Karl Marx's view of the tension between the early capitalists and the aristocracy is not always borne out when one examines the early days of capitalism. There was often a blurring of class distinctions between the aristocracy and the capitalists, and this was particularly true in Italian city states. Venice's linkages extended transnationally to the fairs in France, where they required cooperation with the nobles there. Venice and Genoa supplied the fairs with items from the East as well as from southern Islamic civilization.

In the early days of these cities there were few class distinctions among the traders within these walled enclosures. All were members of the bourgeoisie, a class designation that applied equally to merchants, bankers, and artisans. As time went on, however, only the most wealthy of these burghers were included in the rising bourgeoisie; their wealth began to rival that of the nobles, and they were a threat to those nobles unable or unwilling to take part in the capitalist revolution.

It was during this period that Europe first felt the death tremors of feudal society. Many monarchs joined into alliances with the new urban rich, who gave money to them for protection against raids by the landed aristocracy and feudal lords.[5]

*Supermacro and macro war-making, centralization, and
parliaments in Latin Western Christendom*

An atomic particle of Latin Christendom was the institution of
knighthood. A village, not large enough to be a city, was often
connected to a manor, and the knight was the head of the
village-manor atomic unit.

The privileges and duties of the warrior-knight were given to
the oldest son of the manor. If he was unsuitable for the role,
due to some health condition or obvious physical or tempera-
mental flaw, the responsibility would fall to one of the younger
sons, who otherwise may have been destined to become a
priest. The training of the knight, a duty not taken lightly by
the landed classes, usually began before the age of ten, when
the noble family would send their son to the estate of a relative
or a neighbor for training; it lasted until the formal ceremony
of knighting around the age of 20.

Because being an active warrior was the whole reason for a
knight's professional existence, he was automatically socialized
into a culture of violence. It was difficult to prevent him from
fighting friends, foes, and even relatives; there were also many
incidents in which knights attacked and murdered the helpless
serfs. The church in Western Christendom slowly brought
under control the knightly activities of raiding churches,
marauding monasteries, and killing unarmed people, and made
some progress in getting the knights to abstain from attacking
and sexually assaulting women – at least noble women.

There was really no success, however, in preventing knights
from killing each other. This Hobbesian state of "war of all
against all" created an arms race; nobles competed with each
other for both armaments and fortifications. To choose the
alternative, not to compete, was to run the risk of being conquered by one's neighbors, or by armies from other civilizations.

The violent lifestyle and the emphasis on the military had
ramifications for the class structure of feudal Europe. In the
early Middle Ages, nobility was based on bloodline and
wealth, but by the end of the Middle Ages, crowns often
knighted mercenaries and made them nobles because of military prowess, landholdings, or wealth. Thus, by the end of the

Middle Ages, it is not always easy to distinguish the differences between the growing middle classes and the landed classes.

Some of the nobles gained enough power to challenge the crowns of Europe. Many dukes and counts were far more powerful than the Capetian crown that emerged by the end of the tenth century in France, but the Capetians were able to endure in spite of threats from nobles who rivaled their power. The uninterrupted power of the Capetians was the result of a battle between the descendants of the Carolingians and the Robertians, the latter descendants of Count Odo of Paris. The nobles voted Count Odo king, but he gave up his lineage to his successor Charles the Simple. When Charles the Simple was unable to return the crown to the descendant of Count Odo – most specifically to his son Robert – Robert's descendants, vying for the throne, plagued the apparently stable regime of Carolingian descent. Eventually the ascension of Hugh Capet, a Robertian, ended the reign of the Carolingians. During these internal struggles, the Capetians also had to fight off Magyar and Saracen raiders.

The strength of the Capetian crown came from several factors. The support of the Catholic Church gave the Capetians a certain immunity from the gaze of nearby land-hungry nobles, because the nobles of Catholic Europe took the threat of excommunication very seriously. Moreover, even the most land-hungry nobles did not consider the Capetians' landholdings prime real estate. Another advantage was that the Capetians, not wasting meager resources on wars to determine the rightful heir to the throne, had worked out the problem of succession. They had a remarkable period of dynastic succession, and the eleventh century and part of the twelfth was a period of consolidation for the Capetian throne. In this time they maintained a coalition with the Catholic Church, consolidated their hold in the Ile de France, and maintained relative order in the transition from one monarch to the next.

Nor did they systematically seize their neighbors' land during this consolidation period. It was not until the thirteenth century that the Capetians made real attacks into the domain of nearby nobles, moving under Philip Augustus to embrace Normandy and a large part of the Languedoc. The growing mobilization of the Crusades had the added effect of enhancing the growth of Capetian power, starting in the late eleventh century, when the Capetians were able to quietly expand in the absence of the powerful nobles who were crusading in the East.

The relative decentralization in England, the product of the Viking invasions, was to witness a turnaround toward centralization with the Norman Conquest. Ironically England's destiny was shaped by descendants of the Vikings in France. William, Duke of Normandy, known universally as William the Conqueror, one of France's most powerful nobles and descendant of Rollo, declared that it was he and not Harold Godwinson, the current monarch, who should be the ruler of England. The legitimation for this declaration was that William of Normandy was a cousin of King Edward the Confessor, whom Harold Godwinson had replaced after Edward the Confessor's death in 1066. William backed up his claim by invading England in the autumn of the same year. In the battle of Hastings, the two armies clashed. Despite the resistance of the Anglo-Saxon knights, the Norman descendants of the Viking warriors who inhabited Gaul succeeded in crushing the defenders. In 1066 William I ascended to the throne of England.

The Norman Conquest caused a radical transformation in the status of nobles in England. Until William, the state did not dominate indigenous nobles, but he was ruthless in extracting land and consolidating English society under his rule, procuring about 20 percent of English land for his royal landholdings. Nobles now held their lands at the discretion of the king, and church lands became fiefs of the crown and its vassals. If nobles wished to keep land, they had to supply conscripts to the royal army, a great sacrifice because, although the indigenous English knights were warriors, they had to fight for their conqueror – a conqueror the knights still very much hated.

The great vassals subject to the crown dominated the lesser vassals in turn. To divide and conquer, William built fortifications throughout all of England, posting his more loyal conscripts in these fortifications to prevent revolutionary movements from forming. He made some Normans his sheriffs, a strong arrangement that consolidated William's power; at the same time, it ensured stability from loyal local sheriffs who, through their office, gained power over existing English society. Building this system upon an earlier system, but making it more centralized and efficient, William the Conqueror used this structure to extract more tax revenues than the previous extraction mechanism. His son Henry I (1100–1135) further rationalized the taxation system of England.

During the reigns of William I and Henry I, the English throne was the most powerful monarchy in Europe. Yet there were certain political contradictions in this governing situation: the new King of England was also the Duke of Normandy and a subject, at least in principle, of the French crown.

After the death of Henry I there was a period of civil war. Henry II (1154–1189) ended these wars. He was the most powerful ruler in Western Europe, expanding his domain to become the ruler of all of England plus a large part of France. He married Eleanor of Aquitaine after she divorced Louis VII, and at the time of his marriage he already controlled or acquired through this marriage Aquitaine, Anjou, Maine, Poitou, and Normandy. To be sure, in principle the King of England was subordinate to the French crown, but in terms of wealth, landholdings, and military might, the English monarchy was more powerful than the throne of France.

Another means by which Henry II increased both revenues and power was to alter the structure of the court system. Before the establishment of a strong royal court, a large part of a noble's power and revenue had flowed through the court system of each manor; the noble families made judgments that often entailed fees from their subjects under litigation. Henry II set up a royal court of appeal, to which those litigants unhappy with lower manorial decisions could apply, and which could then overrule the manorial decision and extract new revenues from the guilty party. Should a noble object to this new ruling, the armies of the crown stood ready to attack and decide the situation in favor of the throne. Reforms of this nature reduced the domination of manorial law, which was gradually replaced by a great volume of "common law." Common law not only replaced manorial law, but began to challenge the canon law of the monastic lands and churches as well.

In contrast to Henry II's state-building successes during his reign, King John (1199–1216) encountered stiff resistance in his efforts to control and subordinate the landed elites and to extract even more taxes. Philip Augustus, the King of France, further complicated King John's life by conquering Normandy. John was unable to recapture his ancestral home. The lords in England, opposing his taxation efforts and seeing a political opportunity in the military disorganization and devastation after King John's defeat in Normandy, went into open rebellion against him and demanded certain rights.

This resistance resulted in the document known as the Magna Carta of 1215. The document, while deliberately left vague and expansionary in order for the nobles to develop a flexible strategy against the monarch, demanded certain rights: it provided that the monarch could not confiscate a noble family's land; it granted inheritance rights to all nobility, promising that the estate would stay within the family and not be absorbed by the crown; and it outlawed the hiring of mercenaries by the monarch should the lords not agree to wage war. It also limited the power of the monarch's control over the church.

The Magna Carta's provisions for city dwellers demonstrate an instance where both the burghers and the nobles agreed to constrain the crown. Sharing many similarities with the town charters that granted certain freedoms to cities, the Magna Carta promised that English cities, particularly London, would have economic freedom and not be subjected to customs imposed by the monarch. Finally, the king agreed not to tax nobles without approval of the Great Council, composed of landed magnates.

Henry III (1216–1272) lost further power to the nobles during his reign. Edward I, his son, once again moved to subordinate the landed elites. With military and administrative force, he centralized his control over England and subordinated Wales, Scotland, and Ireland, beginning a process that led to the early establishment of an English empire. He created a sophisticated administrative and military structure in which the crown again forced the landed elites into the royal militia, financed the military through a series of taxes, supplemented this army with mercenaries, and established a centralized control apparatus with strong fortifications.

Edward I succeeded in creating a modern structure of courts, treasury, financial system, and administration. He required that knights serve in the royal militias, and used lords to oversee the running of the financial arm of the royal administration. As an exchange for this greater control of the nobility, Edward I gave the landed elites more power in national affairs by convoking the first English general assembly.

Parliaments, spreading throughout Europe in the period between the thirteenth and fourteenth centuries, were perceived as beneficial to both monarchs and nobility. From the perspective of the landed elites, parliaments prevented the crown from arbitrary taxation or land confiscation without the permission of the nobles themselves. Monarchs, however, viewed parliaments as tax-raising institutions. The Parliamentarian movement that spread throughout Europe often meant that monarchs were calling together the nobles to tax them. Parliaments were called during times of great financial need, particularly during times of war. This was true in both Spanish and Hungarian parliaments during this period. The armies across Europe became more proletarianized as time went on. As can be seen by their real agendas, however, the presence of parliaments in a society did not always connote more democracy for all of its citizens; peasants and artisans had no representation at all.

Germany did not move in the same direction of a monarch ruling with a parliament as in England, but developed a more decentralized system. Despite his exalted title, the German emperor could not trust the powerful nobles, who prevented the rise of a powerful monarchy. Instead, church officials became the royal administrators of the imperial estate, in charge of executing imperial decrees. This arrangement, an improvement over the alternative, could still be problematic for the emperor, because many of the church officials were the younger sons of the landed elites in Germany. The emperor therefore could not tolerate the power of the pope to appoint bishops who might be in league with the German nobility. Further complicating the political mix, the papacy and high church officials in Italy were resistant to the German emperor's designs because of the threat that Italy would be annexed into the German empire, and for fear that the emperor's insistence on his personal selection of bishops and other church officials would undermine the centralized church. The church, with the coming of the so-called Investiture Controversy, fought imperial power for the sole right to appoint high church officials.

From the time of Otto II in the late tenth century, the German imperial forces tried to dominate northern Italy. The German emperor was in mortal combat with the Italian nobles as well as the papacy. Numerous civilizations vied for power in this northern Italian area: Ottoman Islamic, Middle Eastern Islamic, and Byzantine civilizations, as well as the earlier Lombards, all invaded the territory.

The Italians hated the German Frederick I Barbarossa (Redbeard) (1150–1190), who had been elected emperor by the German princes after he had consolidated his position as the most powerful lord from the Swabian house of the Hohenstaufens. Frederick I engaged in a creative plan to increase his power over the German princes: he searched for additional resources and income from adventures in Italy, increasing his reputation much as Julius Caesar gained power by Roman perceptions of his alleged military victories in foreign lands. Frederick's goal was to establish an empire much like the ancient Roman empire. He was to have a new "Holy Roman Empire." Germany was to be Frederick's kingdom, but he would rule it from Italy, like a true Roman emperor.

To engage in his quest, Frederick I had to leave Germany in the hands of someone he could trust. His cousin Henry the Lion, the Duke of Saxony and Bavaria, assumed power while Frederick turned his gaze southward and led his army into Italy, scoring a series of quick victories in northern Italy. Before long, however, Frederick found it was easier to conquer the cities of northern Italy than to rule the bishops who governed these cities. After his attacks, they swiftly formed a military network, the Lombard League, officially condoned by the pope, who was not at all happy about Frederick I's invasion. After all, Germany's presence in northern Italy was a threat to the papal states to the south. The Lombard League was effective enough to stop Emperor Frederick I at Legnano in 1176, where he eventually worked out a cease-fire and left.

Frederick's welcome in Germany was not the triumphant Caesar-like return he had envisioned. Henry the Lion had broken his vow of loyalty and permanently assumed power. His resistance was short-lived, and Frederick I regained the throne.

After consolidating his power in Germany, Frederick I moved again towards the south into Italy. The league of cities, realizing that Frederick I would never give up his ambition to conquer Italy, agreed to pay him a tribute to remain autonomous city states. This concession gave Frederick I the financial base on which to consolidate his power over the German princes and, in yet another imitation of Caesar, to establish the so-called *Holy Roman Empire*.

Frederick II (1212–1250) grew up in Sicily. Islamic attacks on Italy had endowed Sicily with a rich mixture of European and Islamic culture. He carried this multicultural background into his ruling style, even to the extent of having Muslim scholars in his court and Muslim mercenaries in his army. A well-educated person, Frederick II spoke several languages, sang and composed music, and surrounded himself with learned scholars, artists, and authors. Perhaps with limited justification, some historians have credited Frederick II with developing a nationalism based on territory rather than on imperial power. In 1220 he became the Holy Roman Emperor.

The tension between centralized and decentralized power continued to shape European history. No matter how zealously German emperors attempted to centralize and enhance imperial power, they were never so strong that they did not fear German nobles joining nobles throughout Europe to resist the growth of centralized power. The French monarchy in the eleventh century was less successful than was England in constraining the power of the nobles, but during the early thirteenth century the throne built the foundation of the powerful French administration. The Capetian dynasty used the Inquisition to gain noble lands through force, though, to be sure, the crown did return some of these lands as a means of appeasement.[6]

## Centralization of the European State System: Universal-Level Conflict with Islamic and Byzantine Civilizations

Internal conflict within Western European civilization was dangerous in that it diverted Europe from responding to threats over the eastern horizon. The people in Western Christendom knew nothing about the dangers they could face from the Steppe and Turkish civilizations. It was true that the monarchs and nobles desired domains in Byzantium and the Middle East; their quest for land was a natural development, given the knights' propensity for war-making activity, spreading outside Western European boundaries. But one political step was needed first: universal-level war required a unified Europe. Leaders, finding that unifying principle in religion, formed a transnational "Army of Christ."

Scientists, scholars, and students who try to discern if these actions were secular or religious miss the cultural point, that medieval society was a fusion of Christianity, Roman culture, and the warlike cultures of the Franks and Vikings. Knighthood was a religious as well as a secular vocation. Regardless of the motive, the result was conquest and conversion by the sword.[7]

### Civilization-level warfare: the First Crusade and the unification of the decentralized state system of Western Christendom

Although the European nobles often entertained the idea of attacking the Islamic Middle East, they needed a pretext, a perceived threat, or a crisis to rally support for such a massive mobilization. The crisis came in 1071 when the powerful Seljuk Turks defeated the Byzantine emperor at Manzikert. This devastating defeat brought the Islamic empire to within striking distance of Western Europe and led to a series of envoys between the Byzantine rulers and the papacy. These diplomatic exchanges laid the groundwork for a new centralizing dynamic in Europe, in which the papacy, as the only international institution capable of conducting negotiations with the crowns and ruling families throughout Europe, was the focal point.

The result of this civilization-level coordination was the First Crusade. Europe, a series of farms and small urban areas during this period, was to face in battle the great Islamic civilization, a full-blown combination of urban, rural, and desert life. Giant cities came into existence during the Islamic Middle

Ages, including Cordoba in Andalus, and Baghdad and Cairo in the Middle East, bordering vast expanses of desert.

The new military, cultural, and economic power of the Islamic empire, about to become a fateful force in Eastern and Western Europe, was growing in several directions at once. The Abbasid caliphate was able to make inroads into Turkish-held territories in the east. The caliphs – the political, military, and religious leaders of this civilization – were impressed by the military qualities of the Turks and gave these Turkish Islamic "converts" the status of superior slaves. The caliphs promoted them throughout the ranks of military and political society.

Around the same time, however, opposition to the reigning Sunni sect would affect the strength of Islam, and have repercussions for the fate of Europe during the Crusades. A rivalry with the dominant Sunni sect occurred with the rise of a new sect within Islam in 910. A military leader named Ubaydullah, after arriving in Tunisia with a powerful army, claimed to be descended from the Prophet's daughter Fatima. He declared himself Caliph, and started the Shiite dynasty controlled by the Fatimids.

The Fatimids launched attacks against Baghdad, the center of the Sunni dynasty. Unable to gain control of the area that is now Iraq, they were nevertheless successful in establishing their kingdom in the Nile valley. The city of Cairo was their creation. Warring factions of Sunnis and the Shiites divided the once-unified Islamic empire, a division that has had political ramifications well into modern times. The Sunni Abbasid caliphate was able to resist takeover, but the Fatimids continuously challenged their power.

The power balance between the Fatimid Shiites and the Sunni Abbasid caliphate bore directly on the fate of the universal-level wars with the West that were to become known as the Crusades. So successful were the Fatimid Shiites, consummate warriors with a strong mercenary army, that they became even more wealthy than the Sunni Abbasid caliphate. Egypt became the new center of trade for the Islamic world.

The Fatimid army had its own esprit de corps; one group within them, the Seljuk Turks, grew in power and solidarity. The term Seljuk came from the Turkish nomad chieftain named Saljük, who was already dead by the time of the Seljuk sultanate. The Seljuks eventually threatened the Fatimid regime centered in the lavish court of Cairo.

The Seljuk Turks were successful in their attacks against the Abbasid caliphate, and in 1055 penetrated into Iraq and conquered Baghdad. The conqueror gave himself the title of Sultan. The Turks, though violent, were politically astute enough to leave the existing Abbasid caliph as the religious leader of the Sunni religion. Nonetheless, the Seljuks still subordinated the Abbasids, and took firm control of the political and military levers within Islamic Baghdad. In short, after its defeat by the Seljuks, the Abbasid caliphate became a figurehead institution.

The Turks used this new base of power to make their presence felt throughout the Byzantine empire, all the way to the borders of Eastern Europe. Opulent Baghdad was the center from which Turkish power emanated. Though initially slaves of the Fatimids, the Seljuk Turks turned on their former masters, threatening the very walls of Shiite Cairo and attacking the Byzantine empire as well. The Seljuk empire expanded into southwest Asia.

The Seljuk Turks made their initial contact with Europeans through commerce. A central feature of their commercial success was by means of the caravan. They established trade with the Italians and the French. The Seljuks, heavily influenced by Persian culture, enjoyed prosperity and trade with parts of Europe.

How, then, in spite of the trade with Europe, could the rise of the Seljuks put Islamic civilization on a collision course with Byzantium and, indirectly, with Western Christendom? Initially, the Seljuk sultans wanted no part of a war with the Byzantine empire. The neutrality of Byzantium toward the Seljuks protected the sultanate from attack by the Franks in Western Europe. The Byzantine empire served as a blockade for the land-hungry Franks who were promoting a war with the Middle Eastern followers of the Prophet. Moreover, the Seljuk sultans were in the process of a southward sweep of the Islamic world. A protracted war with Byzantium and Europe would be a diversion from this immediate military objective.

The Seljuks did not wish to expend their forces in a

protracted war with Byzantium until there was a unified Islamic empire. Nonetheless, Sultan Tughrul Beg eventually waged war, attacking the state of Armenia within the Byzantine empire. It was after this that the Seljuks victoriously defeated the Byzantine emperor at Manzikert in 1071.

Buoyed by these military successes of Islamic civilization, the Seljuks attacked Anatolia. Even with Byzantium in a state of contraction, Emperor Romanus IV Diogenes could not allow this attack on his empire to go unanswered. The counterattack he launched into Armenia collapsed under Islamic military power in Manzikert. Here the Seljuks defeated the Emperor's army, and Sultan Alp Arslan (Brave Lion) captured the Emperor.

Dealt a mortal blow, Byzantium never achieved its previous grandeur and power. Byzantium's defeat altered the course of world history; it led to the Turks' being admitted into Asia Minor on a permanent basis. The Turks established the Sultanate of Rum as a state in Anatolia.

The course of history was almost altered once again, but the papacy missed an opportunity to contain the Islamic empire when Emperor Michael VII asked Pope Gregory VII for aid in ousting the Islamic forces from Anatolia. Because of his disputes with the Holy Roman Empire, Pope Gregory VII was unable to mobilize a Crusade against the Turks. In the absence of action from Western Christendom, the sultanate increased its power by intervening in Byzantine succession struggles.

The coming to power of the Comnenus dynasty saved the Byzantine empire, at least for the time being. This dynasty was successful in ousting the Normans from the Adriatic area and slowed the expansion of the Seljuk Turks in a confrontation in Anatolia, as well as making peace with Sultan Suleiman.

After battering the Byzantine civilization, the Eastern Islamic civilization was on the threshold of expanding into Europe. The papacy attempted to rally Western Europe to defend the Byzantines against the "infidel" Turks. Pope Gregory VII, whose long-term goal was to reunite the Orthodox Church back under the Roman Rite, saw an opportunity to gain leverage in his dealings with the Byzantine Orthodox Church. Towards the end of the eleventh century, Turkish threats provided the Pope with the rationale to unify all of Western Europe to crusade against the "infidels."

The Pope's ambitions happened to coincide with those of the European nobility. The crowns and nobles of Western Europe had some cause for hope of success against Islam: military victories in Spain and the success of the Normans in throwing out the Muslims in Sicily added bravado to their dreams of the acquisition of land. The Iberian peninsula in the thirteenth century became more integrated into the European community after a series of these "Christian" military victories. When the two Christian Iberian kingdoms of Aragon and Castile became military powers, one of their objectives was to conquer Islamically controlled Andalus. Castile conquered a good part of Andalus toward the south, and Aragon ousted the Islamic forces in Valencia. These wars created an enhanced tax extraction mechanism for both Aragon and Castile, one that would serve Spain well under the rule of Isabella and Ferdinand. Although European forces succeeded in conquering Islamically controlled lands in Andalus, the reconquest of the Iberian peninsula was not total; the Islamic powers were able to hold on to Granada in the southeastern Iberian peninsula.

How did these disparate cultures work together? The treatment of the Islamic people conquered by the Europeans varied, depending on the military leader. The knights often demanded either conversion or death by the sword. Some of the Islamic farmers continued to work the land, but the new rulers taxed the farmers heavily. King Alfonso X, the ruler of Castile, who called himself the King of Three Religions, adopted the most tolerant approach. Christians, Jews, and Muslims had a relative escape from state-guided religious persecution. It is highly probable that Muslims and Jews faced more discrimination, given that Christians controlled the power structure.

On the positive side, the wars in Spain had a considerable impact on the development of Western learning. The interchange among these three faiths in Andalus contributed to the intellectual revolution that occurred at the University of Paris, a cultural exchange that supported the Christian–Aristotelian fusion known as scholasticism. This synthesis was led by Albert the Great and by Thomas Aquinas at the University of Paris, from where it spread to other German and Italian centers of higher learning. It was a revolution which drew originally on Islamic documents, particularly translations of Aristotle's writings from Averroes of Cordoba, as well as a translation from Persia. Jewish scholarship from Andalus also contributed to the educational advancement of medieval Europe during this period.

The Crusades, launched from the papal pulpit, accelerated the trend away from Carolingian disintegration, and helped crystallize the centralizing international theocracy: Latin Western Christendom. The German, French, and English monarchs welcomed the Crusades not only for religious reasons, but because the nobles' foreign responsibilities kept their knights away, resulting in more power for the monarchs who stayed at home. To orchestrate such a massive war, the crowns were able to raise taxes from the nobles and send the knights off to fight. The Crusades slowed the bloodshed at macro and supermacro levels between one noble family and another and one crown against the other.

The legitimation of the powerful monarchy was also the by-product of the Crusades, because the monarchs of Europe were eventually responsible for coordinating the military designs of the popes and other religious leaders. Royal coordination led to a further subordination of the landed elites on the battlefield and a depletion of the nobles' wealth to finance the Crusades; on returning to Europe, they were obliged to assume a role of subservience to the crown. Even countries whose centralizing dynamic had little to do with the Crusades, such as England, profited from the legitimation granted to the monarchy as an instrument of divine providence.

It was during the period of the Crusades that Europe was the closest to being a true theocracy, with the warrior pope as the leader of a multinational Western Christendom. Nobles established Crusader kingdoms in and around their Holy Land. The institution of the papacy and the entire church structure, including the monasteries, reached an apex of power during this period.

The Cistercian monasteries, for example, were remarkable forms of social organization, the most economically effective units in Europe and perhaps in world history to this date. Monks worked in factories, constructed a complex of hydraulic mills that ground corn, and operated forges for producing iron.

The Crusades were brewed from many economic, cultural, political, military, and religious factors. Urban II and Bernard of Clairvaux saw the crusade as a positive way to halt the "disgraceful coreligionist warfare" throughout Europe and harness the energy to a just cause. Pragmatically, Urban II saw control of the crusade as a way of controlling Europe. The knights saw opportunities for booty, land, and glory; if the knight's war-making spread Christianity, so much the better.

At first simply a "holy war against Islam," as time passed the Crusades took on many different forms. The Europeans launched the Crusades on two fronts: one in the Middle East, the other to the west, in Islamically controlled Iberia. The monarchy and landed aristocracy in Spain formed an alliance with the common objective of ousting the Islamic overlords. The Spanish cities tolerated the existence of a landed nobility and the crown to a degree unprecedented in either France or England; their thinking was that it was better to deal with Spanish monarchs and nobles than with Islamic overlords.

The actual precipitating event of the First Crusade (1096–9) was the request to Pope Urban II from Alexius I of the Comnenus dynasty, the Byzantine emperor, for help (primarily for resources) against the Seljuk Turks. Urban II saw opportunities in this situation that may not have occurred to Alexius, ways of increasing his power both temporally and religiously. It appears that he (like for that matter the crowns and nobles of Western Europe) was optimistic about the possibilities of victory against the Islamic empire. The Normans had already been successful in reconquering southern Italy, although it took them 30 years before they conquered the Islamic outpost of Sicily. Islamic Italy had come under siege when Count Roger I, his brothers, and other Norman knights and mercenaries planned a surprise attack on the area. Roger was able to oust the Muslims in the period between 1060 and 1075, and the surrender of the last Muslim stronghold occurred in 1091. Roger II, his son, was crowned King of Sicily in 1130. Once again the Normans made certain concessions to the existing cultures, and tolerated practices of both the Jewish and Islamic faiths. Scholars translated the documents introduced by the royal court into Arabic, Greek, and Latin.

On the papal throne, the politically astute Urban II did not ignore the Christian victory in Toledo, or the Norman success in ousting the Muslims from Sicily. The Pope flattered the Franks, publicly declaring that they were special in the eyes of the Creator because of their heroic deeds and dedication to the Holy Church. He rallied the Franks as the "chosen people" in Western Christendom to lead the Crusades. The Franks had historically been far more dangerous to the papacy than had the Muslims (until the rise of the Ottomans), a fact that may not have escaped the Pope. The Crusades would provide a fine diversion to keep the Franks away from their propensity for conquests in Italy.

Once the "chosen" Franks had been rallied to the Pope's cause, his call for a war against Islam spread like wildfire throughout Western Europe. Not only nobles but also pilgrims, religious leaders, and even children heard the call of this holy war. Peter the Hermit, a charismatic religious leader, formed a rag-tag crusading army composed of poor pilgrims with a few knights; he persuaded them to follow him by producing a letter reputedly descended from heaven, stating baldly that it was God's will that the pilgrims should defeat the Muslims, and promising that the Christians would be successful in ousting the Muslims from the Holy Land. The knights attempted to forge these poor people into an army; as other groups joined Peter in his march toward Constantinople, they engaged in battles, pillaged, and created havoc in the Christian countries and market towns they passed through. When the Poor People's Crusade arrived at the doorstep of Alexius I, he protected New Rome (the Byzantine name for Constantinople) by providing this marauding band safe passage to within striking distance of the Sultanate of Rum. Finding themselves in a Byzantine fort named Civitot, on the Sea of Marmara, under-armed and disorganized, Peter the Hermit's army quickly became the first victims of the Islamic forces.

While the Sultanate of Rum's forces in Anatolia were preparing to slaughter Peter the Hermit's Poor People's Crusade, Urban II was doing the serious recruiting for battle, from the knighted warrior class of the Franks. As the Frankish army of well-equipped knights, many of whom had seen battle against the Byzantines themselves in the recent past, finally descended on Byzantium, one can imagine the doubts that

Alexius I must have had as this group of Western European nobles marched into Constantinople. If we imagine ourselves by the side of Alexius I, the Emperor must have seen thousands of nobles stream into Constantinople, soldiers of fortune with no loyalties to Byzantium. After some initial violence, looting, and murdering, Alexius I was able to cajole the Franks into a vow of loyalty to him before the Crusaders made their way into the Holy Land. Alexius I had spared Constantinople, if only for the time being, from the swords of the Crusaders.

The carnage from the First Crusade was among the greatest that humanity had ever seen up to this point. On 17 Rajab 490/1, July 1097, the Crusaders with their larger force, reversing the loss of Peter the Hermit and his followers, defeated the Seljuks in the Sultanate of Rum in Anatolia. The Frankish army then conquered Antioch and the Seljuks who controlled this area, vulnerable because of their own war with the Fatimids.

Indeed, the Fatimids at the early stages of the First Crusade were cooperating with the Franks to destabilize the Seljuks, but it became clear to them early on that there was no room for religious diversity in the praxis of the Franks' spirituality. Conversion or execution were the choices for the Fatimids, when the Europeans gave them a choice; more often than not, execution was the only option given to the Muslims. As the Crusaders plowed through Tripoli and into Palestine, the Fatimids realized that they had become the target of the Franks' swords, and turned against the Crusaders, but with only limited effect. The Franks captured Beirut and continued bearing south, reaching Jerusalem in the year 1099 and wresting it from the Fatimid (Arab and Sudanese) garrison in July after a five-week battle.[8]

### The establishment of Crusader states

On conquering the Holy Land, the Crusaders immediately repudiated their vows of loyalty to Alexius I, and refused to turn over the conquered lands to the Byzantine emperor as initially planned. The Crusaders' efforts to keep Alexius I from exerting any influence in the lands that the Byzantine empire originally claimed, particularly in Anatolia, resulted in a dispute with the Byzantine empire that cut off the land lifeline linking these new Crusader outposts to Western Europe.

The great noble families of Western Europe, represented by the Crusader knights and nobles, lost no time in establishing settlements in the Middle East. The Crusaders set up four feudal systems, formally four kingdoms under Frankish rule, in the conquered Holy Land: the principality of Antioch, the kingdom of Edessa, the kingdom of Tripoli, and the kingdom of Jerusalem.

Since their Byzantine land routes had been cut off by the dispute with Alexius I, the Crusaders relied on the merchant marine of Italy and port cities to get supplies. The cities of Genoa and Pisa increased their wealth as they became the principal suppliers of goods to these Crusader kingdoms. Venice merchants, observing that there would be a Western European victory by 1099, joined in the fray and obtained a share of the commerce in the Holy Land.

Once word of the Crusader kingdoms had reached Europe, pilgrims flocked to Jerusalem. Ostensibly as a system of protection for the pilgrims, a violent quasi-religious institution developed at this time: the knight clerics. The Knights Templars, for example, were a group of knights who took religious vows. Baldwin II, the King of Jerusalem, gave these knights rooms in his palace, the Templum Salomonis, and they became known as the Knights of the Temple. Another cleric knight group was the Knights Hospitallers (the Knights of St John the Baptist). Originally part of a Christian hostel community that Italian merchants had founded for pilgrims and traders around the year 1070, this group managed, after the First Crusade, to free itself from the direct control of the Benedictine monastery of Maria Latina in Jerusalem. It came under the direct control of the pope and evolved into the Knights Hospitallers, who helped the pilgrims with their needs, while the Templars served as a military escort for travelers. The church hierarchy recognized these groups as legitimate orders, but the knight clerics served as role models for the development of another violent and expansive order: the Teutonic Knights.

The isolation of the new Christian kingdoms in the Middle East – connected to each other and to Europe by a very fragile lifeline – and the refusal of these kingdoms to affiliate with their Byzantine neighbors created a logistics problem. The powerful Shiite forces to the southwest, at Cairo, and the Sunni forces to the east were dangerous threats to these kingdoms. The Mamluks of Islamic civilization would eventually reclaim these states through warfare, seeing their struggle as a legitimate reclamation of conquered land. The European civilization, hearing of the fall of the Christian kingdoms, saw it otherwise: an assault on their rightful claims to the Christian Holy Land.[9]

### The Second and Third Crusades: the growing tension between the papacy and monarchs

The call for a Second Crusade – to recapture these falling Christian kingdoms – did not come from pope, monarchs, or knights. The monastery was the source of the new exhortations for battle, a rather ironic development given the other-worldly mystique of the monastic institution. The famous Abbot Bernard of Clairvaux urged the knights of Europe to take up their cross and throw the infidels out of the Holy Land.

To be sure, the Pope had already issued a papal bull, and King Louis VII developed a plan to engage in a new Crusade, but both of these plans remained dormant until the distinguished intellectual figure and church politician Bernard of Clairvaux gave his approval, and with his great eloquence mobilized the European nobles for battle. As for motives, Bernard may have taken up the cause to prevent King Louis VII from usurping papal authority. Royal leadership of the Crusades would have inflicted a blow to the prestige and temporal power of the church.

After some prodding from Bernard of Clairvaux, Emperor Conrad III of Germany agreed to join King Louis VII of France in the new Crusade. Their combined forces were the engines of the Second Crusade (1145–9), but there was so much animosity and friction between these two groups in terms of military objectives that there seemed to be no hope of providing a unified military front against the Islamic empire. The trouble between these two camps began while they were still trying to work out the logistics of battle.

A further complication of the Second Crusade was that the actual "Holy Land," the kingdom of Jerusalem, was still a viable Christian state, and had even established diplomatic relations with the Islamic leadership in Damascus. This valuable ally, however, was alienated when the Second Crusaders attacked Damascus (unsuccessfully). In addition, the question as to whose side the Byzantine empire was on – Islamic civilization or European Western Christendom – became unavoidable when the guide supplied by Emperor Manuel I of the Byzantine empire led the Crusaders into a surprise attack from the Seljuk Turks.

Because of these issues and the better organization of the Islamic Seljuk Turks, the Second Crusade was a failure. Bernard of Clairvaux, retreating into his religious dicta, argued that the Crusaders failed because of the wickedness of the Christians and the inscrutable judgments of God. He also said that he preached the Crusades in obedience to orders from the Pope, implying that the Pope, and not he, should bear the responsibility for the failed Crusade.

The period following the Second Crusade was not good for Western Christendom's dream of a presence in the Middle East. In 545/1150, an Egyptian fleet prevented supplies from entering the Crusader states by way of Italian supply vessels. In response, Baldwin III, King of Jerusalem, launched attacks to capture the port of Ascalon, a base for raids into the Crusader states and a means of support for the Islamic blockade. In 548/1153, after seven months of using both naval and land forces, Baldwin III captured Ascalon, which reversed its military role and became a Christian base for raids into Egypt.

A real impediment to a Christian presence in the Middle East came in the form of a resourceful Muslim leader. In spite of their enthusiasm and the power of their armies, the Crusaders and Crusader states were faced with a formidable enemy in Salah al-Din, known as Saladin to the Crusaders. Salah al-Din helped unite the entire Muslim world, both the Shiites and the Sunnis, against the Crusaders, in a *jihad* or holy war. This unification became the Ayyubid dynasty, named after Salah al-Din (Salah al-Din b. Ayyub was his full name), lasting in Egypt from 1169 to 1252, in a section of western Arabia to 1229, and in Syria to 1260. Salah al-Din was also responsible, along with his uncle and their armies, for the collapse of the Fatimid caliphate.

Salah al-Din's first goal, on coming to power, was to centralize and extend his rule, centered in Egypt, to the areas surrounding the Crusader states in Syria. Whereas the First Crusade had caught the Islamic forces by surprise, this was not the case with either the Second or the Third Crusades. His initial wars, a phase lasting a little over a decade, were with other Muslims, but he soon turned his attention to the evil from the West, capturing Jerusalem after the Second Crusade.

The Third Crusade, a direct response to Saladin's capture of Jerusalem, gained support from three well-known figures in European history: Emperor Frederick I Barbarossa of Germany (1152–1190), Richard I the Lionheart of England, and Philip II Augustus, the King of France. They personally led their own armies into battle, moving against the East in a politically volatile coalition. For example, an odd alliance between Frederick I and the Islamic leaders in Anatolia warred against the Byzantine empire and the Salah al-Din alliance. But at the same time the Turkish tribes in Anatolia who were outside the control of the centralized Anatolian state harassed Frederick's forces; these were the tribes who later founded the Ottoman empire.

Although the Christian forces achieved some tactical success, the Third Crusade suffered from disorganization and plain bad luck: Frederick I Barbarossa, marching through the smoldering heat while avoiding the Taurus mountain range, drowned trying to cool himself off in the Saleph (Calycadnus) river. Philip II, after scoring modest victories against the Islamic forces in the coastal cities of the Mediterranean, returned to France prematurely. Sidney Painter speculates that he may have felt that his military accomplishments were inferior to those of Richard I. Richard, however, stayed on long enough to reach a compromise with Salah al-Din; the latter, despite his reputation for military brutality, demonstrated his religious tolerance (and won a de facto victory) by granting Christian pilgrims special visiting rights to Jerusalem.

In 589/1193, Salah al-Din died of natural causes in Damascus. He had united Middle Eastern Islamic civilization and captured Jerusalem; although Antioch, Tripoli, and Tyre weathered the Islamic storm for the time being, Salah al-Din smashed the Crusader states, which never again regained their powerful presence.

After Salah al-Din's death, his brother, known to the Crusaders as Saphadin, was the next great "architect" of the Ayyubid political apparatus. After 1238 the Ayyubid dynasty began its decline. By 637/1240, there was a succession struggle among the Ayyubid princes, where one faction formed an unlikely coalition with the Crusaders to defeat the other faction. After the Third Crusade, the Crusader kingdoms began to fall. The only tangible successes of the bloody and brutal Crusades were the pilgrims traveling freely to the Holy Land, and the ghostly castellated ruins of European architecture dotting the landscape – like the Crusaders' hopes, abandoned and out of place.[10]

## Universal-level conflict and the power of the Italian city-state system

While the Crusades were being fought in the East, the city states on the Italian peninsula were becoming more and more powerful, their wealth growing in large part as a product of the Crusades. By the fourteenth century, Venice, profiting from commerce with the Crusaders' Christian kingdoms, had emerged as the center of the capitalist world economy. As mentioned above, the Crusades also served Italy well by providing a diversion for the European knights, who might have viewed the Italian peninsula as a fine addition to their landholdings.

The northern Italian towns were still city states, politically and militarily independent, during the period of the Crusades. They could unite into loose federations if necessary for the preservation of the city-state system. Toward the end of the thirteenth century, cities gradually became the core for larger regions, which were dominated by the city.

Another form of protection emerged as a two-edged sword: in the fourteenth and fifteenth centuries the Italian city states found refuge, and sometimes danger, in the military power of mercenaries. The *condottieri*, the equivalent of generals for hire, were given power to recruit their own armies, often acquiring both an infantry and a mercenary cavalry. Unfortunately, when mercenaries were out of work (during a lull in wars), they would pillage adjacent areas; it was usually easier to pay the mercenaries off than allow them to continue looting.

Also due in no small part to the Crusades, communes came into existence in the eleventh century in the booming economic areas of Tuscany and Lombardy. The bishops governing the towns were often in conflict with the landed elites who lived on the outskirts of these areas. As a consequence, the latter sometimes became the mercenaries for the merchants in the cities, forming communes that were actually coalitions of merchants and landed elites.[11]

### The Teutonic Knights attack Eastern Europe

The relative decentralization of Germany did not result in a more peaceful class of nobles. Although blocked to the south by the Islamic empire, Western European nobles could still make forays into Eastern Europe.

The Teutonic Knights were founded in 1198 as the Order of the Teutonic Knights of Saint Mary's Hospital in Jerusalem. Believing they were continuing the tradition of their ancestor Charlemagne, their original "apostolate" was to protect the Holy Lands against "pagans." These pagans were usually the Muslims, although Jews, too, could suffer from attacks from these knights.

What justified in their minds the marauding of Christian Eastern Europe? Apparently they also viewed the Slavic people as pagans, perhaps because the Slavs' earliest religion had elements of worshipping a god of the sun (if indeed the Teutonic Knights were aware of these spiritual practices). Of course, setting aside religious argument, they also hoped to gain land in the process. The knights seized areas around the Baltic Sea previously controlled by the Lithuanians, Livonians, and Prussians. They conquered the Eastern Slavs. In Hungary, they were given land in exchange for warding off the Cumans (although the Cumans and Hungarians eventually established an alliance). The Teutonic Knights established an empire in Prussia.

During the thirteenth century, these violent knights were also quite successful in "converting" those Russians who doubted the true Sonship of Christ. During this period, the Teutonic Knights formed an alliance with the Knights of the Sword and their religious-military activities were formidable indeed. They finally met their match in Alexander Nevsky, who resisted the knights in Russia.[12]

### The Fourth Crusade and conflict with Byzantine civilization

The state of European affairs took a new turn with the development of the Fourth Crusade, the result of the political/entrepreneurial activities of Pope Innocent III and the crowns, merchants, and European nobility. The death of Salah al-Din in 1193 led Europeans to the erroneous conclusion that the Islamic civilization would suffer from a leadership crisis, and that an opportune time had come for the Europeans to launch another Crusade. This time it was Innocent III who called Europe to arms. France and the Netherlands responded; the merchant marine of Venice offered ships to the new crusaders.

One of the central consequences of the Fourth Crusade was an attack on the Byzantine empire. The West and Islamic civilizations attacked the Byzantine empire. This civilizational attack occurred after the death of Basil II. With the passing of Basil II, at the beginning of the eleventh century, the Byzantine empire declined. The Byzantine strategical leadership, diplomatic expertise, commercial operations, and military power were in a downward spiral which weakened the resistance of Byzantine civilization to attacks from the Seljuk Turks and the Franks.

Emperor Manuel I met with a disastrous defeat in 572/1176 in his effort to expel the Seljuks from the previously controlled area of Anatolia. So devastating was this defeat that it would have been possible for the Seljuk army to destroy the Byzantine army, but as in Manzikert and for reasons that remain obscure, Manuel I and the Sultan worked out a peace arrangement. The decline of the Byzantine empire continued throughout the twelfth century. As Islamic warriors conquered parts of the Byzantine empire, the Sultan extracted taxes and he enforced obedience to the Islamic empire. As a result of this decline, Western scholars were beginning to call Anatolia Turkey by the late twelfth century.

In the west, Byzantium had been assaulted from the Norman and Frankish invaders even before the Fourth Crusade, attacks that accelerated with the empire's growing implosion of power. Competition between the rural magnates and the urban aristocracy within Byzantine society intensified with this withering of Byzantine imperial control. The large estates were able to become independent. This further reduced the administrative capacity of the Byzantine state, and increased internal dissension. Byzantium was caught in a destructive spiral: since the centralized government was no longer able to finance its well-trained military sufficiently, it became even more vulnerable to attacks from the east and west.

Developments from within, however, paved the way for the Fourth Crusade. A momentous turn of events occurred as a struggle broke out over the succession to the imperial throne. After centuries the precise causal sequence of the events is difficult to unravel, but we know the Crusaders intervened in this succession struggle (through Byzantine and perhaps Italian intrigue), and attacked Constantinople in the spring of 1204. The Crusaders killed, looted, raped, and pillaged their way through the entire city; they gutted New Rome and stole or destroyed countless artistic and religious treasures. The Franks were able to maintain control of the city until 1261.

The sack of Constantinople was the most successful attack in history against Byzantine civilization. It was a startling military victory, given that this campaign succeeded where the Islamic forces and Steppe warriors such as the Bulgars failed. The explanation lies in the duplicity of the relationship: the attack was successful because the Franks were ostensibly allies admitted to the city, whereas the other warriors were enemies. The Franks were also successful in establishing temporary systems of domination in areas of the Byzantine empire.

The conquest of Constantinople ended the unified efforts of the Fourth Crusade; the nobles, hastening to establish a new empire in Byzantium, rapidly decentralized this new territory as they fought each other and defended themselves against some of the more powerful Byzantine elites who were able to hang on to their power and offer strong resistance.

In 1261, the constant dissolution of these fragmented, continually warring islands of Western European power allowed a Greek general, Michael VIII Palaeologus, to reconquer the area of Constantinople and reestablish Byzantine rule.

But Byzantium was only a shadow of its former self, and never again the great military, political, cultural, and economic power it had once been. Byzantine civilization did not suddenly die; these attacks from the Crusaders, Steppe warriors, and Bulgars were part of a general period of decline. This weakness was evident when Serbia and Bulgaria were able to gain independence from the central Byzantium state, a decentralizing dynamic that would have been impossible during the height of the Byzantine civilization. The empire during this period pulled out of the far eastern sector, to Asia Minor, where the Greeks continued imperial rule throughout the period of decline. The Islamic empire was able to splinter the adjacent Byzantine kingdoms and hence isolate them from the rest of the Byzantine empire. By the eleventh century the Islamic Turks were bearing down on the Byzantine empire from the north and south.[13]

### *The Fifth and Sixth Crusades and their aftermath*

Innocent III once again saw the papal interests served by encouraging fighting with the so-called Fifth Crusade, the last real Crusade of the thirteenth century. The papacy, along with its monastic leaders, had been the chief movers and shakers in the Crusades, and would suffer a decline in temporal power with their passing. Indeed, even as early as the Second Crusade the crowns were attempting to gain control of them. The civilization of the Christian Middle Ages lost power to the growing power of the monarch.

The Pope faced a propaganda problem in his call for this Crusade, because the target was Egypt. The warriors of the Fifth Crusade were to attack the Islamic center in Egypt, hoping to conquer the Holy Land by way of the destruction of the Ayyubid state in Cairo. This indirect plan lacked some of the appeal of earlier Crusades. In spite of its place in biblical history, Egypt did not have the same symbolic power to motivate warriors as did the Holy Land. The Pope had more difficulty in rallying Europe than before.

Eventually the Fifth Crusade was launched. The strategy was to conquer Damietta, located in the eastern Nile delta, and then from this outpost to destroy Cairo. The initial part of the plan was successful and the papal legate Pelagius captured Damietta in 1219. Yet the occupying force waited in vain for Frederick II to send in the reserves that he had promised. However, even without these reinforcements, the crusading forces were still able to make inroads toward Cairo. The Islamic forces, frightened by the Crusaders' initial success, offered territories in Syria, an appeasement agreed to by the King of Jerusalem but not by the Crusaders, who wanted a total surrender of the Islamic forces. After some setbacks, the Europeans worked out a treaty. The momentum of power had turned, however, and the Ayyubid empire couched the treaty in terms favorable to themselves.

When the infamous Emperor Frederick II finally appeared in the East, he was the author of the most bizarre Crusade of all: the Sixth Crusade. Only the Poor People's Crusade and the Children's Crusade are close competitors. Frederick II had already alienated the church by refusing to lead a Crusade after promising to do so. Since 1215, every year for five years, Frederick II had had some excuse why he could not crusade. The most plausible reason for his unwillingness was that he had established a friendship with the Sultan of Egypt. Indeed, the Sultan had cemented this friendship by giving Frederick II a giraffe.

Previously Frederick II had directed his expansionist drives toward the Italian peninsula, choosing to attack the papal states rather than crusading against Islamic Egypt. In 1220 he moved his base of operations to Sicily, part of an unsuccessful plan to link Sicily with Germany by conquering the papal lands and the independent city states.

The animosity between Frederick II and the papacy is another example of how internal macro conflicts interacted with external supermacro and universal-level conflicts to shape the European political system. It began when Frederick returned from an earlier Crusade, claiming illness, and it led to his excommunication from the church by Gregory IX. At the center of the controversy were Frederick's own doubts about the Pope's spiritual authority, and about the nature of the soul. Frederick had conducted some gruesome experiments with living human subjects to determine if the soul left the body after death. After the deaths of the victims of his experimental theology, he believed that the soul did not leave the body, and perhaps because of this, Pope Gregory IX's threats of excommunication and (according to the theology of the Middle Ages) damnation did not bother him. In point of fact, Gregory IX excommunicated Frederick II as a way of humiliating him and possibly thwarting his designs on papal territory. The Pope knew that Frederick II would have to resort to extreme measures if there was not to be a revolt in Germany. One such extreme measure would be for Frederick II to agree to lead a Crusade to demonstrate his loyalty to the Church of Rome.

Despite his distrust of the Pope's spiritual authority, Frederick II finally agreed to launch a Crusade, landing his troops in the area near Jerusalem in the year 1228. Since there was no strong armed opposition to meet the Crusaders, he engaged in negotiations with the Sultan of Egypt for the return of the Holy City, as well as Nazareth and Bethlehem, to the Christians. On March 18, 1229, without bloodshed and even without the Pope's approval, in the Church of the Holy Sepulchre, Frederick II added "King of Jerusalem" to his list of titles. The coronation of the excommunicated Frederick II must have been a bitter pill for the Pope to swallow.

Frederick's success, however, was short-lived. His major goal, putting the Italian peninsula under German rule, was still unrealized. He had a restless nature and, perhaps bored with the role of King of Jerusalem, decided to leave and begin a new campaign in Italy. The Christian landed elites took over control of Jerusalem, but after only a short period, the Sultan, relying on Turkish mercenaries, reconquered the city.

Although history never precisely repeats itself, there was a certain irony in the attempt of Frederick II to conquer Italy. Like his namesake, Frederick Barbarossa, the new Frederick ran into a similar strategical situation. The Pope joined forces with the northern city-states in defense of the country.

Although the coalition suffered some defeats, in the long run they destroyed Frederick II's plans. By 1248 the Pope's forces, and those of the rebel German princes, had defeated Frederick II's army outside Parma. Frederick II died in 1250, politically isolated, at Castel Fiorentino near Lucera.

After Frederick's death, the Hohenstaufen dynasty collapsed, and with it the dream of establishing a new empire in the manner of ancient Rome. Since Frederick II had been preoccupied with establishing an empire, the barons remained strong in Germany. The battling between Germany and Italy, combined with the election of one domestically weak German emperor after another, resulted in Germany and Italy remaining largely decentralized. After Frederick II's death, the princes chose a successor whom they perceived as yet another weak ruler: a lesser noble by the name of Rudolf of Habsburg. These princes underestimated the ambition of the person they had selected: he used his new position to acquire some important holdings of his own, the duchies of Austria, which would later be the cornerstone of the Habsburg dynasty.[14]

## The final Crusades

By the middle of the thirteenth century, much of the political and economic impetus for continuing the Crusades had diminished. The last two Crusades were both led by Louis IX. In the first of these, in 1248, the Crusaders aimed at gaining Palestine by way of Egypt, the seat of power for the Ayyubids. The Islamic forces defeated Louis IX in this campaign, imprisoning him and the other survivors, and demanding and receiving a huge ransom for their release. Undaunted, Louis IX remained in the Holy Land, consolidating his power there, until 1254, when problems of rule in France forced him to return home. He launched a second Crusade in the year 1270, but this time he and a large number of his troops died during the Crusade from the plague.[15]

## The Failure of the Crusades and the Crisis of the Manor–Church Coalition

During these turbulent times, the Crusades and other foreign activities led to exchanges with the Islamic world. The constant war-making also transformed the European community into a fortified system designed to protect it against its own internal enemies, and to repel warriors from other civilizations. The nobles continued to build castles after the threats posed by the Vikings and Magyars subsided. As for the monarchs, with the Crusades acting as a catalyst, the thirteenth century was a watershed for the monarchy in Western Europe. At home they strengthened their grip against absent nobles, and, taking advantage of their growing military power, gradually took over the control of the Crusades from the papacy.

By these means, England and France developed the two most powerful monarchies, militarily absorbing opposition groups and setting up systems in which subjects were dependent on the monarchy for their continued prosperity. German emperors were somewhat less successful, too distracted by their attempts to conquer Italy to control the internal situation within Germany. The rural areas of Hungary, Poland, Sweden, and Denmark had weaker monarchs, in part because these thrones lacked the rich clientele from whom monarchs could extract taxes. Italy never developed a monarchic system of government, due to the temporal might of the popes, the constant intervention of the northern imperial powers which disrupted unification, and because of the warring towns, with their own entrenched elites.

Below the monarchy and nobility, the peasants went about their labors, tenaciously clinging to their land. Even with the growth of monarchies in Europe, peasants held portions of land well into the eighteenth century. The peasants' insistence on the possession of land weakened the monarchy, particularly in Sweden. Poland could not gain the resources necessary to run a wealthy unified crown because of protracted wars with the so-called pagan tribes in Pomerania and other Slavic territories, supported by the more powerful German crown and magnates who systematically undermined Poland's power. The szlachta dominated the state in Poland, a knightly class opposed to the development of an infantry, which they viewed as undignified.

The most successful resistance to the growing general movement toward centralization was the league of city states that checkmated Frederick II's dreams of an empire that stretched from Sicily to Germany. The situation in Germany and Italy remained somewhat atypical compared with the trend toward growing monarchies in Europe during this period of the Crusades. At home, Frederick scored military successes against the cities in Germany, breaking the autonomy of Berlin, but the emperors in Germany remained weak. With the voting power of the princes, Germany chose emperors who would be so distracted by foreign affairs that they posed little threat at home.

The other institution deeply affected by the Crusades was the church. In spite of all the efforts of the Crusaders, Islamic civilization was able to resist them and even expand. By 1291 the armies of Islamic civilization had driven the last Europeans out of the area of the Christian Holy Land. With the failure of the Crusades, the church met its first major strategical setback since the fall of the Roman empire. The unifying cultural umbrella of Western Christendom suffered a crisis of legitimacy. With the erosion of this cultural unity, the real divisions between the ecclesiastics, manorial elite, capitalists, and the crown became more pointed. The local power of the manor came into conflict with the ecclesiastical structures, and both were at odds with rising urban power and the crown.[16]

### Conflict with Mongol Civilization and the Further Containment of the State System of Latin Christendom

The next grave dilemma facing the West was how to contain the civilization of the Steppe warriors. The groups from the Asiatic Steppes included the Avars, Bulgars, Huns, and Magyars. The Steppe warriors had no written language, but they were superb fighters who used complex military strategies. The Mongols were the most militarily successful of this whole group. The fighting between the papacy and Frederick II prevented the necessary coalition to deal with the Mongol invasion of Europe.

The only civilizations to escape from the Mongols, among the fiercest warriors in history, were those they could not reach on horseback. Like all Steppe warriors, the Mongols organized themselves around a tribal system. Warriors learned to ride their horses and wield their weapons while they were still children. This civilization expanded when they literally sought greener pastures for their horses and animals. Urban areas became rich targets for these marauding armies.

One great warrior was able to conquer and unite these Steppe fighters. Genghis Khan was from the clan of the Borjigin, born into the equivalent of a noble family, the son of a petty chieftain. Genghis Khan created a formidable confederation of fighting forces, which included the Keraits, Merkits, Naimans, and Tatars, as well as his own tribe, the Mongols. This Mongol confederation also included Turkish clans, who ruled eastern Asia under the Uighur's confederacy in the second half of the eighth century and into the ninth.

Through both cooperation and violence, Khan united all of these tribes, composed of clans, into an army of giant proportions under the Mongols, the collective name for "all the tribes who live in felt tents." Linguists have linked the term Mongol to the word *mong*, meaning brave, daring, bold. *Genghis* Khan may mean "Ocean-like" Khan. Mongol civilization fused the clans and army into a civilization on horseback, in contrast to the stationary, sedentary civilizations of Europe and China, although with time the Mongol civilization, too, developed a sedentary core.

Genghis Khan's *tartars* or *tatars* (a name given by the Eastern Europeans and Russians to the Khan's forces) became a dynasty of effective and ruthless warriors, always on the move. The Mongols were able to conquer China, Korea, and Persia during the first third of the thirteenth century. They destroyed the Ayyubid caliphate, a formidable achievement when we consider that the Ayyubids had earlier parried Western Christendom's attempts at conquest.

The Mongol warriors expanded like a military tide throughout the Middle Eastern, Asian, and European continents. At first, waves of Mongol invaders would appear and retreat.

With each successive wave, there was a more enduring Mongol presence, creating a more centralized structure. The initial centralizing dynamic occurred when the Khan's army was able to form a confederation among the various tribes of the Steppes. As the tide grew, the Mongols vanquished Russia, Poland, and Hungary. We see the Seljuks of the Sultanate of Rum and Persia crumbling under the swift cavalry and rains of arrows. Anatolia also became a Mongol colony. The Mongols even defeated the fierce Teutonic Knights with the speed and coordination of their cavalry, a harbinger of the same strategy Napoleon would use centuries later.

The Mongols were ruthless in attacking their enemies and could be quite brutal in their treatment: they might pour molten silver in the eyes and ears of the leaders of their enemies (this was the fate of a Persian ruler); the Prince of Kiev suffocated in a box while the Mongols banqueted, using this box as a table. At other times, however, if defeated soldiers showed great courage, daring, and ingenuity, they might be made generals in the Mongol army.

Those people the Mongols neither slaughtered nor used for other purposes were forced to fight for them, serving in prisoner colonies that might become fluid and transient as they were absorbed into the larger Mongol army. The Mongols appointed Seljuk princes, or sometimes an oligarchy, to be figurehead sultans who answered to the Mongol occupational army in Anatolia.

With time, the Mongols turned their horses to the West. Mongol civilization made its first contact with Western Europe in the thirteenth century. The first Western Europeans to see them were Venetian traders near the Sea of Azov. The Mongols, led by Khan's military geniuses Jebe and Subedei, had just slaughtered the Cumans, or Qipchaqs, Turkish-Mongol warriors who formed a power bloc in the Steppes between the Danube and the Volga rivers. Though ruthless in war, the Mongols had a code of honor and had no interest in destroying the unarmed Venetians. They typically, though not always, gave their military targets warnings before declaring war. War with the Persians, for instance, occurred only after the Persians killed a Mongol ambassador who was attempting to establish peace.

The Mongols used this accidental contact with the Venetians to collect knowledge from them about the unknown civilization of Europe. The Venetians in turn saw glimpses of a sophisticated civilization; they were impressed by the translators who moved with the Mongol army, by the silk clothes and well-crafted weapons of the Mongols. Following a long series of sumptuous banquets, the Venetians and Mongols signed a remarkable treaty under which the Venetians were to be propaganda machines and intelligence officers for the Mongols; in return, the Mongols would destroy all trading centers they passed and would give the Venetians exclusive trading rights in these areas. Throughout the coming Mongol assault on Europe, the Venetian merchants would continue to act as spies for the Mongols.

As friendly as the Mongols were to the Venetians, this treaty did not mean peace with all Italian city states. Shortly after, the Mongols pillaged a Genoese trading center. The survivors of the slaughter, returning home, told tales of the Devil's Horsemen who cruelly killed all who crossed the Horsemen's path.

The Mongols launched their attack on Europe by way of an assault on Eurasia. They conducted a daring reconnaissance mission in Russia in 1223. During this mission, with a dazzling display of strategical and tactical pyrotechnics, the Mongols destroyed an armed council of princes who had formed a coalition with the surviving Cumans and Russians located around Kiev and Chernigov. The Mongols used blinding speed, tactical retreats, and archers with whistling arrows to divide and conquer the greater number of Russian troops.

The conquest of Russia was to be the first step in the campaign to conquer Europe. Although the Franks were successful in thriving in a more decentralized structure, such was not the case with Kievian society; it had disintegrated into over ten principalities. Under these circumstances, it was virtually impossible for the warring principalities to fend off attacks within the Ukrainian area. The Kipjchalk Turks had subjected the principalities to assaults and gained sovereignty in this area in the eleventh century. By the middle of the thirteenth century, Kiev was under attack from the Mongol empire. A campaign of conquest was planned to integrate Russia, disorganized by internal dissension. The Kievian ruling families could not work out a system of military cooperation. Instead, they fought each other for the total domination of Kievian society, even in the face of the Mongol threat.

The Mongol strategy for this war of conquest was to portray the attack on Russia as a raid and not a true campaign. Too late, the Russians realized that the true motivation of the warriors was to annex Russia into the Mongol empire. In the winter of 1237, undetected by the Russians, a Mongol army emerged from the forest on the west side of the Volga. The campaign started with a demand for the surrender of the small vassal state of Riazan in Suzdal. When the Russians refused, the Mongols demonstrated the power of their siege technology and the brutality of their army, annihilating the Russian forces and murdering the people of Riazan. The Mongols spared some Russians to work on military construction projects, specifically a series of wooden palisades around towns and cities under assault. Cities would be isolated by these structures, and archers and artillery were stationed outside them, together with catapults capable of launching rocks at the inhabitants, as well as missiles and rockets (not very effective), burning tar canisters, and grenades that, like the rockets, elicited more terror than damage.

The collapse of Moscow (which was not the huge metropolis that it was to become in later centuries) followed in 1238. After these series of victories, the Mongols prepared for their final onslaught on Russia. The Mongols had succeeded in disrupting the major trading routes of Kievian society around the Black Sea, a trading outlet for the Byzantine empire and the Islamic world to the south and southeast. In the summer of 1240, the attack on Russia began anew. Kiev, the so-called mother of all Russian cities, fell in December of 1240. The Mongols plundered and razed the city.

In the middle of the thirteenth century, Russia collapsed, caught in the pressure cooker between the West and the Mongols. The Mongol Khans enforced a tax policy, but allowed the Russian nobility to keep their power: the nobility could control their subjects, but had to submit to the wishes of the Khans.

After conquering Russia, the Mongol army, arguably the

best in the world at this time, made inroads into Eastern
Europe. A typical Mongol gambit was to attack with a speedy
but small force, luring the defenders from their fortification,
and then to assault them with a surprise ambush from a second
Mongol cavalry on the enemy's flank. The same strategy was
used on Poland. As the overconfident soldiers from Cracow
and Sandomir followed the small band of retreating raiders,
the Mongols ambushed the Polish soldiers with a shower of
arrows. The Poles abandoned Cracow on March 24, 1241; the
Mongols burned down the city.

Also in 1241, another Mongol army, led by Batu, Khan's
son and one of his key generals, was meeting more serious
resistance in Hungary. Batu faced the Templars and the well-
trained Hungarian soldiers, formidable opponents and the
most powerful army in the Mongols' years of war. The
Mongols lost many soldiers to the Hungarians before finally
overcoming this coalition, although the Hungarian soldiers,
too, suffered heavy losses.

The destruction wielded by the Mongols in Poland in 1241
and Hungary in 1241 and 1242 spread fear through the people
of Western Europe, breeding a host of myths about these
unknown warriors, fueled by fictitious reports and real atrocities. The presence of Nestorian Christians in the Mongol army
created the myth that the Mongols were a crusading Christian
army. Some Europeans thought that the Mongols marched
with a cross and were intent on punishing the Russian
Orthodox Church for leaving the Latin Church. Other
Europeans believed a new King David led the Mongols, making raids in the Middle East to free the Holy Land. Again, the
religious cultural practices of the Nestorian Christians were
probably the source of this myth. Some witnesses described the
Mongols as part animal, and swore that the Mongols ate their
dead enemies. Another tale was that Batu was in league with
demons who conquered armies for him.

With the Mongol troops streaming across the European continent, what saved Western Europe from becoming a Mongol
colony? An accident of history in Karakorum, the capital of the
Mongol empire, may have prevented the Mongol's conquest of
Western Europe. It had been Genghis Khan's desire that his
son Ogedei should rule after his death; from Genghis Khan's

perspective, he displayed a mixture of shrewdness, easy-going demeanor, and warm-heartedness that would make him an effective ruler and diplomat. But Ogedei's reign was brief. After succeeding Genghis Khan, Ogedei died, perhaps from a convulsion from drinking too much alcohol, or perhaps assassinated with poisoned wine. His death left the Mongols without a clear ascendant, and it was the custom for all Mongol commanders to return to Karakorum to elect a new leader. The Mongols postponed the European invasion to attend the council, and it is likely that this custom prevented the Mongol army from attacking all of Europe.

The postponement of the invasion was in this case permanent. Toward the middle of the thirteenth century, Khan of the Golden Horde of the Volga area converted to the Islamic faith. The term Golden Horde referred to the troops of Batu, whose empire stretched from Russia to the borders of Hungary, and northward toward the gulf of Finland. In geographical area it greatly surpassed its only historical rivals, the ancient Roman empire and Alexander's empire. Until the British empire in the nineteenth century, the Mongol civilization was the greatest in history in terms of geographical reach.

It is open to debate whether the Mongols could have destroyed Western European fortifications. Europe had fortified itself with castles and walled urban areas, the most effective means of fighting a cavalry. In open combat certainly the Mongol cavalry would have defeated the Western European cavalry. If, on the other hand, the Western Europeans could have resisted the typical Mongol gambit of luring their opponents out of their fortifications, and instead relied on their castles, the Europeans would have stood a better chance. But the Mongols were also the greatest exponents of siege warfare in history. Finally, we should note that it is likely that England would have survived. The Mongols had no navy to speak of.

Perhaps a Mongol invasion would have amalgamated Europe quickly, because a unified European army would have given Europe its best chance of resistance. Given the tensions between Frederick II and the papacy, however, Europe was not likely to forge a unified army. After Hungary collapsed, the only hope of saving Europe was in the hands of Louis IX, the only monarch with an army powerful enough to provide any resistance to the Mongols whatsoever. There is no doubt that Louis IX was well aware of the Mongol threat and appreciated their military prowess. His effort to establish diplomatic relations with the Mongols and to launch a joint Crusade failed because after Louis IX suggested that the Khan become a Christian, the Khan demanded that the Pope become his vassal.[17]

## Europe's Early Conflict with Ottoman Civilization by way of the Collapsing Byzantine Civilization

As Europe expanded to the east in the early days of the Crusades, the question arose as to who would be able to conquer the remains of the Byzantine empire. The most likely candidates were the Ottomans, the Serbs, and of course, the Franks. Even though the Ottomans were formally the subjects of the Seljuks, they were actually independent of Seljuk direct rule, even after the Mongol takeover.

The Ottomans started as a small branch of the Oghuz Qayi Turks who settled in northwestern Anatolia during the Seljuk conquests. The expansion of Mongol power may have caused the gathering of these Turkish tribes by driving a wave of immigrants southward, expanding to the Turco-Byzantine border toward the end of the thirteenth century. The Ottomans, descendants of the Turkish Oghuz clan, derived their name from that of their leader Osman (the later term, the Ottomans, stemmed from the original term, the Osmanlis). They held land for grazing animals next to the city of Merv. The Seljuk Turks dominated this area and spoke the Persian language.

The Ottomans were able to advance toward Europe through the weakening of both the Seljuk Turks and the Byzantine empire. By the middle of the thirteenth century, the Seljuk Turks were the figureheads of the Mongols in Anatolia. Osman capitalized on the disarray of Byzantium and the loss of part of the Byzantine empire in Anatolia, where he was able to expand his territory. The Byzantine leadership, struggling internally within Constantinople as well as with the powerful

Germiyanids in western Anatolia, could postpone a response to the threat of such a seemingly minor opponent as Osman.

Gradually, Osman's people gained more territory, until an Ottoman state governed a part of Anatolia. Osman was not only a skilled military commander but also, like Genghis Khan, a creative builder of organizations and a charismatic administrator able to gain worshipful respect from his followers. Talented warriors and administrators did not make Osman feel insecure; instead he used them to build the Ottoman state. By 1278, the threat of the Ottomans was so apparent to the Byzantine empire that it could no longer be ignored; an unsuccessful attempt was made to form a coalition with the Mongol army to attack the Osmanlis.

When the son of Osman, Orkhan, became ruler of the Ottomans he continued the process of empire-building. Orkhan extended his power into the Byzantine empire by giving troops to Emperor John Cantacuzene, who was the usurper of the legitimate throne of the child emperor, John Palaeologue. The marriage of John Cantacuzene's daughter Theodora to the Ottoman Sultan Orkhan formalized the Cantacuzene–Ottoman alliance, and the added military muscle allowed Cantacuzene to conquer the coastal cities next to the Black Sea, to plunder Thrace, and to launch an attack on Constantinople.

As the Ottomans inched their way into Eastern Europe by way of the collapsing Byzantine empire, they attacked the feudal nobles and incorporated the serfs into the centralized Ottoman sultanate. Slaves owed their allegiance to the sultan, the ruler of the Ottomans, himself; the sultan prevented the rise of feudalism by keeping his control centralized and by not giving land grants to nobility.

Through a combination of marriage, great military patience, and slow gains of territory, the Ottomans established forces in Europe by the middle of the fourteenth century. The rise of Ottoman power threatened the outer Christian states such as Bulgaria and Serbia. These states, feeling betrayed by Byzantine leadership and recalling that Sultan Orkhan was also John Cantacuzene's son-in-law, rebuffed the call of John Cantacuzene for help against Orkhan's attacks. As he could no longer maintain social order, Cantacuzene abdicated his throne, retiring to a monastery and becoming a distinguished historian for the last 30 years of his life, under the pseudonym Joasaph.

The successor to Orkhan was Murad I, a great general, political leader, and empire-builder. Murad I's initial invasion, of Eastern Europe in 1360, led to the de facto subordination of John Palaeologue, who became the Sultan's vassal. The Turks expanded farther and farther into Eastern Europe, absorbing Bulgaria, Macedonia, and Serbia, and ultimately attacking Hungary.

This attack on Hungary could not be ignored by Western Europe. Hungary's strong relationship with the Roman Church, and fear that the threat from the Ottomans heralded the collapse of all of Europe, caused Pope Urban V to encourage the raising of forces, including Serbs and Hungarians, to oust the Turks. In 1363 the Christian troops were driven back by the Ottomans, and failed in their attempt to liberate Eastern Europe. Amadeo of Savoy tried again in 1366, but conflict between the Greek Orthodox and Latin Church leaderships interfered with his effort.

Through a religious and social policy of tolerance toward the conquered warrior classes, the Ottomans were able to keep rebellion at a minimum. The negative side of this situation, however, was the reinstitution of slavery for those classes who could not be of immediate use on the military front. The Ottomans forced many widows and daughters into becoming either their concubines or their wives. They also enslaved those Christians who would not convert to Islam; it is easy to see why there was such a high conversion rate.

Murad I surrounded himself with an elite guard, known as Janissaries, the Yeni Cheri, or "new troops." When territories were conquered, children from their populations were educated into the Bektashi order of dervishes, personally blessed by the Sheik Haji Bektash. The Ottomans paid this guard more than all other soldiers, but prevented them from marrying or owning land. The Janissaries, in short, were military slaves who answered only to Murad I. By the reign of Bayezid I, the sultan was using these slaves of Christian descent for guarding and administering the affairs of state. Through this system, the now sedentary Ottoman nomads solved a problem of rule that had prevented the nomadic Avars from dominating the Slavs for more than 50 years, or the Western Huns from controlling the Hungarians for a century.

When Murad I, at the age of 70, conquered Bulgaria, Hungary helped the Ottoman cause, leading a Crusade into western Bulgaria to convert the Eastern Orthodox "heretics." The Prince of Serbia and his forces initially defeated the Ottoman forces at Plochnik, but Murad I later avenged the defeat, in a battle on the plain of Blackbirds at Kossovo, where Serbia, Bosnia, Albania, and Herzegovina intersect. So confident was Murad I of victory that he ordered that the infrastructure of cities and castles be maintained even before the Ottomans engaged the Serbs in battle. Prince Lazar's Serbian forces were defeated, weakened by division within the ranks. Murad I, his elder son Bayezid, and his younger son Yaku Mura were the field generals in this battle.

The family of field generals was soon to experience tragedy, however. Probably it was Milosh Obravitch, Prince Lazar's son-in-law, who assassinated Murad I either during or immediately after the battle on the plain of Blackbirds at Kossovo. Earlier, Prince Lazar had accused him of being a traitor, and Obravitch may have committed this assassination to demonstrate his loyalty to his father-in-law.

Murad I's elder son Bayezid I replaced him on the battlefield of Kossovo. However, the family violence continued: about six months later, Bayezid murdered his brother on ascension to the sultanate, so that there would be no succession struggle.

After Bayezid I defeated the Serbs, he formed an alliance with Stephen Bulcovitz of Serbia, the son of Prince Lazar. In exchange for troops and silver from the Serbian mines, Bayezid I allowed Serbia to remain an autonomous vassal state, not formally incorporated into the Ottoman empire.

Bayezid, lacking the military patience of his father, experienced setbacks against the European Knights Hospitallers, and was unable to take Smyrna from them. Since the power of the Venetian fleet prevented the Ottomans from controlling the Mediterranean Sea, Bayezid I eventually decided to deal with Hungary and his foe there, Sigismund. With the aid of the Wallachians, who wanted independence from the Hungarian state, Bayezid launched various raids across the lower Danube.

King Sigismund countered these raids by mustering his own attacks on Bulgaria, a vassal state of the Ottoman empire. Bayezid I, not trusting the loyalty of the ruler of Bulgaria, Sisman, had him executed and formally incorporated Bulgaria under the Ottoman imperial government.

King Sigismund tried to drum up support in Italy for a Crusade against the Turks, who were threatening to conquer Hungary. The Italian city states rebuffed Sigismund because they did not wish to jeopardize trade with the Ottoman empire. He received words of consolation from the Pope, but no material support from the papal coffers to support his efforts to fight the Ottomans.

When Sigismund turned to France, King Charles VI, suffering from spells of insanity and in no shape to lead a Crusade, referred Sigismund to his uncle, the Duke of Burgundy. The Duke saw the chance of increasing his fortunes by organizing an international army against the Ottomans, and agreed to support Sigismund's effort with the help of knights and mercenaries. The Comte de Nevers, the Duke's son, would lead these forces. This time the goal of raising an army was easier, because there was peace in the Holy Roman Empire and high unemployment among the mercenaries after the Hundred Years War. An international force composed of knights and mercenaries from Bohemia, England, Flanders, Germany, Italy, Lombardy, Savoy, Spain, Scotland, and Poland prepared to face the Ottomans.

On landing in Hungary, however, the international force found no Turks. They erroneously concluded that the Ottomans were raising troops in Cairo. In fact, not content with the Byzantine empire as a vassal state, Bayezid I had launched an attack on Constantinople, which he renamed Istanbul, a variation on the Greek phrase "is tin poli": "to the city." Manuel II, Emperor of Byzantium, was able to stay in power, but only at the discretion of Bayezid I. Finding no Ottomans, and anxious for action, the international force attacked the very land it had come to defend, the area around the Danube.

At first it met no strong military opposition, but eventually the force ran up against fortified structures. Without siege equipment (the plan had been to fight the Ottoman cavalry), it made little headway against the fortress at Nicopolis. Hoping to starve out the residents of the fort, for two weeks the European multinational army of Christian knights feasted outside this fortress, raped women, and murdered inhabitants in the general vicinity of Nicopolis. Then, almost out of nowhere, the troops of Bayezid I's army appeared and the Crusaders were caught in a trap. The Crusaders had never before met such a mobile cavalry. The armies of the Turks annihilated the European international force, and the survivors hastily returned to the West with tales of the invincible Ottomans. After the defeat of Western Christendom's best army, Emperor Manuel II was unable to raise troops in the West to protect the Byzantine empire from another attack against the Ottomans.

The only thing that prevented Bayezid I from a complete takeover of the Byzantine empire was the invasion of Timur the Tatar, which diverted his resources and attention away. Timur the Tatar, from a small tribe in the area between Samarkand and Hindustan, was successful in creating an empire that bordered the Ottoman empire. It was obvious that neither Timur nor Bayezid I would submit to the other. Timur, with the help of Genoese resources and other aid from Europe, succeeded in defeating the Ottoman army, capturing Bayezid I, and displaying him like an animal in a cage. Bayezid died in Timur's captivity, perhaps by suicide. Timur, after slaughtering, enslaving, and extracting resources from the Ottomans in Anatolia, apparently saw his feat of conquering the Ottomans as less than an important victory; he made plans for the conquest of China and left the Ottomans to govern themselves. After a succession struggle and a civil war, Mehmed I won control of the Ottoman empire, though his rule lasted only for a brief period.

New Rome, the jewel of the Byzantine empire, still eluded the Ottomans. To capture Constantinople, the new sultan, Mehmed II, one of the key engineers of a centralized Ottoman state, spent time overseeing the building of "super-cannons" and catapults that could launch projectiles powerful enough to collapse the walls of Byzantine fortifications. In addition, Mehmed II quite rightly believed that the earlier attacks on Constantinople had failed because warships did not support the army. He went about building a navy that surpassed the Byzantine navy, with five times as many ships.

Seeing these preparations, New Rome's emperor, short of troops and money, sought allies in the West. The Ottomans' war with the Byzantine empire was of great concern to Italy, the Ottomans' main rival for naval supremacy in the Mediterranean. Consequently, ships and troops from Genoa and Venice were sent. A famous Genoese expert on walled fortifications, Giovanni Giustiniani, became the commander-in-chief of the defense against the Ottomans' assault on Constantinople.

At first the Byzantine emperor tried to strike a peace, but it was to no avail. The Ottoman siege began during the Octave of Easter in 1453. Thanks to the ingenious defense system of the Venetians and the Genoese commander-in-chief, the first Ottoman–Byzantine encounter was a standoff. A string of wooden floats across the harbor of the Golden Horn foiled the Ottomans' naval assault on Constantinople. Next the Ottomans pursued a novel, and successful, idea: moving ships on land to avoid the floats. Oxen pulled ships on roads built by Ottoman engineers. After a gallant defense, the city fell, with Emperor Constantine last seen, as legend has it, stripping off his royal identification. An unknown assailant killed the Emperor in hand-to-hand combat. The Ottomans captured Constantinople on May 29, 1453, following up their victory by pillaging, killing, raping, and by taking slaves.[18]

## The Impact of Civilizational War: European Expansion and the Implosive Formation of National States in Latin Christendom

From the civilization struggle perspective, we see how a gradual transformation occurred in Europe, from feudalism toward centralized states, usually headed by a monarch. The change started internally at the macro level, from the social structure that arose in battling the Vikings, as manor fought manor. Gradually the winners of these lesser battles expanded into ever-widening circles of territory.

Eventually the crowns' outward expansion became conflict at the universal, intercivilizational level, with the arrival of the

Crusades. The initial successes and ultimate failures of the Crusades, tied to the fate of the papacy, were engines of state-building. The monarchs, who eventually led them, were able to enhance their power through taxation and through the structure of the crusading army, which enabled them to dominate the nobles. With the rising power of Islam, the Crusades failed, and the Islamic warriors ousted the Crusaders from their outposts in the Middle East. The apparatus then turned inward, back to the supermacro and macro levels, as the states of Western Christendom expanded by battles waged between manors and with other nearby societies. In the arena of religious power, the failure of the Crusades eroded the authority of the papacy, and the enhanced power of the thrones at the expense of both nobles and the papacy set the stage for the Reformation. At the same time, the crowns were subject to some limitations through the formation of parliaments.

During the period between the eleventh and thirteenth centuries, increasingly rich burghers laid the groundwork for modern capitalism, profiting either directly or indirectly from the Crusades and other intercivilizational war-making. By 1300, Western Europe had developed a consciousness of itself, both in cultural and religious terms, an awareness which was the product of the civilization of Western Christendom. The wealthy merchant class was able to fund armies that warded off threats from the nobility and the church, often through the medium of the crown. As the townspeople became rich, the church attempted to extract more resources; it was a situation that put the church and townspeople in a more antagonistic relationship, further fuel for the Reformation.

Considering the civilization struggle thesis, war-making was a central engine in the transformation of Europe. The Mongol and Ottoman invasions of Asia minor, Russia, Eastern Europe, and the Middle East prevented the eastward expansion of Latin Christendom. The extension of Ottoman forces into Eastern Europe began an era of Western European retrenchment. This containment of European society after the failure of the Crusades also created a recession: the great banking houses of Italy, which had made fortunes by simultaneously financing the Crusades and establishing trade with the East, failed one after another.

This implosion in turn reverberated throughout Western Christendom, and a general social crisis shook the foundations of feudal society. It exacerbated class conflicts between peasant and noble, stirred up combat involving cities and manors, and produced pressures in monastic capitalism, tensions among the landowners, the crown, and the growing merchant class, and a growing discontent with Catholicism and the papacy among certain elites in Europe. Europe faced threats from the Middle Eastern, Byzantine, Turkish, and Mongol civilizations, and contained them, but not before these civilizations had transformed and eventually conquered much of Eastern Europe. The aftermath of the collapse of Western Christendom is the topic of the next chapter.[19]

# 5

# The Renaissance, the Reformation, and the European State System

## Overview

The civilization struggle model provides a mechanism with which to view the relations among civilizations, and how they shape state systems. The failure of the Crusades, combined with the encroaching military frontiers of the Byzantine, Islamic Middle Eastern, Mongol, and Islamic Ottoman civilizations, led to the implosion of the European state network. Moreover, this situation fueled the Reformation and religious wars, interacting with the ongoing wars with the Ottoman civilization and destroying Latin Christendom. The military clashes among civilizations, and the failure of the West to beat the so-called infidels, made the Reformation a viable political reality.

The failure of the Crusades provided the spirit for the success of the Reformation. By granting the nobles and the crowns the authority to lead giant armies in the name of God, the papacy had legitimized the throne as an instrument of divine providence. This precedent had the unintended consequence of putting the throne in direct competition with the Chair of Saint Peter as the instrument of God, and further legitimized the idea of the divine right of monarchs.

The civilization struggle thesis is a conceptual lens through which to gain an understanding of internal European developments. In a surprising turn of events, the Ottomans were partially responsible for the success of the Reformation and the collapse of Latin Christendom. The war with the Ottoman empire and the power of the German landed nobility prevented the Habsburg empire from conducting an all-out oppression of the Protestants in Germany. Once the Reformation took hold in Germany, it spread quickly throughout Europe, not only as a religious revolution but as a political, military, cultural, and economic one, which completed the destruction of Latin Christendom. The Ottomans' economic support of the Reformation countries, and of other allies who would help the Ottomans in their efforts to destroy Spain, contributed to the success of the Reformation when Charles V made a truce with his bitter enemies, the Lutherans, to fight the Ottomans.

The social earthquakes that became known as the Reformation and the Renaissance occurred in the fifteenth and sixteenth centuries. Wars shook Europe during this period, and Italy in particular suffered from war. The result of the wars that ravaged the Italian peninsula during the Renaissance was the development of a very decentralized system of sovereign duchies surrounding city states. Because the decentralized Italian city-state system was not conducive to forging a unified foreign policy, the city states were subject to attacks from other European states and Islamic civilization.

Although the Reformation transformed Europe, there was still much continuity between Latin Christendom and the emerging structures. The culture, realms, and kingdoms of Renaissance and Reformation Europe shared many similarities with the states and culture that had developed during the latter Middle Ages. The Renaissance state became a national state: it is during this period of the Renaissance, Reformation, and Counter-Reformation that the monarchs formed the so-called "absolutist" states – something of a misnomer, since monarchs in even the most powerful states still faced opposition from factions of the landed aristocracy. The development of the absolutist states led to the separation between political and economic institutions. The decline of the papacy, the strengthening of the monarchy, and the development of proto-nationalism crystallized. During this transition, the power of parliament increased in England, and the bourgeoisie grew stronger in England and many other European societies.

A central development of this period was the continuing implosion of Western European power to the east and the southeast. Many factors contributed: the failure of the Crusades, the wall set up by the Mongols to the east, the growing presence of Ottoman power in the Mediterranean, and Ottoman intervention into Europe. The Eastern European societies continued to play their historically tragic role as military buffers for Western Europe; the Ottoman and Russian attacks, as well as international war, kept the polities in these Eastern European nations in disarray and decentralized.

Europe had more success in the west; the Spanish Reconquista subordinated the remains of Islamic power in Iberia, and the establishment of a Western European state structure filled the void. Moreover, the growth of Portuguese sailing technologies put the Islamic naval forces on the defensive throughout the Mediterranean. There European forces caused Islamic defeats in North Africa.

Islamic, Mongol, and Islamic Ottoman civilizations set up a wall against further European expansion to the east and south. This enclosing wall added fuel to the Reformation, internalized European war-making and centralization, and aided the development of full-blown monarchies in Europe. Blocking European civilization to the east, the Ottomans continued their expansion in the Mediterranean by skillfully playing European powers off against one another.

As monarchies grew, the institution of the papacy declined. The failure of the Crusades created a legitimation problem within Latin Christendom, since the papacy had blessed the efforts of the Crusades, even declaring that the Crusades were the will of God. The various popes, who had used up much of their political capital during these military failures in the Holy Land, could no longer intervene in the affairs of the nobles or the crowns with impunity. Crowns, nobles, dissenters, thinkers, and artists reexamined the church and all its activities, including its beliefs and institutions.

The disillusionment of the Europeans in the aftermath of the Crusades was the soil in which the Reformation could take root. Ottoman support of England and France dashed the Habsburgs' dreams of restoring a unified Catholic Europe, providing a clear example from the civilization struggle perspective

of the way that universal-level war between civilizations interacts with the supermacro level of international politics and
with the macro-level national states to change state structures.
The wars with the Ottomans linked through to the
Reformation, destroying the last remnants of Latin
Christendom and transforming the economic and political
landscape of Europe.

Interacting with the Reformation, wars of religion and class
conflict transformed, altered, and destroyed institutions of the
Middle Ages. It is not always possible to know whether these
wars were religious or political, or how much of the violence
was triggered in the name of religious reform and how much
came from a drive to protect the civilization of Christendom.
The open rebellion against the centralized church meant that
the state could now ignore the church's religious and political
dictates, with Protestantism accelerating the demise of papal
political power. The Protestant merchant class would emerge
as the dominant class in many European societies.

During the Counter-Reformation, Catholics were able to
gain new converts, in spite of the church's decline in political
power. The Jesuits, the "Pope's personal army of God,"
became expert preachers and helped gain many new converts.
They also acted as agents, sometimes perhaps inadvertently, in
failed attempts at European empire-building in Russia, Japan,
and China.

The nobles who subscribed to the Protestant faith undermined the legitimation granted to the Habsburg ruling dynasty
by Catholicism. Ottoman trade supported the reformers working to undermine the power of the dynasty without worrying
about the formal sanction of the Catholic Church. What we
see, then, is the destruction of the hegemonic world-view of
Latin Christendom (to be replaced by a multitude of alternative
world-views), and the splintering of the political alliances, the
economic relations, and the unified knowledge base of the civilization of the Middle Ages.

Between 1560 and 1650, states transformed the system that
unified Latin Christendom. Leaders of the new state system
were not necessarily obedient to the papacy on either secular or
religious issues. In spite of the unevenness of the situation, in
certain states the development can be seen of that army of civil

servants that makes up the modern bureaucratic state. In England during these centuries, the development of the classes of the gentry and yeomen consolidated, and early industrialization continued to expand.

State-building continued in the aftermath of the Crusades, the intercivilizational war with the Ottomans, and the Ottoman-supported religious wars. By the middle part of the seventeenth century, a cluster of centralized "nations," not always recognized as nations by their inhabitants, enforced the homogenization of life within their social structures, as monarchs replaced local and canon law with royal law and royal authority. Although the structures that emerged took the form of nation states, it is not clear that there was formal nationalism within them. The nation state coalesced around the competing entities of towns and new cities, merchants, feudal structures such as manors, and the crown. After centuries of struggle, the ultimate political losers were the Catholic Church and the manors.

In line with the civilization struggle thesis, it is important when examining developments in one civilization to observe intercivilizational relations as well. Many scholars have argued that the times between the fifteenth century and the seventeenth century were "the European centuries," but they were also the centuries of other civilizations too. The Western Europeans made only symbolic inroads into Chinese and Japanese civilizations across these years. Meanwhile Russia was expanding into Siberia, and the Ottoman and Middle Eastern civilizations were also advancing, often at the expense of Western Europe. The Islamic empire continued to move into Eastern Europe, India, Asia, and parts of Africa. To be sure, Islamic civilization ran into stiff resistance and lost some ground during the seventeenth century, but this fact should not obscure the general pattern of the Islamic increase in power during these centuries, particularly Islamic Ottoman civilization.

The great civilizations in China, the Middle East, and India resisted European expansion for the time being. In the fifteenth and sixteenth centuries, the Europeans left largely unscathed the South Sea Islands, Australia, and the Amazon. Northern parts of North America also temporarily escaped the conquering armies of Europe. The great structural and military wall built up by the other civilizations increased the pressure on Europe to follow the line of least resistance, to expand its maritime power and extract resources from what we now call American Indian civilizations, since they lacked the military prowess to defeat the stronger adversaries. Let us look in some detail at this pressure toward westward maritime expansion.[1]

## War and the Structure of States in Renaissance Europe

The Renaissance was partially a by-product of the neo-Aristotelian revolution that started at the University of Paris during the high Middle Ages. With their emphasis on human reason, and human beings as the measure of all things, Renaissance thinkers built upon the Paris revolution and took this movement even further.

The Catholic Church was undermined as a political institution during the Renaissance through challenges to church doctrine, in part because the church sometimes contested scientific discoveries, and in part because the endless papal proclamations that the war with Islam would end in a glorious Christian victory made thinkers see all papal pronouncements in a more skeptical light. In addition, the corruption of the papacy in the Renaissance, including the capturing of the papacy by rich Italian families, reduced its credibility in the eyes of the European intelligentsia. For example, the son of Lorenzo de' Medici was virtually able to buy the papacy: he was an archbishop at eight and a cardinal at 13; he ascended to the papacy at the age of 37.[2]

### Spanish state expansion against Islam during the Renaissance

A central trend in the Iberian peninsula during the fifteenth century was the ousting of Islamic power and the establishment of a Western European state system. The political marriage between Ferdinand of Aragon and Isabella of Castile was the beginning of the Spanish empire. The union coordinated the two kingdoms, which maintained their political independence (even their parliamentary systems) after the royal marriage. Castile, however, played the dominant role in this partnership. Both leaders strengthened their hold on their kingdoms. Indeed, Ferdinand and Isabella were ruthless in centralizing their power. The Spanish Inquisition, on the surface a religious purge of the unfaithful, was often a euphemism for the elimination of political enemies in Castile and Aragon.

This coordination of Spanish royal power with the papacy, not found in such bold relief in either France or England, where the papacy and the crowns were often at odds, was also quite successful in increasing internal power. In the case of Spain, the papacy legitimized the ecclesiastical courts, which worked in conjunction with the royal families in seeking out alleged heretics, who were often the enemies of national rule.

After this political marriage, the crowns ousted the landed elites from state positions, increased royal power over the cities, and linked cities and urban areas to the power of the thrones. Queen Isabella was successful in dissolving the royal council, which had been made up of nobles, and this gave her more centralized power. The crowns, who quite rightly believed that these nobles were enemies of the Castilian–Aragonian union, replaced them with middle-class lawyers whose fortunes were dependent on their favor. As a result, there developed a fierce loyalty to the crowns among the lawyer courtiers.

In spite of the formal political separation between the nations, this marriage created a cultural fusion of Aragon and Castile into a new society. The state-building activities of Isabella and Ferdinand also extended to the church. While still remaining on good terms with the papacy, they were able to wrest from it control of clerical appointments; with time, they built up a church hierarchy in their kingdoms that supported the crowns at the expense of the church. Demonstrating consummate political skill, the Spanish rulers achieved their aim without the battle between the crowns and the papacy that occurred in other European states under similar circumstances.

The marriage of Isabella and Ferdinand had fateful consequences for the Islamic presence in Iberia. The consolidation of power in Aragon and Castile allowed the Spanish rulers to challenge the last remnants of Islamic control in the peninsula.

Although it is true that the Crusades were born and died with the Middle Ages, similar activities carried over into the Renaissance and the Reformation. The target of these Crusades often changed, but the opponents were usually the followers of Muhammad. These Christian holy wars were just as sacred to the Christians as the *jihad* was for the Islamic warriors. By the middle of the fourteenth century in Spain, the only remaining remnant of Islamic power was the kingdom of Granada, across the Mediterranean from what is now Morocco and Algeria; Granada fell to Spain's superior artillery in 1492.

There followed an era of westward maritime expansion by the Spanish that was, by the end of the Renaissance, to secure Spain's place as a world geopolitical force. Isabella financed the voyages of Christopher Columbus, an Italian *condottiere*, in his efforts to find shorter trade routes to the east. A similar outward expansion occurred from Portugal. The Portuguese were successful in conquering parts of northern Africa during the last part of the fifteenth century and the beginning of the sixteenth. The Islamic forces, still expanding in the Balkans, were attacked in the Mediterranean. By the late fifteenth century, not even the legendary Islamic sailors were a match for the Portuguese captains who had emerged after Henry the Navigator. The European sailors, thanks to their new instrumentation and navigational skills, did not lose their bearings even in the most inclement weather.

Their vessels, too, were particularly suited to their dual roles of trade and war. The European galleon was a hybrid of Arab and European technology. The speed, flexibility, maneuverability, and military capability of the European warships, superior to all others, bewildered the Islamic admirals. A small fleet of European ships could defeat a larger fleet of Islamic ships. The battle of the Arab Sea near the Indian coastline of Diu, won by the Europeans against a much larger Middle Eastern force, demonstrated to the Islamic sailors the superiority of the European vessels. The tactic of ramming and boarding that had served the Middle Eastern captains so well was useless against these new European ships; it was impossible to board a ship that could not be caught. On those occasions when the Middle Eastern ships were close enough to come alongside, they were destroyed by the cannons of the European vessels.[3]

## Italy, warfare, and city states during the Renaissance

The growing might of the Venetian military had become a threat to Genoa. The growth of Venetian and Genoese commercial power was positively correlated with the era of Venetian Genoese city-state wars that started in the thirteenth century.

To understand conflicts of this kind, we should realize that a weakness of the Italian city-state system was that these kingdoms, duchies, republics, and territories were subject to invasion from European states and Islamic civilization. The system also had to deal with great threats from the Ottoman empire. Yet there was no common foreign policy that could prevent an invasion. A balance of power developed in which loose alliances between various city states emerged. In 1454, for example, the development of the treaty known as the Peace of Lodi gave this informal coalition legal significance, and temporarily stopped the bloodshed that had occurred over the past centuries. But these temporary defense leagues between and among Italian city states were not always effective. Naples and Sicily in the south of Italy, for example, never really experienced the Renaissance, because the wars waged over controlling this area prevented any cultural flowering. Outside states, particularly France and Aragon, launched attacks on southern Italy, leaving in their wake poverty and severe oppression of the peasants, whose lives in this area mirrored in many ways the conditions of the oppressed and impoverished peasants in Eastern Europe.

The precarious lack of a foreign policy became a real problem for the Italian peninsula in relation to its Christian neighbors as well. However wealthy the city states, they could not resist the powerful forces and mercenaries of the external crowns, or the onslaught of Islamic civilization. The papacy had especial trouble keeping control of the papal states during the fifteenth century. The areas of Bologna, Ferrara, and Urbino escaped from the papal administrative system and set up independent governments. With constant war a way of life for the Italians, the *condottieri* reached the apex of their power during the fifteenth century. By then, the various Italian duchies, republics, and kingdoms had slowed their expansion – it was no longer possible for Italian city states such as Venice to expand any further without engaging in wars of attrition that were not worth the expense. In 1494, for example, the Duke of Milan worked out an agreement of military cooperation with King Charles VIII of France, who brought a force of more than 25,000 troops to conquer the southern kingdom of Naples. This action started a battle for control of the entire Italian peninsula between Spain and France.[4]

### Renaissance Europe, wars and the growth of the monarchy

The term "the Renaissance" is misleading because the movement did not exist in many European nations, and where it did exist it is difficult to argue that it showed much similarity to the Italian prototype. The Italian Renaissance saw the consolidation of the city-state system, but other parts of Europe experienced the growing power of the monarchy. This occurred after setbacks in the first 50 years or so of the fifteenth century, setbacks that were the result of the financial devastation and erosion of the universal or intercivilizational power of the monarchs in the aftermath of the Crusades. On the macro level, however, the second half of the fifteenth century saw the monarchies of England, France, and Spain reverse the trend and expand their power.

The external civilizational enemy had played a large role in the growth of the early nation state, and initially crowns fashioned this license for their power by emphasizing threats from Islamic civilization and other countries. After the Crusades, the revenues continued to flow to the crowns, but once there were no Crusades to fight, they could turn their attention and resources toward controlling the landed aristocracy within the territory of the state. The European crowns were very successful in gradually undermining the papacy's power, gaining new resources by raising taxes, and shaping their territories into nations through a powerful ideology according to which its citizens owed services and money to the crown.

In Eastern Europe and Germany the landed aristocracy, still the dominant class, controlled the decentralized political institutions. In the case of Poland, the monarchy had gained power earlier, when in the fourteenth century the marriage of Jagiello, the Grand Prince of Lithuania, to the Polish Queen Jadwiga created a Lithuanian-Polish society. This marriage resulted in a huge victory of the crown over the landed elites. Ottoman warriors eventually absorbed the Polish territorial gains in the south. The landed aristocracy struggled with the crown and steadily eroded the power of the throne. Bohemia, although formally a part of the Germanic Holy Roman Empire during the fifteenth century, was not fond of the Germans. The Bohemians attempted to create alliances with the Slavs to the north. For a period in the fifteenth century, King Matthias Corvinus of Hungary was able to dominate the landed elites and establish a powerful monarchy in the largely decentralized Eastern Europe. His rule shared similarities with the rising crowns during the Renaissance: as with Elizabeth I in England, he became a patron of the arts and sciences and immersed his court in Renaissance culture. After his death, the landed elites decentralized the government once again.[5]

## The Final Collapse of Latin Christendom: Civilizational War, the Reformation, Wars of Religion, and State-Building

The crisis of Latin Christendom after the financial, cultural, and political devastation of the Crusades culminated in the Reformation. The religious wars that were the result of the Reformation interacted with the threat from the Ottomans to destroy Latin Christendom and create a new Europe.

Latin Christendom was a largely decentralized manorial structure, held together by the secular and cultural power of the papacy and the culture of Catholicism. The whole reorganization of the centralized church meant that the state could now dominate and/or ignore the church. The fates of the church and the landed elites were intertwined with one another. The destruction of the church as the hegemonic ideological power led to the decline of those landed elites who were not able to protect and expand their fortunes by linking themselves to the emerging capitalist economy. It also meant that the merchant class could challenge the dominant class, replacing nobility of blood with the nobility of wealth.

The Reformation, through those barons who adopted the Protestant faith, eroded the legitimation granted to the Habsburg and other Catholic ruling dynasties by the Catholic Church. Due to the intercivilizational war with the Islamic civilization of the Ottomans at the same time, the Habsburgs (particularly Charles V, and to some extent Philip II) did not attack the reformers. Protestant monarchs worked to undermine the wealthy Catholic Church and confiscate the lands of the Catholic nobles; they also undermined Catholic nations at every opportunity. What one sees culturally, then, is the destruction of the hegemonic world-view of Latin Christendom, and a splintering of the political knowledge and economic thought of the Middle Ages.

We cannot continue our discussion of the Reformation without looking carefully at an important precipitating event. In 1517 an Augustinian friar in the German town of Wittenberg altered the history of the world. He may or may not have hung the famous 95 theses at the castle church of Wittenberg, but he definitely circulated these theses privately. The friar, of course, was Martin Luther, and his act polarized the conflict that Erasmus, More, and other Catholic Renaissance humanists had started previously with their controversial writings.

For Protestants a central concern was the corruption of the Catholic Church. Luther galvanized a social movement based, in part, on the idea that eternal salvation came through the sheer mercy of God. This, of course, was well within the guidelines of Catholic theology, but Luther's argument was that salvation was *exclusively* through God's mercy. This argument undermined the role of the Catholic Church as a divine instrument of salvation through the priestly administration of the sacraments and as sole arbiter of doctrine.

When the Catholic Church excommunicated Martin Luther, he responded by publicly burning the excommunication papers. Politically, to protect himself from the Habsburg emperor, Luther sought support from the German barons and from the dying institution of knighthood. With the arrival of mass armies and capitalists, knights were discontented and embattled. Those commoners who interpreted Luther's doctrine as a social revolutionary manifesto misunderstood him. Luther was against the hierarchy of the Catholic Church, but he supported traditional political authority, even the barons' power. The peasants who believed in revolutionary Protestantism and viewed Lutheranism as an attack on all authority were probably influenced by a former disciple of Luther's: Thomas Müntzer. The peasants organized uprisings, but Luther stunned them when he published a pamphlet urging the barons to crush the so called *hordes of peasants*. Yet in this pamphlet Luther blamed both the peasants and rulers.

There was one aspect of Lutheranism, however, that could be interpreted as politically revolutionary. One of the great appeals of the Reformation to the barons and thrones of Europe was the idea that the state had the responsibility of supervising the church. This Protestant teaching, of course, was diametrically opposed to the Catholic Church's teaching that the church had primacy in both spiritual and temporal matters. Certain Reformation states such as Sweden interpreted this new teaching as permission to use the clergy as their instruments.[6]

### Islamic civilization and the European state system

While the Reformation was gaining ground in Europe, the success or failure of this mobilization was influenced by events that were taking place thousands of miles away and tied to the fate of Islamic civilization, continuing to expand its empire. While the containment of the European forces led to internal conflict and state-making in Europe, Islam, after the defeat of the European Crusaders, was safe from European designs of conquest. The expansion of Islam occurred in India, where the existence of a powerful military Islamic force in the south was successful in establishing its rule. It overthrew the powerful and wealthy Hindu-based Indian state of Vijayanagar. In Java, the Islamic forces overthrew the Hindu ruling castes and established a state that was more clearly Islamic. A European threat came at the hands of the Portuguese military in Africa, but even in this apparent setback, in terms of military control of territory, the Islamic warriors expanded inward into the mainland of Africa; the Portuguese did not follow because they were inferior to the Islamic warriors on land.

In spite of the greater scope and power of the Islamic empire when compared to Europe, Islam too was experiencing its internal problems, and their eventual consequences would enhance the power of the Asian, Eurasian, and European civilizations. The factionalization within Islam differed from the type of factionalization that developed in the Christian world during the Reformation. We recall that the Reformation was caused, at least in part, by the struggle between a sacramental-based Christianity (Catholicism) and a scriptural-based Christianity (Lutheranism). It was a doctrinal debate, but one with profound political consequences: if God predestined a person to either salvation or damnation, as Luther argued, then the worshippers' use of priests had limited value at best and was illegitimate at worst. In contrast to the debate of the Reformation, the Sunni–Shiite conflict was over the question of who was the legitimate heir of Muhammad. The Shiites had established a power base with the Buyid rulers in Baghdad, and believed that the rightful successor to Muhammad was the son-in-law of Muhammad: Ali. The Sunnis, on the other hand, argued that the rightful heirs to Muhammad were the caliphs, who also claimed to be members of the Prophet's family.

This division between the Sunnis and the Shiites, which had a telling impact on the long-term future of Eastern and Western Europe, became more complex with the development of the mystical sect of the Sufi. The Sufi embraced the early caliphs Abu Bakr, Omar, and Othman as the legitimate institutional heirs to Muhammad. The Sufi spirituality, however, was more like the Shiites. The mysticism of the Sufi, with their emphasis on their special election and a more experiential mystical tradition, drew large numbers of followers to this branch of Sunnism. At the organizational level of this dispute, the Sunni caliphate possessed a stronger bureaucratic organization than did the minority Shiites. The tension between the Sunnis and the Shiites made it far more difficult to unite, even in the face of the Christian military threat.[7]

## Civilizational warfare: Ottoman civilization, the Habsburg empire, and the European state system

The Ottomans, who helped hasten the final destruction of Latin Christendom, claimed allegiance to the Sunni tradition. But the Shiite influence could not be eliminated: the mystical dervishes were embraced and this group was used to further the organizational cause of the dominant fifteenth-century Ottomans. The division between the Sunnis and the Shiites obstructed any Ottoman goal of conquering Europe. The Ottoman Sunnis could not underestimate the power of the Shiite minority. The militarily brilliant Isma'il Safavi scored a series of Shiite victories around his home by the southern Caspian Sea, and it threatened the ruling power of the Ottomans. Isma'il Safavi became the self-proclaimed shah; within the first 15 years of the sixteenth century, the Safavid dynasty dominated Persia.

This division within Islam protected Europe from a unified Islamic enemy. Ideologically, Isma'il I was a superb propagandist and inspiring leader. The ideology of his war-making and leadership was religious, based on the claimed superiority and authenticity of the Shiite beliefs and himself as the Shadow of God on Earth. Isma'il tried to conquer, rout out, torture, and murder the Sunnis. This charismatic hero inspired the entire Shiite community. He even created conflicts indirectly by inspiring warriors of the Shiite faith who were not under his direct control.

Isma'il was a great general, but, perhaps for reasons of chivalry, he refused to adopt artillery and handguns. He consequently suffered a stunning loss to the Ottoman forces and never again personally led troops in war. However, after quelling the Shiite uprising, the Sultan of the Ottomans decided to destroy its source. His forces continued eastward with the goal of defeating the core group of Safavis, but even after many victories, the Ottomans were still unsuccessful in crushing them.

The Safavid dynasty's empire threatened the Ottoman empire throughout the sixteenth century and impeded expansion into Europe. The Shiites were not at all ecumenical, and their idea of dialogue was war. They unabashedly supported the overthrow of the Ottoman empire and the crushing of the Sunnis whenever possible. The Shiite empire was able to consolidate its geopolitical advantages and solve the problem of the legitimacy of successors. Through Shah Abbas I of the Safavid dynasty, sometimes referred to as Abbas the Great, the Shiites reached the full extent of their power toward the end of the sixteenth century and retained it well into the seventeenth century. The Ottomans were successful in institutionalizing the Sunni branch of Islam in the east, but in the west the Shiites remained a viable force.

The threat to Europe from the Ottomans was more centralized than that from the Viking onslaught. In his challenge to Europe from the fifteenth century, the supreme leader of the Ottoman empire maintained an imperial household of non-Muslim slaves loyal only to the sultan. The Abbasid caliphate in Baghdad had used Turkish slaves in a similar manner in the eighth century.

The Ottomans' major opponent in Europe was the Habsburg dynasty, whose crowns wanted a unified Europe, and whose ambition it was to sustain and increase the power of the Spanish Catholic empire. While the scope of this ambition exceeded their realistic reach, the Habsburgs were nevertheless successful in establishing a great empire and political dynasty by means of shrewd political and economic marriages, turning them into military and political power.

The Habsburg leader most responsible for defending Europe against the Ottomans was Charles V. The marriage of the Ferdinand/Isabella family into the Habsburg dynasty shaped Europe. The union of these two powerful families put fear in the hearts of the English, French, Italian, and Scandinavian ruling elites.

Charles V began his royal career as Charles I of Spain, the offspring of Philip of Burgundy and the grandson of Emperor Maximilian I. Charles succeeded to the throne on the death of his maternal grandfather, Ferdinand of Aragon, to become King Charles I of Spain, and to establish the most powerful European empire of its time. He became the Holy Roman Emperor Charles V, arguably the most powerful emperor since Charlemagne. He ruled Spain and its colonies, and still held the Habsburg lands of Bohemia, Germany, Hungary, and the Low

Countries, as well as Naples in the southern part of Italy.

Many of the desires of the papacy coincided with the projects of the Spanish military, until the Habsburg–Valois wars. The papacy and the Habsburgs profited by ousting the Protestants from their footholds in Italy, mobilizing against the Reformation in Europe in what was to become known as the Counter-Reformation.

Charles V was not content with the worldwide empire that he and his grandparents had established. His vision of becoming the new Holy Roman Emperor led to a crisis within the Spanish crown. Charles V's goals were very simple to enunciate, but exceedingly difficult to institute. He wanted to maintain his empire, destroy the forces of the Reformation, and restore Europe under Catholicism. He saw the Catholic faith as a way of creating a spiritual and ideological community in much the same manner that Catholicism held together medieval Christendom. He would find, however, that the turmoil unleashed by the Reformation handicapped his goals. His project was fraught with difficulties from his conflicts with other German landholders, the political disruption of the Reformation, and the threat in the east from the Ottoman Turks. Conflict with the papacy, as well as wars with the French, also frustrated his designs.

The development of the standing army supplied the Habsburg empire with a significant advantage over the feudal army, where only nobles could be soldiers, a tradition dating back at least to the tribal confederation of Germany. Unfettered by this requirement, Spain and other societies had a numerical advantage over the armies of nobles. The sophisticated arms and war-making skills of the nobles were as nothing compared to the sheer power and numbers of mercenary armies.

Charles V exemplified the dilemma of internal macro versus external supermacro and universal tensions. He spent a great deal of his time and resources defending his empire against the Ottoman Turks as the Reformation gathered steam, while at the same time the enduring competition between the ruling families of the Valois and Habsburg dynasties caused other wars. Charles V's fight with the French was against Francis I, who was supported by the Ottomans, further complicating this situation. As we now perceive the various motives in this war,

France's goal was to obtain Habsburg territory. Francis I accurately foresaw the danger that France would be squeezed out of existence by the empire of Charles V. Although the attack never occurred, the latter had in fact signed the secret Treaty of Windsor, calling for England's Henry VIII to participate in the invasion of France.

The two ruling houses of the Habsburgs and the Valois also prized Italy as a trophy. By 1540 the Habsburgs controlled Milan and Lombardy, and the French controlled Savoy and Piedmont. Venice and Genoa had lost their preeminent positions but were able to maintain their oligarchic system of rule. Pope Clement VII, afraid of Charles V's aspirations in Italy, sided with Francis I; however, Charles's troops sacked Rome, forcing Clement VII to give up the papal states.

The Habsburgs brought one other skill to their efforts: their ability to raise capital would determine the success of this struggle, and the success of their wars with the Ottomans. Throughout the sixteenth century the Habsburgs and other thrones of Europe needed bankers to finance wars; and one clear way for a banker to make a fortune was to form alliances with the most powerful monarchs and make them loans. One of the wealthiest banking families during the sixteenth century was the Fuggers of Augsburg, who were originally merchants. Along with wealthy banking families of Italy, they engaged in lending money to monarchs, primarily to finance war-making operations. The Spanish crown financed the expensive Spanish Wars with loans from Antwerp, backing them up with Spanish "new world" resources. Thus once again we see the interrelationships among the defeats of the Crusades, the internal struggles of European monarchs, and the effect of explorations of the New World on European consolidation.

As the Fuggers learned, loans could work to the advantage of the lender, but could also lead to disaster: monarchs were notoriously fickle in repaying their debts. The case of Jacob Fugger the Rich, who was the banker of Charles V, illustrates the danger. Initial repayments from Charles V allowed Jacob Fugger to make a fortune in precious metals from mines, but later Charles V decided not to repay a loan, which drove Fugger into bankruptcy.

By the fifteenth century, European civilization was bracing

itself for an assault from the Ottomans, who were challenging the powerful Italian sea force. They launched a series of attacks against the Republic of Venice that lasted 16 years. In 1477, in one siege, the Ottomans made a land assault and reached the Italian peninsula; they were so close to Venice that the Venetian senators could observe the Ottoman campfires and the flames from the villages that the Ottomans had set on fire. In another attack against Italy, the Ottomans captured Otranto, in the south. Venice and Turkey were in the early pangs of a protracted conflict (the Venetian–Turkish War of 1499–1502) that would give the Ottomans one of the most dangerous footholds in Europe; indeed Venice lost a number of trading outposts in the action.

The Ottomans solved many of their own internal problems when they found a great general in Selim the Grim, whose success in consolidating Islamic power provided a viable threat to Europe. Selim the Grim's Ottomans faced many obstacles during their years of expansion: they had to contend not only with the Shiite soldiers in Morocco, but also with the forces of Spain that were militarily active at the beginning of the sixteenth century. Selim's central religious goal was to eliminate Shiism. He defeated the Shah of Persia, and, with a single military expedition, his forces conquered and ended the Mamluk dynasty in Egypt. During this period, the Ottomans also conquered the religious centers of Islam: Mecca and Medina. Selim I's forces were also able to gain parts of Africa. The caliphate had passed to the Ottoman sultanate; Selim I was now Islam's most powerful leader.

Suleiman the Lawgiver, or, as he was known to the West, Suleiman the Magnificent, had ascended to the sultanate in 926/1520, after the death of Selim I, and he would earn both respect and fear from all surrounding civilizations. The Sunnis in the Ottoman empire and the Mogul state in India had established theocratic bureaucracies. Suleiman the Lawgiver refined theocratic rule in the Ottoman empire. Internationally, he immediately began to erode Habsburg power by establishing friendly ties with Venice and France and granting trading rights to Francis I. His coalition with France hurt his great Habsburg rival, Charles V, who spent a great deal of his time and resources battling Suleiman the Magnificent.

The Ottoman Turks were able to penetrate into the Byzantine empire. By the middle of the fourteenth century they controlled large areas of Byzantine territory and the Balkans. In 1453, as we explored earlier, they backtracked and conquered Constantinople. After this victory, they turned their sights on the West, targeting Austria, Bohemia, Hungary, and Poland. Force was exerted on the Danube region, all around the area of Turkey and Greece, and in the Mediterranean as well.

During these wars the Ottomans captured many Christian prisoners and large areas of Europe came under their control. Up until the seventeenth century, they continued the practice of taking away male children of their Christian prisoners or conquered populations and training them to be either soldiers or courtiers. This policy served the political purpose of solidifying Ottoman rule with the Christian inhabitants. The Christians could at least see some of their relatives in the Ottoman court, and perhaps also see some of their interests reflected in the policies enacted there. The Ottomans could be very tolerant of other religions, just as long as the tax revenues continued to flow. Indeed, during the sixteenth century, Jews who suffered persecution from Christians found refuge in the Ottoman empire. It was possible on occasion for some Jews to rise to the level of court official or advisor in the Ottoman state, particularly in the fields of finance and politics.

The Ottomans conquered large expanses of Eastern Europe, attacked Hungary and other states in the general vicinity of the Black Sea, and absorbed Bosnia. The execution of Stephen of Bosnia, who had ties to the Latin Church, was viewed as an attack on the Catholic West by Rome.

It was in 1526 that the Ottomans, led by Suleiman the Lawgiver, overran Hungary and killed Louis II of Hungary and Bohemia. With this foothold in Eastern Europe, Suleiman the Lawgiver pressed on into Austria. It is not clear what prevented Suleiman from overrunning Vienna (after taking Güns 60 miles away), but it is clear that Suleiman wanted to engage Charles V's army. Finding no imperial army to attack he waited three weeks for Charles V's forces to engage him, then retreated. Perhaps it was the strong defenses that he had come across, the heavy losses he anticipated in taking Vienna, or the coming of winter that caused his withdrawal. With Suleiman the Lawgiver's offensives, however, the Ottoman empire reached a new pinnacle of power. Suleiman used Venetian envoys for intelligence rather as the Mongols had used the Venetians in the thirteenth century. To the dismay of the Emperor's brother Ferdinand, Archduke of Austria (and since January 1531 the so-called King of the Romans), the Emperor conceded Hungary to the Ottoman empire, although Charles V held a small frontier there.

Alongside rational military considerations was the battle of egos. Suleiman the Lawgiver tried to reduce Charles V's empire because he feared that Charles V, and not himself, would be the "Lord of the Age." For his part, Charles V, recognizing the Ottoman threat to Europe, came to terms with the Lutherans for military purposes because of his conflict with the Ottomans. Ironically, then, the Islamic Ottoman empire became an asset to the Reformation. With the attack of the Ottomans in Hungary, Charles V established the Peace of Nuremburg in May 1532, a peace that ensured there would be no state convictions for religious practices or beliefs without a council being held to investigate these charges.

With the support of this resolution by the Protestants, it was possible for Charles V to counter the Turkish threat by raising the largest army ever seen in Europe, comprised of both Catholics and Protestants. With this, Austria would be liberated. The meeting of the two great generals never took place. Charles V did not launch an offensive attack; the Christian forces waited for Suleiman I 200 miles from Vienna, up the Danube in Ratisbon. To the relief of the anxious Christians, Suleiman, perhaps realizing that the army that Charles V had amassed was larger than the force that had previously deterred his advance on Vienna, did not put the situation to the military test, but instead returned to Istanbul.

The Ottomans saw another Western threat in the form of the Knights Hospitallers, based on Rhodes, which the Ottomans had earlier attacked without success. The knights had become pirates, attacking and plundering Ottoman ships. After a siege of Rhodes, the Ottomans obtained their objective when they established peace with the Knights Hospitallers on Ottoman terms, between late 1522 and early 1523. One concession the Ottomans made was to allow safe passage to the Grand Master of the Hospitallers from Rhodes.

After the non-battle of Vienna, Suleiman I still had the ambition of beating the "King of Spain" to be the "Lord of the Age." He shifted his strategy from using his land-based forces to building a navy, realizing that the Ottoman naval forces were lagging behind the navies of non-Ottoman Europe. Indeed, the European naval forces began to poach on Ottoman territories through a series of raids led by the brilliant Genoese Admiral Andrea Doria, a recent ally of the Habsburgs.

In this effort, Suleiman recruited the great Khaireddin Barbarossa as his head admiral. As part of an all-out ship-building effort, and to slow and reverse Habsburg expansion into the eastern Mediterranean, Suleiman I and Barbarossa established a coalition with the French that counterbalanced the powerful Habsburg navy.

As the first gambit in the naval battle, the Ottomans launched a string of diversionary attacks in Italy and the Kingdom of Naples. Their real objective was to secure a network of harbors throughout the southern Mediterranean, thereby controlling the entire north African coast from Gibraltar to Tripoli. Tunis was the key that united the network to the east and to the west. Barbarossa succeeded in capturing Tunis in August of 1534, making it his naval base of operations.

Charles's first move was political. Discerning the deeper pattern beneath the diversionary attacks, he saw that, should the Ottomans achieve their aim, they could strangle Sicily and with it Habsburg control of the Mediterranean. Initially preferring intrigue to actual war, Charles V tried a three-pronged envoy/spy strategy to break up the Ottoman harbor chain. With the help of the deposed ruler of Tunis, Muley Hassan, Charles V sent one of his Genoese envoys to act as a spy and organizer. The envoy's goal was to organize an insurgency movement against the occupying forces of Barbarossa. Should this plan fail, the envoy would attempt to bribe Barbarossa, or, depending on the circumstances, assassinate him. Unfortunately for Charles V (and his envoy), Barbarossa's forces uncovered the plot against the Ottomans and killed the

envoy. Now open conflict was necessary for the forces of
Charles V to break the Ottomans' naval bid to control the
Mediterranean.

Andrea Doria led an international fleet against the
Ottomans at Tunis. During the naval battle that ensued, many
of Barbarossa's ships were destroyed. Barbarossa himself
escaped and linked up with a reserve fleet. In a bold move
requiring great military ingenuity, Barbarossa avoided re-
attacking Tunis, instead heading northwest to the Habsburg-
controlled Balearic Islands. Cleverly disguising the Ottoman
ships by flying Spanish and Italian flags, Barbarossa's forces
sacked the harbor town of Mago and made the Christians
prisoners. Barbarossa destroyed the military capacity of the
harbor and took back to Algiers the treasures he captured.
The message was clear: the defeat of Tunis had not decisively
changed the strategical balance in the western Mediterranean
in favor of the Habsburgs; Barbarossa could still strike with
impunity.

The Sultan set out to replenish the ships destroyed by the
Habsburg forces in this contest. By 1537 he had built a new,
larger fleet. The new plan was to conquer Venetian landholdings and eventually Venice itself. Once again Charles V assem-
bled a huge international armada. Barbarossa, perhaps a
student of history, used the same strategy Octavian had
applied 1,500 years earlier to defeat Anthony and Cleopatra
in the battle of Actium. But Andrea Doria did not want history to repeat itself. He did not enter the gulf beyond the point
of Actium, where the greater number of his European ships
would lack mobility and be faced with fire from the Turkish
galleons. Likewise, Barbarossa did not leave the secure gulf,
where the greater number of European ships with their superior warfare technology would be waiting.

The result of this standoff was a de facto victory for the
Ottomans. The Europeans had failed to eliminate the
Ottoman threats to Venice, which had to withdraw from the
Habsburg alliance and form a new strategical configuration
with France and the Ottomans.[8]

*Civilizational and macro warfare: the Reformation,
religious wars in Europe, and the decline of Catholic state
power*

Charles V's need to forge an international army to fight the
Ottomans, combined with his weak control over the German
princes, gave the Reformation a good foothold in Germany. In
spite of the religious differences and mutual animosity between
Protestants and Muslims, it is logical that one of the planks of
Ottoman    international    strategy    was    to    support    the
Reformation. Offers of military support were made to the
Lutheran princes in the Low Countries and other territories
under Habsburg control.

The Diet of Worms in April 1521 focused the complexities
of Charles's position. While Charles V denounced Luther, the
powerful Elector of Saxony protected him. Charles V did not
want a war with Germany, given his other problems with
France and the Ottomans and his precarious financial situation, but his only hope was to use force to end the German
Reformation.

The Reformation rapidly crossed national boundaries and
spread    throughout    Europe.    In    Switzerland,    where    the
Zwinglian Reformation had its origins, political units known
as cantons warred over the religious issue. Although ordained a
priest, Zwingli denounced the Catholic Church in his theology,
becoming one of the leading figures in the Reformation in
Switzerland. To spread the doctrine, Zwingli and his followers
turned one of the most successful Catholic apostolic strategies
to the reformers' advantage. During the high Middle Ages, the
Dominicans had publicly challenged the "heretics" to debate
theology with them. In a similar manner, the followers of
Ulrich Zwingli called on Catholics to debate the Catholic
Church's position on central issues. The reformers had a huge
advantage in these debates, in that the Catholic Church had
centuries of corruption for the Zwinglians to criticize. With no
such historical record themselves to defend, the Zwinglians
were able to convert controversy into victories in debate, in
turn transforming these victories into popular and political
power, pressuring the canons to legitimize the preaching of the
Zwinglians.

Zwingli's reform movement was particularly successful in the urban areas of Switzerland, where his teachings appealed to the wielders of power. They could use these reforms to prevent the Catholic Church meddling in their economic and political affairs, emphasizing its corruption. Zwingli's message, however, was not so compelling to those in the Swiss rural areas who heard his cries for reform. There was a strong feeling of solidarity among parishioners, and loyalty to the Pope: many of the Catholic priests were relatives of the parishioners in such areas.

The Habsburgs, who were eager to defeat the Reformation, saw this difference in strength of support as a possible opening in which to create dissension. To counteract the Habsburgs' divide-and-conquer strategy in a number of Swiss cantons, Zwingli's forces attempted to thwart the alliance between Habsburgs and rural cantons by putting in place a countervailing balance-of-power approach. His forces attempted to forge political and military alliances with German barons who would act as protectors and advocates of Lutheranism. Thus the existing threats to both the German and Swiss reform movements from the Catholics in general, and Habsburgs in particular, initially served as an aid to cooperation among the reformers.

Given this ferment, a civil war broke out in Switzerland between the forces supporting Catholicism and the reformers supporting Zwingli. The defeat of the Zwinglian forces in the fall of 1531, and the death of Zwingli in battle, slowed the expansion of the Reformation in Switzerland, but did not stop the movement entirely. In retrospect, we see that the Zwinglians lost their real battle earlier, in religious debate, when they could not forge a successful theological agreement between the Lutherans and themselves. The Zwinglians believed in only a symbolic presence of Christ, whereas the Lutherans believed in the real presence of Christ in the bread that Protestants used to recreate the Last Supper. Because of their failure to agree on theology, no permanent political or military alliance was possible.

Let us now take up again the factors that resulted in the French wars of religion during the sixteenth century. In France the Valois monarchy was strong; through the leadership of Francis I and Henry II, the House of Valois skillfully used a mercenary army to expand their power. In addition, by controlling appointments within the national church hierarchy, it was able to keep the power of Rome at a minimum without resorting to breaking with the Catholic Church. The Valois were also able to work out an effective taxation system. The complexion of this situation changed with the accidental death of Henry II at a tournament in 1559. Although he was eventually succeeded by his sons, they were rulers in name only: Catherine de' Medici, a member of the famous Italian banking family, wielded the true power as the virtual ruler of France for two decades.

The French crown, highly intolerant of the growing Reformation, persecuted the reformers but failed to stop the spread of Protestantism. Once the Protestant Reformation had started, it continued until about half of all the French nobles became Huguenots – including the House of Bourbon, next in the line of royal succession to the Valois.

The House of Valois viewed the Protestant Bourbons as dangerous rivals. Regent Catherine de' Medici tried to keep peace by working out an agreement in which religious tolerance would be a central feature of her rule. The problem she faced was that the contesting religious parties were unwilling to compromise. At one extreme, the powerful Guise family, supported by the Pope, bought an army of mercenaries to help them lead the ultra-Catholics. While the stated intentions of this papal/ultra-Catholic alliance were to oppose the Huguenots, it threatened the Valois ruling family as well.

These political developments at the macro level in France had ramifications at the supermacro and universal levels. The Huguenots fought the Catholics and the nobles challenged the monarchy because, with no stake in the crown, they were eager to join a movement that promised more power. Internationally, Spain had a king who supported the Guise family's ultra-Catholic position: King Philip II, who had succeeded Charles V. The English under Elizabeth I, on the other hand, were pro-Protestant. She sided with the Huguenots, even though there was no love lost between her and the Calvinists. It was just a convenient way to drive a wedge into the ruling coalition of the Valois monarchy, and to strike at Philip II's ambitions to overthrow Elizabeth I. Since the ultra-Catholics were against the more moderate strategy of dialogue, reconciliation, and compromise advocated by the Regent Catherine de' Medici, her efforts failed. The ultra-Catholics and Huguenots mobilized for war.

In England, Queen Elizabeth I's strategy of quietly supporting the Protestants was successful in hurting the French monarchy. First, the conflict between the ultra-Catholics and the Huguenots prevented the expansion of the French abroad. Second, the international ideology of religion for a time eclipsed the growing national identity that the French had forged during the Hundred Years War with England.

War finally commenced in the year 1562, when the Duke of Guise attacked a group of Huguenots. This short-lived victory for the ultra-Catholics did very little to eradicate the Huguenots, who were well armed and well organized and put up strong resistance. The Huguenots posed no threat to the French monarchy: they could not possibly defeat the coalition of ultra-Catholics, with their support from Philip II, Jesuits, the Pope, and the ample resources of the French throne itself. Still, even with the crown's forces and the ultra-Catholics and their supporters ranged against them, the Huguenots were powers that kept the Valois – attempting to keep the various groups under royal control – in a state of disarray.[9]

### *The Reformation wars in England, and the eradication of the political system of Latin Christendom*

The Reformation in England was the direct result of the battle between King Henry VIII and the papacy over Henry VIII's attempts to get the church to legitimize his divorce. As the Pope refused to recognize the divorce, Henry VIII broke with Rome, and the Tudor monarch became the official leader of society, the state, and the church, a centralizing dynamic that was to bring England into modern times. Henry had the power to absorb the lands held by the Roman Catholic Church and Roman Catholic nobles. Centralization reached a feverish pace when the architect of the new kind of state, Thomas Cromwell, moved to consolidate Henry VIII's power by violently taking over church lands. Henry VIII, now the undisputed ruler of all England, was able to increase the holdings in his treasury as

Cromwell absorbed the noble's resources into the King's coffers.

In 1553, the Catholic, Mary I, the new Queen of England, taking a course decidedly at odds with the direction of her time, alienated the English people by marrying one of the enemies of Protestant England, Spain's Philip II. In the attempt to restore Catholicism as the official religion of England, her methods earned her the name Bloody Mary. She set about ruthlessly killing Protestants, ordering the execution of several hundred "heretics" who refused to accept Catholicism. By the time of the crowning of Elizabeth I, Mary I's strategy had greatly increased social solidarity among reformers, and provoked hatred toward Catholics.

The English religious wars spread to the supermacro level with the rise of Elizabeth I, Henry's daughter from his marriage to Ann Boleyn, and Elizabeth's battle with Philip II and the throne in France. With his marriage to Jane Seymour, Henry VIII was finally able to get the male heir he had long desired, the future King Edward VI, but in spite of this great happiness, it was Elizabeth Tudor, not Edward VI, who was responsible for England's enlarging its empire, and who proved to be the most effective ruler among Henry VIII's offspring.

Elizabeth I was as shrewd as any monarch in history, a great woman known for her political acumen. She continued the Tudor policy of forming a coalition with the gentry against the barons; her foreign policy was masterful; and during her reign she was a major patron of the cultural flowering of the English Renaissance. Unlike Mary I, of whose policies she was a prudent observer, Elizabeth I had learned to promote religious tolerance while at the same time increasing her population's devotion and obedience to the throne. Her goal was to restore the political stability that both Edward VI and Bloody Mary had lost during their reigns. Although the Act of Uniformity made Protestantism the state religion, the informal position of the throne was one of tolerance.

While promoting religious tolerance, however, Elizabeth I denied the Catholic Church's authority in matters of state. In the case of any conflict over religious or political issues, Elizabeth I and not the papacy would decide the fate of England. The Act of Supremacy emphatically stated that the throne was the sole arbiter in things temporal and religious.

Elizabeth's political tolerance was the official state policy, but social dynamics did not always put that tolerance into practice. Protestant nobles and commoners had suffered extreme persecution under the reign of Mary I; they were not ready to forgive and forget. The supermacro climate also worked against the normalization of relations between Catholics and Protestants. The Puritan branch of the Anglican Church, fast becoming a powerful social force in England, argued that the Church of England would have to purify itself from its last traces of Catholicism. Puritans believed there was still too much hierarchy in the church, and held that the Church of England was merely Catholicism in a new package.

Elizabeth I recruited talented aides in her efforts to deal with Catholic/Protestant tensions and supermacro and universal level politics: Sir William Cecil and Sir Francis Walsingham were the successors of Thomas Cromwell, whom Henry VIII had executed. She kept the dissatisfaction of the landed aristocracy at a low ebb, limiting the power of Parliament so effectively that it convened only 13 times during her rule.

One other important political strategy of the Queen should be noted: war was the sport of monarchs, but Elizabeth I preferred the nonmilitary growth of her supermacro power, and tried to strike a public pose of neutrality in this arena. In reality, however, and in private, she was far from neutral. She was able to maintain a massive intelligence network by means of which she promoted clandestine war in the form of piracy. She also provided covert resources to her allies, the Huguenots in France and the Calvinists in the Spanish Netherlands. Through this aid, she eroded the power of both France and Spain. In her public pronouncements and in her formal diplomatic moves, she continued to feign neutrality until 1585, when she broke this stance and engaged in formal military actions against Spain.[10]

*The Reformation, the Ottoman empire, and the failure to restore a Europe-wide Catholic political structure*

English Protestants viewed the Spanish king, Philip II, the son and the heir of Charles V, as the true face of Catholicism. His stated goal was to conquer England, and in addition, like his father, he aimed to create a Catholic empire. In the latter, Philip II succeeded, ushering in the Golden Age of Spain, the age of the country's international leadership in both the political and cultural realms. Like his father, he was also the target of Ottoman intrigue, since the Ottomans covertly supported England, the Netherlands, and Protestants in general in their struggles with Spain.

During the first 20 years of his reign, Philip II had to deal with Islam at the universal level of conflict. The Ottoman threat in the Mediterranean, as well as the allied Barbary pirate attacks on Spanish galleons, drained the already troubled Spanish economy. The Ottomans and the Barbary states had formidable navies, and only the harsh winters kept them from eliminating Spanish shipping in the Mediterranean. After defeat in a battle with a Turkish fleet in which over 40 ships were lost, Philip II mobilized Italian shipbuilders to rebuild his massive navy, and hired additional naval forces from Italy and Portugal. By 1564, Spain had regained the initiative in the western Mediterranean; after 1565, the Ottomans could no longer claim naval supremacy in that area.

By 1566, a crisis had developed in one of Philip II's most prized possessions, the Spanish Netherlands, a crisis that complicated the situation at the universal level and prevented a total war against Islamic Ottoman civilization. From the eleventh to the seventeenth centuries the Low Countries were one of the centers of European economic power. Philip II had very little interest in the day-to-day dealings of the people in the Netherlands; he saw them essentially as a source of tax revenues and wealth. But Charles V's wars had placed Spain in a terrible financial situation, and local members of the Netherlands landed aristocracy, who wielded considerable power, began to oppose the continual tax drain that Philip II used to finance Spanish empire-building.

Returning for a moment to the religious and political dimensions of the Reformation, we note that the nobles of the Spanish Netherlands were ripe for conversion to Protestantism. As other nobles had done throughout Europe, many Dutch landowners who wanted to worship without interference from what they viewed as a corrupt church turned to Calvinism. In the disagreement regarding Spanish taxation, Protestantism created a sense of solidarity among the nobles who opposed Spain.

Again, the Ottomans supported the Reformation to constrain and divert Habsburg attention away from the Spanish–Ottoman confrontation. As the tensions between Spain and the Netherlands mounted, the Ottomans helped the Dutch Calvanists by opening the vast markets of the Ottoman empire to them, thus weakening Philip II's hand in the Mediterranean. This war, now fought on two fronts, was too much for Spanish resources. Philip II moved away from the expeditions of Charles V to contain the Ottomans by fortifying existing fortresses with increased mortar and bricks. With increased Spanish restriction on the Netherlands, Protestants embraced more militantism and radicalism.

Between 1567 and 1568, animosity toward Spain increased when Philip II moved to take over the Dutch-based control of the Catholic Church, and to crush the growing Calvinist movement, adding fuel to the religious/political dispute. The discontent erupted into violence against Catholics and the destruction and desecration of the symbols of Catholicism. Churches, statues, and artifacts within Catholic churches became targets for the reformers. Arriving from Spain in 1567, the Duke of Alba was to become a hated figure in the Reformation circles of the Spanish Netherlands, and a source of increased friction between the Netherlands and Spain. Nobles were already hostile to Spain, and Philip continued to alienate the bourgeoisie by instituting a new sales tax in 1571. This extra financial burden on the economy of the Spanish Netherlands acted as a catalyst for a society-wide liberation movement. It manifested itself in several ways. First, the Netherlands issued state securities to finance military opposition to the Spanish crown. Second, those nobles who sided with the Spanish monarch became particularly hated members of Dutch society. Finally, a nationalist leader was found. William the Silent, who was formally William of Nassau, the Prince of Orange, played a large organizational role in this anti-Spanish and anti-Catholic insurrection. The nobles under his leadership destroyed Catholic churches. Philip II responded by dispatching approximately

10,000 troops led by the Duke of Alba, the general of these mercenaries.

A very powerful secret tribunal in the Netherlands, known as the Council of Troubles, moved to institute a type of guerrilla organization to liberate the Netherlands from Spain. Under the leadership of William of Orange, the Dutch made efforts to regain some of the resources that they had lost as tax revenues. This effort was particularly effective in the north, with the development of a fleet of Dutch pirate ships, the Sea Beggars.

The revolutionary moment seemed to be at hand when William of Orange was able to provide a statement of independence known as the Pacification of Ghent (1576). According to this document, all 17 provinces would unite under his rule. The new independent nation would allow religious freedom. After this failure for Spain in the Netherlands, the Duke of Alba was recalled by Philip II in 1573, then returned to duty in 1580 as the commander of the invading force against Portugal. In this attack Philip II backed up his hereditary claims on Portugal with military might.

The incipient Calvinist revolution, however, had not taken enough account of the ultra-Catholic presence in the Netherlands, which viewed a strong Protestant state as a development worse than a Catholic state under the domination of Spain. The politically astute Alexander Farnese, Duke of Parma, who eventually became the new Governor General of the Netherlands after the Duke of Alba's departure, correctly assessed that the Netherlands was not uniformly under the leadership of William of Orange. He used the ancient political strategy of "divide and conquer" in his efforts to crush the revolutionary movement. He was able to play on the differences between the ultra-Catholics and the Protestants to interfere with the liberation mobilization, a strategy that wreaked religious and political havoc on William of Orange's unified front. The nobles in the southern Netherlands made peace with Farnese, but the northeastern provinces remained independent from Spain.

On the civilization level, once again the Ottomans tried to take advantage of the diversion created by the uprisings in the Spanish Netherlands and the Islamic mobilization against

Philip II in Grenada. In the face of Ottoman expansion, the states in Europe unified to some degree to ward off the Turkish threat. Supported by trade with the Ottoman empire, France and England stayed aloof. In 1570 the Ottomans attacked the Venetian possession of Cyprus. Philip II tried to respond with a hastily put together fleet composed of Italian and Spanish ships, but the "liberation" fleet turned back after meeting bad weather, and after hearing reports of the further success of the Ottomans in Cyprus. Pope Pius V started negotiations with Philip II and his ministers to plan an attack on the Ottomans. His argument to Philip was that the Mediterranean frontiers of the Venetians were buffers that protected Spain. Philip II, bowing to these and other political and financial considerations, agreed; Venice, Spain, and the forces of the papacy eventually formed a military alliance, the Holy League.

Europe was able to halt Ottoman expansion in the victorious battle of Lepanto in October 1571, where a smaller European force destroyed the Ottoman fleet. The resulting Peace of Buda was arguably the first comprehensive peace settlement in modern times, yet within three years the Ottomans were again a power in the Mediterranean.

In England, Spain faced the government of Elizabeth I, which, by 1580, had established cooperation with the Ottoman empire to prevent Habsburg domination of Europe. This coalition had economic overtones as well. Throughout the seventeenth century, Ottoman trade rivaled trade with India in its importance for England. For reasons difficult to fathom, Philip II believed that the English were primarily Catholic, that under Mary I's rule they had been truly happy, but that Elizabeth I's policies had forced Protestantism on the English people. Gradually he came to believe (or perhaps this was just a pretense that legitimized his attack on England) that the English people were waiting for him to liberate them. In a disastrous campaign, Spain unleashed its naval forces against England in 1588. The destruction of the Spanish Armada, though far from ending the imperial rule of Spain, ended Philip II's dream of a Catholic empire that included England. After the failed attack, Protestant threats forced many Catholics out of England.

Throughout his reign, Philip II engaged in state centralization, not always to the benefit of his administration. Perhaps

because of his sense of duty, or his mistrust of the landed aristocracy and staff, he was unwilling to delegate assignments to
his courtiers; his administration often became bogged down by
his empire-wide correspondence and the detailed policy direc-
tives he gave to his subordinates. Unlike Charles V, Philip II
was more truly the King of Spain than the Emperor of the
Habsburg empire. He was successful in gaining control of the
military, which the landed aristocracy had previously controlled, and internally, he furthered political centralization
through his own repressive apparatus. His power was
increased by the legitimation of the Catholic Church, allowing
him to use the Spanish Inquisition to achieve his ends. In addition, he moved toward further centralization through the control of his 66 *corregidores*, who, at least in Castile, dominated
the town councils.[11]

### The aftermath of the Reformation: parliaments, absolutism, and the middle classes as a political force

The aftermath of the Reformation saw the flow of two broad
political currents: on the one hand, the vastly enhanced power
of the crown, and on the other, the increased effectiveness and
influence of the parliament. Of all the nations in Western
Europe south of Scandinavia, only Italy and the Germanic
areas did not develop strong monarchies and their accompany-
ing parliamentary structures. Parliament at this time represented a victory for the landed elites over the crown, although in
the long run, through the power of the franchise, it would help
to destroy the power of the crown as well as that of the landed
classes. Increasingly, the throne had to deal with the landed
aristocracy as a legal and legislative entity, and not as a force
that could be silenced by military might.

The rise of a powerful parliament in England also influenced
the middle classes in France. The revolutionary period in
England between 1640 and 1688 slowed the growth of the
crown. Not precisely a democratizing force in England by com-
parison with modern democracy, parliament to some extent
reinstated the rule of the feudal landed elites as a national
force. In the aftermath of the English Civil War between 1642

and 1648, made possible by the linkages between the nobles and the merchant class, the landed aristocracy was able to put limits on the power of the British monarchy. In France, the English example gave the aristocracy reason to reconsider the position of the landed elite in society: landowners in England had regained power that their French counterparts had lost with the growing centralization of the French crown.

The landed elites were instrumental in the development of a parliament: it transformed them into a viable national political power. Both the crown and the landowners in parliament needed the cooperation of the rising middle classes, or at the very least to be able to coerce them into doing their bidding. It was not always easy to bring pressure on these rich cotton manufacturers, bankers, and traders, including slave traffickers, who were beginning to have an impact on the political process. With their vast wealth, capitalists could successfully lobby parliament, or receive political favors after loans of money, gifts, or bribes to the crown and the parliamentarians.

This parliamentary dynamic tended to give the well-to-do a far more powerful political presence in England than their counterparts enjoyed in the more centralized regimes of France, Prussia, or Austria. In France, it was more prestigious for a commoner to achieve a position as a high state official (which granted de facto nobility) than to accumulate wealth in the role of a merchant or banker. This was not the case in England, where the lines between the landed elites and the commercial and financial classes became blurred.

The seventeenth century was the century of the Netherlands, England, and France in Europe. In France, with the ascension of Henry IV to the throne, the crown was successful in solidifying the control of the monarchy there. Unlike the case of Spain, where the monarch and the Catholic Church worked in tandem, there was tension with the papacy during the expansion of the crown's power. This is hardly to say that the church was without power in France: during the reign of Louis XIII, Cardinal Richelieu served as the chief minister to the crown. Richelieu took sides that sometimes supported and sometimes contradicted the position of the Catholic Church, and when it suited him, that of France as well. His general goal was the expansion of royal power. Richelieu ordered the French army to crush nobles and elements of the capitalist class that tried to resist the growth of the centralized state.

In contrast to the centralized parliament in England and the bureaucratic absolutism of France, Holland had a decentralized form of government in the period between the sixteenth and seventeenth centuries. Holland was a confederation of towns, the products of Holland's Middle Ages, dominated by middle-class burghers who had a strong say in the governing of the state. Whereas in France the crown hired the middle classes but was less willing to give them autonomy in the city itself, in the Netherlands, the power of the burghers made this the first truly capitalist state in the early modern era. In England the balance of these two forces was different: the burghers could not so easily overthrow the landed aristocracy, who were able to hang on to much of their power during this period. There was constant tension between the two groups, and the merchant class did not enjoy the political power of the Dutch bourgeoisie.

At the supermacro level, the international banking firms became the great cross-national power that linked merchants throughout Europe, particularly in the areas of the great banks and their headquarters in Florence, Venice, Augsburg, Ulm, and Genoa. Venetian merchant bankers early in this process created close to a monopoly in international exchange and credit, before the rise of other international banking houses.[12]

## The Blocked and Contracted East and the Line of Least Resistance to the West

The Ottoman land block led Europe to attempt to expand into Asia and Eurasia, yet for various reasons the attempts to build empires in this direction failed for the time being.

### China

The deft political hand of the Manchus limited the impact of Europe in China. The Manchus recognized that Japan, not Europe, was the true threat to China. The whole landscape of Chinese society changed with the rise of a powerful military force in Manchuria and its overthrow of the Ming dynasty, which itself had defeated the Mongols. The Manchurians, the regime that would face both Europe and Eurasia, took much of the seventeenth century to achieve their objective of ruling China. Seeing themselves as military leaders first and foremost, the Manchus had no real interest in governing, and allowed the conquered government to continue to function.

Military troops, not parliaments, enforced the social order of China under Manchu power. These troops – the Banner – answered directly to the Manchu warlord, who was the emperor. The Banner mobilized throughout the Chinese kingdom, and maintained a form of martial law. The Chinese administration that the Manchus had left intact extracted taxes from peasants and gave these taxes back to the emperor. Likewise, the administration and its army of bureaucrats supervised the Chinese merchants who traded with the Europeans; the administration received goods from these merchants, and the emperor then "received" these goods from the administration. The Manchus, however, did not give up their monopoly of military power. While allowing the lower leadership of the military ranks to be staffed by the Chinese, the Manchus reserved the highest ranks for themselves.

Russian warriors challenged China after the Manchus – Manchurian and Tibetan Steppe warriors – had consolidated their power. Cossack soldiers who had moved into Siberia by the seventeenth century viewed China as a potential military target. However, the Russians limited their excursions into the Steppes, the home territory of the Manchurians and Tibetans, in order to avoid a war that would distract Russia from its dealings with Western Europe.

Although China eventually contained the Russian danger, new threats sailed in from Europe and Japan. The Chinese were masters at combining isolation with external coalitions, to protect themselves and to maintain their own independence. An excellent example of this procedure was China's strategy in dealing with European and Japanese threats: they courted the favor of the Europeans, in part because the Europeans were also enemies of the Japanese. The Europeans in turn were eager for this coalition, because the Japanese pirate force was disruptive to European trade.

While the Chinese viewed most Western Europeans as uncultured barbarians, they made exceptions for Western European intellectuals, particularly the Jesuit scientists. The Chinese intellectuals during the Manchu reign were Confucianists. As Weber and others have shown, the reason for the success of these intellectuals in the court was the formalism and manners of Confucianism. This philosophy, whose precepts developed the perfect bureaucrat, impressed the Manchus with its decorum, tact, and obedience, traits so admired that the Manchus allowed it to become the dominant ethical force in the empire. In many ways, the Jesuits were similar to the Confucianists, sharing an understanding of hierarchy and obedience to their superiors. They took part in many of the cultural activities of the Chinese, and were able to adapt well to court life. They were prudent in concealing their missionary zeal, a too visible display of which could cost them their lives.

The Manchu court held these European intellectuals in such high repute that the Jesuits became part of the imperial court, with access to the Emperor himself. They participated in astronomical and other scientific research with the Chinese intellectuals. In sum, there was a distinct type of dialogue that occurred among the Jesuit scholars, the Chinese intellectuals, and the Manchu ruling class.

Europe had few prospects of either conquering China or making permanent economic outposts there. Trade led to growing imports of Chinese goods into Europe and the Americas, and to the development of a larger Chinese industrial base. Italian maritime traders were successful in making fortunes shipping the limited exports from China that the Manchu regime allowed, and soon learned that the bourgeoisie of China lacked the prestige and power of their European counterparts. Internally, the military imperial courtiers and intellectuals had higher standing than did the merchants or craftspersons who made trade with Europe possible.[13]

## Japan

The West was only marginally successful in influencing Japan in political, cultural, and economic terms. Once again Europe made its presence felt through the missionary efforts of the Jesuits. Japanese society of the sixteenth century had an ostensible ruler, more of an illusion than a reality; in practice, the country consisted of a series of feudal fiefdoms constantly battling with each other. A dominant ruling family could not emerge from this never-ending conflict; no existing ruling power was strong enough to intervene.

Because of this war of "all against all," Japanese society was even more militaristic than Western feudalism. Each class, too, was in a state of war with the other classes – one of the central battles was the conflict between the Buddhist monk warriors and the warrior class proper. Members of the samurai class were warriors by profession, and they eventually defeated the opposition force of monks and peasants. The unity of the samurai class broke up, however, as they fought to determine the dominant group among themselves. The military faction led by the samurai warrior Hideyoshi was ultimately successful. Hideyoshi started his career as a young boy who looked after the horses of the samurai. Through patronage, his own ingenuity, and luck, he rose to become the most powerful leader in Japan.

Another powerful leader, Ieyasu, was the founder of the Tokugawa Shogunate, which followed Hideyoshi's successful mobilization for national unity. The rise of the Shoguns had important ramifications for European imperialism. Ieyasu was mentored by Hideyoshi and was always respectful to his senior, even when he succeeded him. However, Ieyasu's ideals and political strategies were different from Hideyoshi's. The latter was an aggressive, conquering warlord; Ieyasu and the Shoguns, on the other hand, were interested in the consolidation of power and protection from both internal and external threats.

Eventually, the Tokugawa Shoguns centralized their political rule across all of Japan by using the Europeans as a foil. They eliminated the pirates who had been plaguing commercial shipping, and instituted Hideyoshi's system of domination. When the Shoguns ended the civil wars that were endemic throughout the Japanese islands, this centralizing peace left the warrior class, the samurai, without any wars to fight. The Japanese capitalist class thrived in this peaceful environment, and gained the wealth to challenge the samurai class.

After the Shoguns banned their military campaigns, the samurai were unable to replenish their dwindling resources. Agrarian based, they could not compete with the growing, less ascetic elite of the new urban upper class, who based their power on trade. The Shoguns were able to turn the samurai into glorified tax collectors; as a class, they never recovered from their defeat.

The Shoguns promoted a policy of isolationism in relation to the West, a policy grounded in political reality. The Jesuits had been successful in converting many of the Japanese people; politically astute, they combined Western Christianity with a large dose of Chinese culture learned under the Manchus, and they were able to play off the warlords who were battling against each other. Ieyasu was a devout Buddhist, so he had a double objection to the Jesuits. Instead of accepting them as true missionaries, he believed that they were in league with the European governments. Ieyasu saw the Jesuits arriving aboard the gunboats, and viewed them as spies who spread religion and poured information back to their European leaders, intelligence they would use to invade the Japanese islands.

In the light of the course of European history and the linkages between the conquering forces and the furthering of Christianity, Ieyasu was politically shrewd in his appraisal of the dangers of allowing missionary activity. Although they had welcomed the Christians in the 1540s, the Japanese under Hideyoshi began ousting the Jesuits in the late 1580s. For fear of alienating the Portuguese powers, however, Hideyoshi recanted and failed to oust all the Jesuits.

Under an ideology built on fear of Christianity, the Shoguns completed the political consolidation of Japan. It is difficult to know the true motivation of their oppression of the Christian communities that had spread throughout Japan. Under the third Shogun the wholesale persecution of the Christians, both of Japanese and European descent, began in earnest. The

Shoguns conducted attacks on cities and villages, rounding up all the Christians in these areas and executing them.

The European dream of conquering the Japanese and incorporating them into a European colony was not possible. The Shoguns limited Western colonization and dealt with Europe on terms that were acceptable to the Japanese. Their power was such that Shoguns were able to rule for more than 300 years.[14]

### Russia

Starting in the thirteenth century, the West's dreams of conquest also motivated Europe's Teutonic Knights to attack the states within Russia. The Mongols were in control of Russia, the khans using the existing power structure of the landed elite to enhance their rule: the landed elites could prosper even under Mongol rule so long as they stayed loyal.

A turning point in Russian history occurred with the ascension of Ivan III. He was able to gather provinces under his control, and because of conflicts within the Mongol empire, he succeeded in liberating Russia from Mongol power in 1480. He also waged wars of conquest in Lithuania-Poland and absorbed the area around Chernigov, Kiev, and Smolensk into his Moscow-centered Russian empire. With the ousting of the Mongols, a new national spirit moved the Russians to attack Eastern Europe. When they tried to expand the scope of their military operations to Sweden and Poland, however, they met stiff military resistance. The counterattacks of the Swedish and Polish armies shrank the Russian empire geographically again.

The glorification of Russian culture acted to insulate the Russians from the West, even if they could not resist militarily. There was a strong reaction against the ways of the West in almost everything – except Western technology, particularly military technology. The Russian ruling elite had a strong cultural identity of their own, and military successes served to increase Russian nationalism, leading to a glorification of Mother Russia's institutions, in the present and the past. Starting in the fifteenth century, the Muscovite Tsars began to establish a more centralized regime, and the trend of cultural nationalism continued.

The strong ideological resistance to the West existed side by side with the efforts of the Russian elites to extract all the cultural benefits they could from Western Europe, even while viewing the Westerners as cultural inferiors. The coalition of the Orthodox Church and the ruling families of the Russian state served to keep the West at arm's length, but during the reigns of Ivan III and Ivan the Terrible in the fifteenth and sixteenth centuries, the West was tapped for economic, artistic, and military resources. Ivan the Terrible put Russia's entire society under a state of siege from the throne. Russia borrowed artisans, traders, and military technologies from the West to transform Moscow. Particularly effective was the Russians' use of artillery, introduced by Ivan the Terrible while capturing Kazan in 1551. Ivan IV attacked the landed elite in Russia with the goal of overthrowing them, and the Tsar was able to confiscate the land and wealth that was in their hands.

After Ivan IV, there came a period that McNeill and others have called the Time of Troubles. It was during this period, which lasted from the late sixteenth century through the first 13 years of the seventeenth century, that the defeated nobility struck back with political intrigue and violence in attempts to destroy the Tsar and restore their lost fortunes. They plundered and engaged in guerrilla-like activities against the Tsar's holdings.

The Russian nobility initiated this counter-revolution in unison with the Orthodox Church. In many respects the church was a cultural microcosm of the events that were occurring within the Russian state itself. The Patriarch of Moscow, Filaret, and later his son Michael Romanov, led the rebellious wing of counter-revolutionaries. After overthrowing the Tsar, they established a state that was subservient to the landed elites at the expense of its imperial rulers.

The early Romanovs were both drawn to and repulsed by the European West. Their influence remained the central source of power for the Russian empire until Peter the Great. They learned much about European war technology, while limiting cultural contact with Europe in other areas.

In sum, after the Crusades, Europe made only limited inroads into China, Japan, and Russia. The failure of the Crusades left the European states in a situation where the crowns turned the war-making apparatus inward in much of Europe. While this internal centralization led to the growth of the crown in France, England, and Spain, the idea of a general European expansion is questionable. Instead, the evidence supports a Europe under siege, particularly in its eastern areas, starting in the fifteenth century. The Ottomans continued to bear down on Eastern and Western Europe during this period; indeed, even Austria was not immune to the Ottoman forces. By the late fifteenth century, Western European civilization was imploding from the expansion of the Ottoman empire. Europe's limited advances into China, Japan, and Russia failed. The only recourse for many societies in Europe was to continue to drain the resources of their colonies in the Americas.[15]

# 6

# The Findings and their
# Implications for the
# Americas

Building on the Tilly–Giddens principle linking warfare to
state-making, and on Toynbee's ideas regarding civilizations as
the key unit of analysis in understanding social change, this
analysis suggests that the civilization struggle model indeed
explains the origins of the modern state system that developed
in Europe between the eighth and the seventeenth centuries.
Great Asian civilizations and Islamic Ottoman civilization
resisted the onward expansion of European civilization even
beyond 1600; the solid configuration of the civilizations in the
Far East withstood the West, at least temporarily. This
research qualifies the idea that Western European civilization
intrinsically and independently exerted an inexorable effect on
the world through European economic and cultural superiority. Underscored by this analysis is the recognition of the role
that these other civilizations played in the rise of the European
state system.

The civilization struggle model connects the origins of the
Western European state system to the social conflict among
civilizations. The conflict amid the European, ancient Roman,
Islamic, Viking, Byzantine, various Steppe warrior, Ottoman,
Native American, Eurasian, and Mongol civilizations occurred
at what I termed the *intercivilizational* or *universal* plane. We
explored how this plane includes the power hierarchy and the

stratification system of civilizations on a global scale. Lower down in geographical magnitude is the *supermacro* level that contains civilizations, society, societies, and networks of societies. Society, societies, and networks of societies are the components of the supermacro scale and are the building blocks of civilizations. As outlined in chapter 1, internal to each society at the *macro* level are the dynamics of class, gender, institutions, states, structures, economies, and people within these societies. The *micro* level is the level of individual actions and face-to-face behavior.

Turning to social dynamics at the most comprehensive level of causality, and invoking the Tilly–Giddens principle, we have seen *universal struggles* that involve conflicts among civilizations. Here we explored how they led to European state-building and state transformation. The structure of warlike behavior was a central mover in fashioning the origins of Latin Christendom, occurring first by the destruction of the Roman empire, and then by the rise of the Carolingian state system as it emerged from the Carolingian's conflict with the Islamic civilization in Andalus. The Carolingians then absorbed contiguous Germanic tribes and routed the Lombards from Italy. Universal-level war was one of the fundamental organizational factors in the West during this period; between the fall of Rome and the rise of the modern binary system, the struggle among civilizations was a central causal mechanism of social change. Likewise, contradicting the predictions of modernization theory, the central dynamic of this change occurred long before the industrial revolution – from at least the origins of the Carolingian system.

The conflict among civilizations was an engine driving the rise of the Western state system. The formation of European civilization was primarily a reaction against the power constellation of Viking, Islamic, Byzantine, multiple Steppe warrior, Mongol, Islamic, and Ottoman civilizations. The conflict with Vikings destroyed the centralized Carolingian state system. The result was a situation in which a decentralized military structure was the most advantageous system for self-defense.

Culturally, at this universal level, the papacy came to represent a unifying force in rallying Western Europe against Islam.

The Crusades created a capitalist boom as Italian city states grew rich from supplying resources to the Crusader kingdoms in the Middle East. This was followed by the eventual failure of these kingdoms, as the expenses incurred by these universal-level mobilizations created an implosion within European civilization. Europe was reeling culturally, politically, and economically from the failure of the Crusades. This whole process led to the decline of the manor and the demise of Roman ecclesiastical power, culminating in the Reformation.

Under the ceiling of greater civilizational struggles, we observed *supermacro struggles* that are lower down the ladder of geopolitical magnitude, where states struggle against each other to defend themselves or to expand their power over other societies. Civilizations at this level radically transformed social structures by militarily absorbing previously external societies, altering the social structure of these societies as well as the civilization's own stratification system. Exploring the internal dynamics within the types of civilizations, we saw differing patterns of social structure, and varying economic systems. The states that emerged within a civilizational conflict generated certain cultural patterns, repressed others, and influenced the degrees of differences allowed within a civilization. We saw how the early European state absorbed other Germanic bands while building the Carolingian system, and how later the warring of the Carolingian superstate system helped dismantle the Carolingian empire and bring on feudalism. We recorded how the attack of the Normans transformed England, and how the war-making of the European states, the various religious wars, and the wars of the Habsburg empire transformed Europe. Similar internal dynamics were seen within Islamic, Viking, Byzantine, various Steppe warrior, Ottoman, Eurasian, and Mongol civilizations.

*Macro intranational struggles* within each society, still lower down the scale of geopolitical magnitude, are where class struggle, social movements, competition among institutions, social organization, and the internal dynamics of each society exist. The Tilly–Giddens principle of war shaped society at this level as elites attempted to maintain their macro power while engaging in supermacro and civilizational level conflict through manifold political, economic, and military means from the early Carolingian system to the rise of the absolutist and the democratic states. If these elites and structures dominated their macro plane, they maintained this domination and expanded into other societies and other civilizations at the supermacro and universal levels. If these classes and structures were ascendant forces at all levels in a given geographical area, then this represented a world historical civilization.

Within the macro societal level, Marxist dynamics came into being where the successions of classes occurred. Even here, however, we witness how civilization-level configurations come into action. The history of Western binary civilization is not only the transformation of state structures by one successive class after another, but the conflict of civilizations through war-making, which imposes exogenous classes on to other structures.

The processes of historical change as theorized by Marx, particularly the importance of class conflict, and by Weber, in the significance of forms of ideologies, cultural patterns, bureaucracies, organizations, and institutions, come into operation at this level and expand upward and downward to other levels. The growing attempts by the ecclesiastical power to extract resources from, own, and control the manorial structure follow along Weberian-Marxian lines. The growing union of town and crown often thrust the adversaries of manor and church back on the same side, in a failed effort to constrain the bourgeoisie and state-builders.

I have argued that the Reformation was a natural result of the causal chain starting as early as the twelfth-century Crusades, and perhaps earlier. The real cause of the rise and success of Protestantism was that it fitted well into the material, cultural, and political circumstances of the emerging binary system that was in the process of exploding the boundaries set by feudalism. The Reformation was in part a product of the failure of the Crusades, when the papacy used up its cultural and political capital in this military mobilization. This failure produced the climate for reexamining the role of the church in the affairs of state and society.

When the leadership of the Crusades slipped from papal and manor mobilization to imperial and monarchical leadership, the papacy was in a situation it could no longer control. For other groups, particularly nobles and capitalists in countries and empires dominated by Catholic monarchs, there was an incentive to defect from the governance of the papacy and Catholic rulers. This was particularly true in view of what the reformers saw as the corruption of the Catholic Church. In previous heretical movements the throne could crush these dissenters; however, in the case of the Reformation the Habsburgs' war with the Ottoman Islamic civilization complicated the situation. This tension provided the soil in which the Reformation could take hold. Ottoman support of monarchs and movements opposed to the Catholic Habsburg monarchs helped the Reformation succeed.

This modifies Weber's early interpretation of the rise of capitalism, in that I have argued that the cause of the success of the Protestant ethic was the previous rise of the state and capitalism. As Weber maintained, the worldly Protestant ascetics then rejected the wealthy Catholic Church and its corruption. This led to a turn of emphasis away from institutional sacramental administration as aids to salvation, and toward belief in predestination and a search for signs of salvation in the life of the believer. Wealth became the outward sign of God's favor. This created the Protestant work ethic. Ironically, from Weber's perspective, the Protestant believers created the greatest wealth-generating system in history: modern capitalism. Because of their asceticism, Protestants kept investing and reinvesting the money that they earned into expanding their capitalist ventures.

In his early theory of capitalism, Weber saw capitalist development as the dependent variable reacting to the rise of the Puritans' cultural belief systems. He placed less emphasis on the events that led to the Protestant Reformation, in particular the early economic stimulus and later failure of the Crusades. Contrary to the brilliantly insightful analysis of Weber, the foundations of capitalist economy predated the Reformation, as argued by Collins. This analysis is in line with the more mature Weber. We have seen how Italian city states developed booming capitalist economies during the period of the Crusades, beginning in the eleventh century.

The struggle between Christendom and Islamic civilizations fashioned the conflict between the European crowns, on the one hand, and the papal manorial structure on the other. The rise of bourgeois civilization required that the Latin Church be constrained. The Puritan, Lutheran, Episcopalian, Zwinglian, and Huguenot ethics all served the same purpose in legitimizing the rise of bourgeois civilization. They promoted liberated or highly independent crowns in relation to papal control, even in those societies such as Spain and France that remained significantly Catholic. At the universal level, the Reformation prevented European unity for the war with the Islamic Ottoman civilization, until Charles V allowed a degree of religious diversity.

Individuals interacted within traditions that structured their everyday behavior, as structuration theory explains. These interactions were important features of this research. At the micro level the interactions between members of families, clans, or even individual soldiers who fought each other were influenced by the civilization conflict at the universal level. There were many examples of these phenomena in European, Eurasian, ancient Roman, Islamic, Viking, Byzantine, Steppe warrior, Mongol, and Ottoman civilizations. Here various family and clan dynamics created wars, prevented wars, led to attempted fratricide, actual fratricide, suicide, and slaughters, and determined legitimate heirs to thrones or theocracies, with ramifications that lasted centuries. Indeed the folkways of a group of people are products of interactions in face-to-face behavior that have been influenced by universal-level conflicts, or send their influence in the other direction; they may also be the result of exchanges among members of the upper classes or the interaction of classes among civilizations.

As mentioned earlier, I have not designed this book to test all the theories addressed. Instead, I use existing theories in a synthetic manner to develop this new theory, building primarily on the work of Tilly, Giddens, and Toynbee. Nonetheless, it may be useful to explore the linkages and ways that the civilization struggle model has integrated theories in light of the historical movements analyzed in the previous chapters.[1]

## Civilizational Conflict and Mann

This research has taken a holistic approach to power relationships, as does Michael Mann. Mann calls the "four sources of social power" the ideological, economic, military, and political (IEMP). As can be seen by the theory offered here, the interplay of these dynamic power networks played a determining role in the development of the European state system. The emphasis in my approach has been to place Mann's ideas within an intercivilizational and civilizational context.

As Mann argues, various power networks can influence all parts of a civilization or society. Military adventures often mean changes to customs that are quite evident in civilizations or societies. There is no question that the events studied here among the ancient Roman, Islamic, Viking, Byzantine, Ottoman, Eurasian, Mongol and various other Steppe warrior civilizations showed that economic, political, ideological and military events at the universal, supermacro, macro, and micro levels may drastically alter the state. Political and military developments at the very top of the civilizational hierarchy have profound consequences for the degree of spatial, political, cultural, gender, or economic freedom that any particular civilization enjoys.

In addition, and adapting Mann's perspective, within a particular civilization or society at what I have called respectively the supermacro and macro levels, we see the various sources of social power and the networks that evolve from these structures. Thus each civilization and society has its own particular configuration of political, economic, military, and ideological sources of social power. The types of social norms and type of stratification system are also parts of distinct forms of social organization and networks, at both the supermacro and macro levels. There are networks related to geographical proximity, or networks maintained through kinship, and other networks that extend beyond the geographically closest societies. Examples of the latter case were the marriages between the elites of the Ottoman and Byzantine civilizations, and the elites of Rome and the Germanic tribes. Other examples include the Ottoman use of Christian slaves at court, and the way the Europeans forced the Avars to convert to Catholicism or die.

Using Mann's network approach, the macro dynamic of class conflict interacts with the civilizational and supermacro dynamics of classes attempting to extend their national domination into international domination. National elites from without attempt to graft their systems of domination on to other societies, networks of societies, and other civilizations. Civilizations, societies, and societal networks incorporate, drive off, or hold in stalemate these external classes. At other times, these external classes are victorious. We saw this occur among the ancient Roman, European, Islamic, Viking, Byzantine, Steppe warrior, Eurasian, Mongol, and Ottoman civilizations. In a similar manner, Mann's typology is useful when we are confronted with entities such as the Roman Church, wielding a power that was at once political, economic, ideological, and, in coalition with the manors during the Crusades, military as well. This represents a sampling of the ways that Mann's work has been utilized.[2]

## Civilizational Conflict and Spengler

Spengler is correct about morphology, but I qualify three factors within his theory: (1) his ideas regarding morphological analogies; (2) his cyclical theory; and (3) the organismic model he proposes. In viewing the rise of the European state system, researchers will find only limited utility in proposing analogies between the West and Rome or Greece, or between Caesar and Charlemagne or Charles V, and so on. History, though lawful, does not repeat itself, and drawing too many analogies does violence to reality. The goal here has been to discern differing states as well as similarities. Likewise, all known civilizations go through transformations, but it is not always useful to call this a death because, as long as humans exist, there are structural continuities offering definite longstanding linkages to previous history. Thus this research also questions Spengler's idea that civilizations are a morphological conclusion of a previous culture. Spengler's theory minimizes the impact of intercivilizational conflict at the universal level. This analysis has shown a structural continuity between the Middle Ages and the modern world that is not totally amenable to Spengler's death analogy.[3]

## Civilizational Conflict and Sorokin

If we disregard Sorokin's three ideal-typical modes of civilization, and concentrate instead on the power of culture in the rise of states, there are many points of agreement with his argument. This theory adds to the idea that the collapse of the Middle Ages was the result of the collapse of a culture, as argued by Sorokin. The transformation of culture created by and interacting with wars at the universal, supermacro, macro, and micro levels of structure developed and changed European states. At the universal level, we see Sorokin's cosmologies existing and his principles in action. Rather than sorting civilizations by these various principles, we can see elements of idealistic, sensate, and ideational principles at work in most of the civilizations that we examine, with the pure types of these principles difficult to find. Culture is a powerful causal mechanism and an important sustaining mechanism in the development of European states. One such example of the power of culture was the role of the culture of Catholicism in holding together decentralized medieval society, and the power of culture in the clash of Islam and Christianity during the Crusades.

When examining the internal dynamics of civilizations, as Sorokin argues, we often see a variety of approaches to religion, reality, and cosmologies. Ancient Roman, Islamic, Viking, Byzantine, Ottoman, Eurasian, Mongol and the other Steppe warrior civilizations, while sharing certain cultural similarities, also differed in their cultural approaches to life. There are, however, defining "Sorokinian moments" when a particular civilization can take on one particular character, or conversely assume various social and cultural principles. For instance, we can see that for a brief period for the educated classes the Middle Ages were a blend of knowledge based on revelation and reason, as Sorokin argued, but in the less educated classes this seemed to be less true, and faith ruled more than reason – as witnessed by Peter the Hermit's mobilization of the poor with a "letter from heaven." Legend has it that Thomas Aquinas asked God for an appraisal of his research. "The Unmoved Mover" (God) responded that Thomas "had written well of him." This and the popes' pronouncements regarding the sure victory of the Crusaders against Islam shared certain characteristics with Peter the Hermit's letter, but no pope made such a specific claim as to say that a tablet from heaven had been received ensuring victory. Likewise Aquinas used reason not "Divine Approval" to defend his scholarship against critics.

Considering Sorokin's work, we can see how war-making activities interacted with particular cultures and in turn had their effect on states. Differing developments linked to cultural products such as religions, ideologies, and world-views occur within these civilizations at the universal, civilizational, macro, and micro levels and interact with wars to shape states. Within the societal level, a society's position in a particular civilization, or its relationship to an external civilization, may cause an intense alteration of existing cultures. One example of this was the tragic fate of the Eastern European societies that acted as buffers between the Western European, Byzantine, Mongol, Ottoman, and Middle Eastern Islamic civilizations.

At the micro level, we saw that religious practices may determine or alter the outcome of a war, and that the religious fates of nations and civilizations may change when the religious beliefs of an individual are transformed through some form of protest, "revelation," or by a conversion experience, and when that person works to spread this experience throughout the society and among civilizations. In the case of Luther and Zwingli, along with Protestant supporters, military measures were used, even at the civilizational and intercivilizational levels, to ensure the survival of their beliefs. We saw how the Protestants interacted with the Ottoman–Habsburg wars, and we saw the origins and development of the Shiite branch of Islam and the subsequent war with the Sunnis. It was an apparent revelation at the micro level that led Peter the Hermit to launch his ill-fated crusade. Nonetheless, these events do not occur in a civilizational vacuum, and throughout this work we have seen how even these micro decisions are linked to the universal and supermacro levels. For Luther this occurred as a result of disillusionment with the Catholic Church, in the aftermath of the Crusades, and because of what reformers, even inside the Catholic Church, viewed as the corruption of the papacy.

Like Spengler's work, Sorokin's theory is brilliant but analogous to Comte's or Hegel's work[4] in that they gloss over the role that war played in the expansion of the contemporary world – although Sorokin was well aware of war as a powerful force for social change.

## Civilizational Conflict, World Systems, Dependency, and Modes of Production Theory

Drawing on the work of Wallerstein and of Frank, but using it with the framework provided by Toynbee, and the Tilly–Giddens principle, we observe that a world system may emerge when one civilization develops a system of hegemony over other civilizations. To be sure, in the strictest sense of the definition, a world system has to have an impact on the entire world. Yet if we relax that definition and explore the "civilizational world system," we can make some fascinating observations. One generalization that can be drawn is that for a large span of human history the world system has been composed of multiple civilizational systems that may or may not overlap. Multiple civilizations have their own powerful economic cores and peripheries. We saw a Mongol civilizational system develop that was to be the largest in existence until the maturing of the European world system after the Age of Exploration. Indeed, the Mongol system dominated China, Russia, much of the Middle East, Eastern Europe, and other peripheral civilizations.

The civilization conflict perspective shows that at other times rival civilizations created partitioned, simultaneous, or overlapping economic systems. This is particularly true where a "power barrier" is formed. At one point the Ottoman system and the European civilizational system formed a power barrier in which the Ottoman civilizational system and the civilizational system dominated by Spain reached an impasse in the Mediterranean, leaving only the Atlantic open for further European expansion. At other times, due to political and historical circumstances, one civilization finds itself unable to make inroads into the markets and political systems of other civilizations, resulting in a partitioned civilizational world system. This was true in most of European history, where most world civilizations never came into contact with each other. Also, civilizational systems may fail to emerge because groups are decentralized and out of touch, for various reasons, with lines of trade or conflict. Again this was true for the American Indian civilizations until the European invasion. Parts of Germanic civilization escaped the fate of becoming a full-blown part of the ancient Roman system because they were so remote and unattractive to the Romans.

Within the civilization proper, the type of lifestyle and material well-being is often determined by the location of the civilization's core economy. It is important to identify whether the civilization is in fact an emanating core civilization or a peripheral civilization. The economic systems of the Byzantine empire and the Islamic empire had trade routes and power that allowed them to develop magnificent trade centers and urban areas, whereas the peripheral European state system was largely austere and rural. Internally, we saw how important it was to explore whether a society was a vassal or peripheral society. This issue arose in the early Carolingian civilization when it conquered and subordinated the civilization of the Avars and others, and with the conquered Christian societies in Andalus and in Eastern Europe.

The economic systems emanating through core portions of the civilization and/or from other civilizations may have a powerful impact on the macro societal level, particularly through warfare. The external civilization's economic system may also change a society. This latter situation was particularly telling in the Italian city-state system, profiting when the Crusaders inhabited the Holy Land. Altering the position of another civilization as a rival, a subordinate, or a partner, and thereby indirectly altering the society through the whole cluster of societies that make up a civilization, also occurs. Moreover, within the supermacro and macro levels we often see states develop, as Porter shows, where the political core is at war with the political periphery of a particular society. State-building in France occurred along these lines.

It is important to track the political developments within a particular society and to see if the point of origin is in its own or another civilizational system. Thus, instead of seeing the society just in terms of one particular political system, depending on the manner in which various civilizations have competed, other parts of the civilizational system may be observed to intercept a society. This is relevant for those civilizations that I examined that started off as small societies but expanded into world-dominating civilizations. We saw this pattern in a number of cases throughout this study: the relative poverty even of Charlemagne's magnificent court was due in no small part to its place on the periphery of Byzantine civilization.

Finally, the mode of production analysis ties the structure of states to the underlying development of classes and the relations of production. From this perspective, capitalism developed states as a by-product of capitalist development. This insight was useful in exploring how civilizations and state networks interacted with modes of production in the rise of the European state system. We have seen modes of production develop by external stimuli, particularly war-making. In addition, I examined how warfare and trade disperse a particular mode of production, or how other civilizations capture, ignore, or borrow it. Similarly, distinct forms of production may develop. Throughout this book I have examined how the conflict among civilizations altered the modes of production and shaped the development of capitalism. This was particularly true when we saw how the Crusades spread the capitalist mode of production, making the Italian city states rich in the process.[5]

### Civilizational Conflict and Technological Theory

Orienting the analysis with the Tilly–Giddens principle and applying the work of Lenski and Lenski, I showed how technological features also played a role in the conflict among civilizations. This goes further than "inventions" and embraces technology in a broader sense. In particular, I inspected the development of military and transportation technologies, as well as social technologies which included stratification structures and banking and market breakthroughs. These technological breakthroughs were used for conquest or defense and gave the advantage to one civilization over another. We examined numerous cases in ancient Roman, Islamic, Viking, Byzantine, Ottoman, Eurasian, and Mongol civilizations. There were occasions when a particular civilization, while having access to a new technology, refused to adopt it, and this decision had ramifications on their fates. Three cases of the rejection of economic and military technologies among many include the nobles who resisted capitalism, the nobles who resisted the proletarianization of the army in Europe, and the way that the Shiites resisted the military advances, giving the Sunnis a military edge in war.

Within a particular civilization, a technological core or a cluster of technological developments may alter its historical path. These developments may be purely technological, or there may be changes that are in the nature of social technologies adopted in response to military threats. European castle-building, various metal-working, shipbuilding, trading and banking innovations, Ottoman centralization, Eurasian borrowing of Western technology, Mongol cavalry technologies, all influenced the trajectory of world history. Sometimes, because of a desire for external expansion, states may develop military and other technologies. At other times, wars do not generate military technologies, but states use technological developments already in existence. In addition, technological advances may result from economic stimuli, or banking and commercial developments may be produced by conflicts with other civilizations. There were many examples. We saw how William the Conqueror developed new social technologies such as vassalage and sheriffs to control the subordinated English population, and we saw bankers and merchants responding to the need for finance for monarchs to wage war.

A society may internally generate technological developments, or at other times they absorb and institute developments by way of the host or external civilization. Internally, Charlemagne developed new war-making technologies, and externally, the Ottomans adopted technologies from European shipbuilders. The particular geographical location of a society also has a bearing on the types of technologies and cultural and economic systems that develop. The austere conditions of the

Germanic tribes led them to develop strategical technologies to plunder the more affluent Roman empire, and the nomadic way of life of the Mongols led them to the social technology of superior horse-riding skills that they used in combat. The Vikings developed ships that were useful for a combination of shallow water and oceanic voyages, due in part to the location of the Norse warriors. Sometimes, a particular society spurns new technological innovations for religious or other reasons. This was the case, again, with that branch of the Shiites who were opposed to using advances in technology for war-making, and with those European knights who believed that war-making should be left to nobles, and with the Europeans who tore down walls, asking God to defend them against the "Godless" Vikings. It was important for us to follow the multilevel nature of all of these changes.

At the micro level, the arrival of certain technologies may transform an individual's life. Yet the actions of various individuals, even those not at the top of the hierarchy, can have a significant impact on society. The transformation of European life with the advent of cities and fortified living, and the proletarianization of war, had critical impacts on the everyday life of individuals, societies and civilizations.

## Conclusions

This research gives additional support to the Tilly–Giddens principle linking warfare to state-making. Universal-level conflict included the battles among European, ancient Roman, Islamic, Viking, Byzantine, Steppe warrior, Ottoman, Native American, Eurasian, and Mongol civilizations. Wars were central movers in fashioning the rise and fall of the Carolingian state system, and in shaping the internal workings of Latin Christendom. As these means of violence turned inward, they interacted at the universal level to create the transformation of the feudal state system, through the absolutist state, to parliamentary states. It was not only internal macro dynamics, but also the interaction of these dynamics with the intercivilizational conflict of the Crusades that promoted state-building.

Universal-level conflict in conjunction with supermacro and macro struggles determined the degree and success of state-building. In England, France, and Germany, the Viking attacks led to a massive decentralization. The lingering impact of the Vikings again transformed Europe; the Normans conquered England, leading to moderate centralization in England. The Crusades contributed to the centralization of France, but the Germans' relative disdain for this activity and their emperors' attempts to conquer Italy at the supermacro level left Germany decentralized, and the barons retained the bulk of the power. The presence of Islamic Andalus led to high centralization in Spain as Castile and Aragon formed a union to match the power of their Islamic foe at the universal level.

Italy and the Netherlands remained largely decentralized. In Italy this was initially because of the papacy's success in striking alliances with the crowns of Europe; later, after the decline of the Carolingian system, the constant state of siege Italy suffered from the rest of Europe at the supermacro level, and from Islam and the Ottomans at the universal level of conflict, also prevented massive Italian centralization. The Netherlands remained largely decentralized because it was under the power of Spain until the burgher class was already well established. Due in part to Spain's universal-level conflict with the Ottomans, Spain eased its yoke and the burghers were able to build on the largely stateless system to keep the Netherlands decentralized.

The English and French went through another period of state-building thanks to the coalitions they formed at the universal level with the Ottomans against the Habsburgs. Parliaments that came into being played twin roles: they were avenues for resource mobilization and tax revenues for monarchs for wars and Crusades, and also for ensuring the rights of the landed aristocracy. The tension between these two often contradictory goals created much conflict and tension between royalty and nobles.

This research has introduced the importance of deep time to add to the revolutionary time of Marx and Weber. The glacial pace of movement in the rise of civilizations and state systems is often striking. A specific event, be it the revolutionary overthrow of the landed aristocracy in Marx, or the overthrow of

Catholic belief systems during the Reformation in Weber, may be placed more meaningfully as the turning point of humanity in the context of the transformation and interactions of civilizations. The conflict among civilizations, often centuries old, was the furnace that forged the Western state system and hence the events that Marx and Weber emphasized.

Focusing on the universal and supermacro structures enhances the work of both Marx and Weber by placing specific macro structural, class, ideological, and religious transformations in their supermacro and universal level settings. By situating in this way the European-oriented view of internal class conflict in Marx and the Reformation in the earlier Weber, an underlying process now links these seemingly unrelated phenomena. Both the Reformation and class conflict could not have occurred in the manner they did without the forge and the pressure provided by the competition with the Islamic, Viking, Mongol, Byzantine and Ottoman civilizations. This conflict had an impact on the fortunes of Europe, particularly the fate of the papacy that led to the Reformation and the class and state structure of feudal Europe, culminating in the European state system. This process demonstrates how war shaped the rise of the West.

We have seen that by the eighth century competing civilizations existed as organized entities that would fashion the future of Europe. The intercivilizational struggle for survival and expansion in the world arena had telling consequences for the structure and development of social institutions and class structures in the Far West.

An advantage of the civilizational approach is that it questions a strict Eurocentrism in understanding the rise of the European state system. The present analysis surveys the critical role that other competing civilizations had in fashioning European civilization and shows how the Western European state system was the result of this struggle. Several patterns can be discerned that represent turning points in the development of states in Europe. The Germanic state system prevailed against the great Roman empire. The Carolingian superstate system collapsed under the weight of the Vikings' attack. The Western European states did severe damage but did not succeed in vanquishing Byzantine civilization permanently. The

Crusades accelerated the growth of capitalism and the capitalist class, yet ultimately Islamic civilization erased any gains the Europeans made in the Middle East. Europe lost ground against Mongol civilization, and an accident of history may have prevented a Mongol Europe. The Ottomans disrupted a unified Catholic Europe and gave support to the Reformation, and expanded geographically into Eastern Europe. In short, Europe had such limited success that even on the eve of the Age of Exploration, Islamic and Mongol civilizations dwarfed Western Europe; Western Europe was part of the "third world" of the globe and held this status from the collapse of the Roman empire through the Age of Exploration.

The encroaching civilizations created the conditions in which the national state and bourgeoisie became the political center of the binary system. The tools that were so ineffectual at making inroads into other civilizations proved mercilessly effective in dominating the civilizations in the Americas and elsewhere, with the development of European maritime power.

The greatness of the European state system was a result of its weakness against these arguably greater civilizations. The walls set up by the Mongol, Islamic, and Ottoman civilizations in the East, the resistance of Asian and Eurasian civilizations to European conquest, and the financial devastation of universal and supermacro level war made Europe dependent on resources in the militarily weaker native civilizations in the Americas.

At the most general level of causality, early European state-building was the result of these universal-level struggles among the European, ancient Roman, Islamic, Viking, Byzantine, Steppe warrior, Ottoman, Eurasian, and Mongol civilizations. These collisions interacted with supermacro, macro, and micro variables and shaped the linkages among military, economic, and political structures, affecting the geographical power of the Germanic bands and later the Carolingian empire, feudalism, and the era of state-building.

Given the Islamic, Mongol, and Ottoman walls in the East, the path of least resistance was maritime expansion to the west. Because of this containment of European civilization, Western Europe used the maritime power it had built up to attack the civilizations in the west. In the late fifteenth and early sixteenth century, Western Europe used a combination of war-making and navigational skills to establish colonies. At the same time, Spain increased extraction to fight the mighty Islam in its Middle Eastern, Ottoman, and Andalusian manifestations.

Unable to make significant inroads on the land in the Middle East, China, and Japan, Europeans were capable of dominating all the Native American civilizations with military operations. They started a trend that would continue throughout the nineteenth century. Europeans would attack and extract resources from those civilizations that could not meet attacks from their sea-based power.

The growing impact of the extension of Western civilization affected the globe, but Chinese, Japanese, Eurasian, and parts of African civilization were able to withstand this impact, at least for the time being. China and Japan used military force to keep the Europeans at bay; particularly in China, geography helped this process along, the vastness of the Chinese empire helping to frustrate European initiatives. Although the Europeans were successful in establishing a slave trade with Africa, the large geographical terrain, the variety of city states, and the more decentralized African structure prevented immediate domination of the African continent.

The European invasion devastated the American Indian civilizations. These American Indians became oppressed underclasses of the European state system. The Europeans also conquered the decentralized confederation of American Indians and relegated them to lower-class status. The power gained by the Europeans increased through the extraction of precious metals, agricultural goods, trade, and taxes. This gave them resources to counter the Ottoman Islamic civilization, which had profited by pitting Spain, France, Italy, and England against one another.

The Western European state system became strong by overseas expansion. This was because of the power and wealth that flowed to states such as England, Portugal, Spain and other pioneers in the Age of Exploration, leading to an age of "competitive colonization" in which the winners would reap big dividends from empire-building. The booty obtained overseas provided the colonial powers with the means with which to increase their military power and wage wars. It should be added, drawing on James Lang, that state-building also resulted from the necessity of managing overseas empires administratively.[6]

The next great period of Western expansion was from the eighteenth through the twentieth centuries. This occurred with the collision of the West with the societies in South America, southern Africa, and Australia. Through the expansion of violence and trade, Europe absorbed other civilizations. The implosion of these great civilizations to subordinate civilizations is an incredible saga. As one looks back across the time horizons, the ascension of the European state system seems remarkable. Its future is, of course, beyond the scope of this research.

# Notes

## Introduction

1 So as not to pepper the text with too many note numbers, I have grouped the references into larger notes. Here, see the following: Abu-Lughod, *Before European Hegemony*; Braudel, *Capitalism and Material Life*, p. 63; Braudel, *Civilization and Capitalism*, vol. 1, p. 57; Collins, *Weberian Sociological Theory*, pp. 2–3, 19, 49, 76; Frank, *Dependent Accumulation*; Frank and Gills, "Five Thousand Year World System," pp. 22–3; Giddens, *Capitalism and Modern Social Theory*; Giddens, *The Constitution of Society*, pp. 236–44, 251; Giddens, *The Nation-State and Violence*; Held, *Political Theory*, p. 2; Huntington, "The Clash of Civilizations?" pp. 22–6; Mann, *The Sources of Social Power*, vols 1 and 2; Mills, *The Power Elite*; Parsons, *The Structure of Social Action*; Spybey, *Social Change, Development and Dependency*, p. 233 and passim; Tilly, *Coercion, Capital, and European States*; Wallerstein, *The Modern World-System*, vol. 1; Weber, *General Economic History*.

## Chapter 1   A Theory of the Modern European State System

1 Abu-Lughod, *Before European Hegemony*; Burke, "The Rise of Europe"; Comte, *Religion of Humanity*; Finer, "State and Nation Building"; Frank, *Dependent Accumulation*; Frank and Gills, "Five Thousand Year World System," pp. 10, 23;

Giddens, *The Nation-State and Violence*; Kennedy, *Rise and Fall*; Mann, *The Sources of Social Power*, vols 1 and 2; Mann, *States, War and Capitalism*; McNeill, *The Rise of the West*; Porter, *War and the Rise of the State*; Sorokin, *Social and Cultural Dynamics*; Spengler, *The Decline of the West*; Tilly, "Reflection"; Tilly, *Coercion, Capital, and European States*; Toynbee, *A Study of History*; Wallerstein, *The Modern World-System*, vol. 1; Wolf, *Europe*.

2 Anderson, *Passages from Antiquity to Feudalism*; Anderson, *Lineages of the Absolutist State*; Chirot, "The Rise of the West," p. 193; Frank, *Dependent Accumulation*; Huntington, *Political Order in Changing Societies*; Lenski and Lenski, *Human Societies*; Sorokin, *Social and Cultural Dynamics*; Skocpol, *Protecting Soldiers and Mothers*; Spengler, *The Decline of the West*; Wallerstein, *The Modern World-System*, vols 1 and 2.

3 Collins, *Weberian Sociological Theory*, pp. 9, 52; Frank and Gills, "Five Thousand Year World System," pp. 10, 23; McNeill, *The Rise of the West*, pp. 538–47; Porter, *War and the Rise of the State*; Spybey, *Social Change, Development and Dependency*, p. 58.

## Chapter 2    Early Foundations of Western European Civilization

1 Franzius, *History of the Byzantine Empire*, p. 43; Hodges and Whitehouse, *Mohammed, Charlemagne*, pp. 67–8; James, "The Northern World," pp. 60–1, 75, 77–9; Le Goff, *Medieval Civilization*, pp. 10–15, 16–17, 29, and passim; Randers-Pehrson, *Barbarians and Romans*, passim, and esp. pp. 81–5, 107, 110, 116, 121.

2 Brown, "Transformation of the Roman Mediterranean," pp. 9–10; Hodges and Whitehouse, *Mohammed, Charlemagne*, pp. 54, 75; Le Goff, *Medieval Civilization*, p. 10; Randers-Pehrson, *Barbarians and Romans*, pp. 217–19, 221, 224.

3 Chirot, "The Rise of the West"; Downing, *The Military Revolution*, p. 19; Franzius, *History of the Byzantine Empire*, p. 153; Gerberding, *Rise of the Carolingians*, pp. 14–18, 173–81; Hodges and Whitehouse, *Mohammed, Charlemagne*, pp. 80–1; James, "The Northern World," pp. 58, 65–6, 89–91; Le Goff, *Medieval Civilization*, pp. 21–3; McNeill, *The Rise of the West*, p. 443; McKitterick, *The Frankish Kingdoms*, pp. 21–2; Spybey, *Social Change, Development and Dependency*, pp. 55–6.

4 Abu-Lughod, *Before European Hegemony*, p. 189; Brown, "Transformation of the Roman Mediterranean," pp. 11–12, 15; James, "The Northern World," pp. 90–1; Downing, *The Military Revolution*, p. 19; Hodges and Whitehouse, *Mohammed, Charlemagne*, pp. 70–1, 81; Hourani, *History of the Arab Peoples*, pp. 22, 25–6, 31–4, 36–7, 41–3; Lasko, *The Kingdom of the Franks*, pp. 68–9; McNeill, *The Rise of the West*, p. 442; Read, *Moors in Spain and Portugal*, pp. 23–4, 40, 48; Spybey, *Social Change, Development and Dependency*, pp. 57, 213; Vaglieri, "The Patriarchal and Umayyad Caliphates," pp. 86–7, 94–5.

5 Franzius, *History of the Byzantine Empire*, p. 153; Gerberding, *Rise of the Carolingians*, pp. 130–45; Hodges and Whitehouse, *Mohammed, Charlemagne*, p. 81; James, "The Northern World," pp. 89–91; Lasko, *The Kingdom of the Franks*, pp. 68–70, 126–7; Le Goff, *Medieval Civilization*, p. 23; McKitterick, *The Frankish Kingdoms*, pp. 30–7, 48, 50–1; McNeill, *The Rise of the West*, p. 445; Riché, *The Carolingians*, pp. 24, 44, 46, 50, 66–7, 69; Spybey, *Social Change, Development and Dependency*, p. 50; Vaglieri, "The Patriarchal and Umayyad Caliphates," pp. 95–6.

6 Franzius, *History of the Byzantine Empire*, p. 153.

7 Brown, "Transformation of the Roman Mediterranean," pp. 24, 35, 45; Bullough, *Carolingian Renewal*, passim, esp. pp. 14–15, 132–9, 207; Franzius, *History of the Byzantine Empire*, pp. 153–4; Hodges and Whitehouse, *Mohammed, Charlemagne*, p. 102; James, "The Northern World," pp. 63, 67, 74–5, 93–9; Lasko, *The Kingdom of the Franks*, pp. 126–7; Le Goff, *Medieval Civilization*, pp. 23, 37–43, 128–30; Logan, *The Vikings in History*, p. 112; McKitterick, *The Frankish Kingdoms*, pp. 21–2, 53–60, 64, 68, 87–8, 91, 145–66, 200–25, 287, 299; McNeill, *The Rise of the West*, pp. 442, 444–6; Read, *Moors in Spain and Portugal*, pp. 51–2; Riché, *The Carolingians*, pp. 85–6, 88–9, 98; Romanides, *Franks, Romans, Feudalism and Doctrine*, pp. 14–15; Spybey, *Social Change, Development and Dependency*, p. 56; Tilly, *Coercion, Capital and European States*, p. 144.

8 Bloch, *Feudal Society*, p. 16; Brown, "Transformation of the Roman Mediterranean," p. 17; Jones, *A History of the Vikings*, pp. 199–200, 224–6; Le Goff, *Medieval Civilization*, pp. 23, 43–4; McNeill, *The Rise of the West*, pp. 420, 443, 445, 447–8; Wallerstein, *The Modern World-System*, vol. 1, pp. 36–7.

9 Collins, *Weberian Sociological Theory*, p. 9; Giddens, *The Nation-State and Violence*; Tilly, "Reflection"; Tilly, *Coercion, Capital, and European States*.

## Chapter 3   Early Feudalism and Competing Civilizations

1 James, "The Northern World," pp. 98–9; Porter, *War and the Rise of the State*, p. 6; Spybey, *Social Change, Development and Dependency*, p. 54.

2 Franzius, *History of the Byzantine Empire*, pp. 193–4; Hodges and Whitehouse, *Mohammed, Charlemagne*, p. 103; Hourani, *History of the Arab Peoples*, p. 38; Kreuger, "The Italian Cities," p. 43; McKitterick, *The Frankish Kingdoms*, pp. 107–8.

3 Brown, "Transformation of the Roman Mediterranean," p. 17; Lewis, "Egypt and Syria," pp. 193–4; McNeill, *The Rise of the West*, pp. 447–8; Whitton, "Society of Northern Europe," pp. 161–3.

4 Abu-Lughod, *Before European Hegemony*, p. 80; Downing, *The Military Revolution*, p. 20; Hodges and Whitehouse, *Mohammed, Charlemagne*, pp. 102–3, 164–5; James, "The Northern World," pp. 92, 98–9; Jones, *A History of the Vikings*, pp. 199–200; Lasko, *The Kingdom of the Franks*, p. 42; Le Goff, *Medieval Civilization*, p. 46; Logan, *The Vikings in History*, pp. 15–17; McKitterick, *The Frankish Kingdoms*, pp. 106, 169–87, 381; McNeill, *The Rise of the West*, p. 448.

5 Bloch, *Feudal Society*, pp. 19–22; Hodges and Whitehouse, *Mohammed, Charlemagne*, pp. 112–13, 121; James, "The Northern World," pp. 99–108; Jones, *A History of the Vikings*, pp. 59–314; Logan, *The Vikings in History*, pp. 15–16, 29–33, 35–57, 114–24, 128–36; McKitterick, *The Frankish Kingdoms*, pp. 228, 231–5, 237–8; Riché, *The Carolingians*, pp. 218–21; Sourdel, "The Abbasid Caliphate," p. 118; Tilly, *Coercion, Capital, and European States*, pp. 134–5; Whitton, "Society of Northern Europe," p. 150.

6 Downing, *The Military Revolution*, p. 20; Jones, *A History of the Vikings*, pp. 248, 262–3; Le Goff, *Medieval Civilization*, p. 43; Logan, *The Vikings in History*, pp. 185–96, 202–3; McNeill, *The Rise of the West*, p. 448; Tilly, *Coercion, Capital, and European States*, p. 138.

7 Logan, *The Vikings in History*, pp. 138–79; Jones, *A History of the Vikings*, pp. 150, 222.

8 Bloch, *Feudal Society*, pp. 8–9, 11–13; Logan, *The Vikings in History*, pp. 15–16; McNeill, *The Rise of the West*, p. 449; Tilly, *Coercion, Capital, and European States*, p. 44; Whitton, "Society of Northern Europe," pp. 138–43, 161–2.

9 Downing, *The Military Revolution*, pp. 23–4; Le Goff, *Medieval Civilization*, pp. 91–5; Whitton, "Society of Northern Europe," pp. 116–17.

10 Chirot, "The Rise of the West," p. 193; Collins, *Weberian Sociological Theory*, p. 38; Frank, *Dependent Accumulation*; Wallerstein, *The Modern World-System*, vols 1 and 2; Whitton, "Society of Northern Europe," p. 119.

11 Downing, *The Military Revolution*, pp. 19–20; Hodges and Whitehouse, *Mohammed, Charlemagne*, pp. 103, 112–13, 167; James, "The Northern World," pp. 99–108, 106; Le Goff, *Medieval Civilization*, pp. 43–5; McKitterick, *The Frankish Kingdoms*, pp. 232–3; Tilly, *Coercion, Capital, and European States*, p. 44.

## Chapter 4   The Manor and Church: Internal and External Conflict

1 Collins, *Weberian Sociological Theory*, pp. 9–10.

2 Abu-Lughod, *Before European Hegemony*, p. 106; Braudel, *Civilization and Capitalism*, pp. 494–5; Guenée, *States and Rulers*, pp. 137–8; Downing, *The Military Revolution*, p. 20; Howorth, *History of the Mongols*, pp. 113–15; McNeill, *The Rise of the West*, p. 538; Spybey, *Social Change, Development and Dependency*, p. 54.

3 Downing, *The Military Revolution*, pp. 20–1; McNeill, *The Rise of the West*, p. 540; Tilly, *Coercion, Capitalism, and European States*, p. 45; Wallerstein, *The Modern World-System*, vol. 1, pp. 36–7; Whitton, "Society of Northern Europe," pp. 118–19.

4 Fossier, *Peasant Life*, pp. 34, 51–2, 127, 149–51; Guenée, *States and Rulers*, pp. 137–8; Whitton, "Society of Northern Europe," pp. 118–19.

5 Abu-Lughod, *Before European Hegemony*, pp. 55–77; Braudel, *Civilization and Capitalism*, p. 492; Brown, "Transformation of the Roman Mediterranean," pp. 28–9; Downing, *The Military Revolution*, pp. 27–31; Guenée, *States and Rulers*, pp. 137–8; Le Goff, *Medieval Civilization*, pp. 74–5; McNeill, *The Rise of the West*, p. 542; Reynolds, *History of English Medieval Towns*, pp. 161–2, 168–71, 204–6, 214–18, 312–16; Spybey, *Social Change, Development and Dependency*, p. 60; Tilly, "Warmaking and Statemaking," pp. 169–91; Whitton, "Society of Northern Europe," pp. 122–4.

6 Bendix, *Kings or People*, pp. 193–7; Chambers, *The Devil's Horsemen*, pp. 104–5; Denley, "The Mediterranean," pp. 222–9; Downing, *The Military Revolution*, pp. 23, 61–2,

74–8, 157–86; Given, *State and Society*, pp. 44–9, 108–14; Guenée, *States and Rulers*, pp. 20–1, 140–4, 172–87; Le Goff, *Medieval Civilization*, pp. 93–4, 97–100, 102; McNeill, *Venice*, p. 26; Reynolds, *History of English Medieval Towns*, pp. 267–70, 296, 311; Tilly, *Coercion, Capital, and European States*, pp. 154–5; Vale, "Courts and Cities," pp. 283–94; Whitton, "Society of Northern Europe," pp. 109–64; Wolf, *Europe*, p. 108; Spybey, *Social Change, Development and Dependency*, p. 55.

7 Whitton, "Society of Northern Europe," pp. 117–19.

8 Abu-Lughod, *Before European Hegemony*, p. 106; Charanis, "Byzantine Empire," p. 213; Denley, "The Mediterranean," pp. 246–7; Franzius, *History of the Byzantine Empire*, pp. 303–7; Collins, *Weberian Sociological Theory*, pp. 9–10, 52–4; Duncalf, "Councils," pp. 241–2, 258–9, 260–3; Hourani, *History of the Arab Peoples*, pp. 39–41, 85; Kinross, *The Ottoman Centuries*, pp. 16–18, 51; Le Goff, *Medieval Civilization*, p. 69; Lewis, "Egypt and Syria," pp. 196–7; Lopez, "The Norman Conquest of Sicily," pp. 65–6; McNeill, *Venice*, pp. 1–3; Morris, "Northern Europe Invades the Mediterranean," pp. 168–74, 194–5, 197–204; Spuler, "Disintegration of the Caliphate," pp. 149–50; Tilly, *Coercion, Capital, and European States*, p. 25; Turan, "Anatolia," pp. 233, 235, 238, 259; Whitton, "Society of Northern Europe," p. 119; Wolf, *Europe*, p. 123.

9 Abu-Lughod, *Before European Hegemony*, pp. 107–9; Denley, "The Mediterranean," pp. 244–5; Franzius, *History of the Byzantine Empire*, pp. 307, 327–8; Hourani, *History of the Arab Peoples*, p. 85; Lewis, "Egypt and Syria," p. 197; Mayer, *The Crusades*, pp. 82–3; Morris, "Northern Europe Invades the Mediterranean," pp. 209–10; Wolf, *Europe*, p. 106.

10 Franzius, *History of the Byzantine Empire*, pp. 324–7; Hourani, *History of the Arab Peoples*, p. 84; Johnson, "The Crusades," p. 114; Köprülü, *Origins of the Ottoman Empire*, p. 79; Lewis, "Egypt and Syria," pp. 200–4, 207; Mayer, *The Crusades*, pp. 96–8, 108–9, 130–4; Morris, "Northern Europe Invades the Mediterranean," pp. 175, 207–8; Painter, "The Third Crusade," pp. 70, 83–5; Spybey, *Social Change, Development and Dependency*, p. 57; Turan, "Anatolia," pp. 241, 244.

11 Denley, "The Mediterranean," pp. 229–37; Downing, *The Military Revolution*, pp. 27–31; Guenée, *States and Rulers*, pp. 140–4; Morris, "Northern Europe Invades the Mediterranean," pp. 216–19; Spybey, *Social Change, Development and Dependency*, p. 64; Tilly, *Coercion, Capital,*

*and European States*, pp. 80–1; McNeill, *Venice*, pp. 69–70; Lane, *Venice*, pp. 231–2.

12 Chambers, *The Devil's Horsemen*, pp. 107–8; McNeill, *The Rise of the West*, pp. 545–6; Tilly, *Coercion, Capital, and European States*, pp. 22–3, 57.

13 Abu-Lughod, *Before European Hegemony*, pp. 109–11; Franzius, *History of the Byzantine Empire*, pp. 349–56; Kinross, *The Ottoman Centuries*, p. 37; Mayer, *The Crusades*, pp. 189–90, 193–6; McNeill, *The Rise of the West*, pp. 30, 515–16, 518–19; Morris, "Northern Europe Invades the Mediterranean," pp. 168–9, 219–21; Spybey, *Social Change, Development and Dependency*, p. 59; Turan, "Anatolia," pp. 243–4.

14 Chambers, *The Devil's Horsemen*, pp. 105–6; Collins, *Weberian Sociological Theory*, pp. 9–10; Denley, "The Mediterranean," pp. 222–9; Guenée, *States and Rulers*, p. 6; Lewis, "Egypt and Syria," pp. 207–8; Mayer, *The Crusades*, p. 229; Reynolds, *History of English Medieval Towns*, p. 300; Van Cleve, "The Fifth Crusade," pp. 377–428.

15 Denley, "The Mediterranean," p. 244; Lewis, "Egypt and Syria," pp. 208–9; Mayer, *The Crusades*, pp. 251–3, 255–7.

16 Abu-Lughod, *Before European Hegemony*, p. 120; Chambers, *The Devil's Horsemen*, pp. 108–9; Downing, *The Military Revolution*, pp. 140–1; Le Goff, *Medieval Civilization*, pp. 102–3; Guenée, *States and Rulers*, p. 165; Tilly, *Coercion, Capital, and European States*, pp. 26–7; Whitton, "Society of Northern Europe," pp. 109–64.

17 Abu-Lughod, *Before European Hegemony*, pp. 141–4, 155–70; Chambers, *The Devil's Horsemen*, passim and esp. pp. 24–5, 27–8, 30–4, 37–8, 56, 62–7, 76, 80–3, 85–7, 89–90, 97–8, 107–9, 111–12, 114–18, 120–9, 134–5, 144; de Hartog, *Genghis Khan*, pp. 31–3, 46, 119–23, 164–83, 185–6; Downing, *The Military Revolution*, pp. 38–44, 48–9; Howorth, *History of the Mongols*, pp. 21, 27, 50–1, 112–14, 116–61; Kinross, *The Ottoman Centuries*, p. 19; Köprülü, *Origins of the Ottoman Empire*, pp. 32–3; Mayer, *The Crusades*, pp. 258–60; McNeill, *The Rise of the West*, pp. 492–3, 514; Phillips, *The Mongols*, pp. 38, 72–6; Spuler, "Disintegration of the Caliphate," pp. 160–1; Spybey, *Social Change, Development and Dependency*, pp. 50–1; Tilly, *Coercion, Capital, and European States*, p. 138.

18 Barkey, *Bandits and Bureaucrats*, pp. 28, 34; Denley, "The Mediterranean," pp. 251–3; Hourani, *History of the Arab Peoples*, p. 214; Imber, *The Ottoman Empire*, pp. 22–4, 26–56, 64–5, 75–6, 148–51, 156–7; Inalcik, "Rise of the

Ottoman Empire," pp. 265, 268, 274, 276–80, 295–6; Kinross, *The Ottoman Centuries*, pp. 23–6, 39–43, 45–53, 57–8, 60–71, 76, 78–81, 100–3, 108–11; Köprülü, *Origins of the Ottoman Empire*, pp. 80–1, 109–10; McNeill, *Venice*, pp. 77, 81, 83; Wolf, *Europe*, pp. 35–6.

19 Guenée, *States and Rulers*, p. 3; Kinross, *The Ottoman Centuries*, p. 45; McNeill, *The Rise of the West*, pp. 541–5, 547; Wallerstein, *The Modern World-System*, vol. 1, pp. 28–32.

## Chapter 5   The Renaissance, the Reformation, and the European State System

1 Cameron, *The European Reformation*, pp. 104, 168–70; Collins, *Weberian Sociological Theory*, pp. 9–10; Downing, *The Military Revolution*, pp. 20–31, 35, 37–8; Guenée, *States and Rulers*, pp. 3, 20–2; Lynch, *Spain under the Habsburgs*, p. 80; McNeill, *The Rise of the West*, pp. 578–9, 591, 607; Reynolds, *History of English Medieval Towns*, pp. 251–4; Spybey, *Social Change, Development and Dependency*, pp. 37, 59, 62, 66, 93; Wallerstein, *The Modern World-System*, vol. 1, pp. 240–50, 260.

2 Cameron, *The European Reformation*, pp. 32–5, 174–5; Whitton, "Society of Northern Europe," pp. 134–7.

3 Denley, "The Mediterranean," pp. 246–7, 263–6; Hourani, *History of the Arab Peoples*, p. 85; Inalcik, "Rise of the Ottoman Empire," p. 312; Le Goff, *Medieval Civilization*, p. 65; Lewis, "Egypt and Syria," pp. 228–9; McNeill, *The Rise of the West*, pp. 571, 613; Tilly, *Coercion, Capital, and European States*, pp. 45, 92; Wallerstein, *The Modern World-System*, vol. 1, p. 29; Wolf, *Europe*, pp. 112–13, 235.

4 Lane, *Venice*, pp. 73–5, 234; Tilly, *Coercion, Capital, and European States*, p. 78; Wallerstein, *The Modern World-System*, vol. 1, p. 171.

5 Garraty and Gay, *Columbia History of the World*, pp. 468, 470; Le Goff, *Medieval Civilization*, p. 63.

6 Cameron, *The European Reformation*, pp. 100, 112, 145–67, 200–2, 207–8, 247, 267–72, 274–6; Collins, *Weberian Sociological Theory*, pp. 9–10; McNeill, *The Rise of the West*, p. 591; Tilly, *Coercion, Capital, and European States*, p. 107.

7 Hourani, *History of the Arab Peoples*, pp. 36–7; Morris, "Northern Europe Invades the Mediterranean," pp. 174–5; Spuler, "Disintegration of the Caliphate," pp. 152–3; Wallerstein, *The Modern World-System*, vol. 1, pp. 327–30.

8 Barkey, *Bandits and Bureaucrats*, pp. 44–5; Cameron, *The*

*European Reformation*, pp. 200–2, 208–52; Inalcik, "Rise of the Ottoman Empire," pp. 311, 314–15, 324–7; Kann, *History of the Habsburg Empire*, pp. 25–8, 35–9; Kinross, *The Ottoman Centuries*, pp. 45, 132–3, 135–7, 166–7, 170–1, 174, 176–9, 189, 191–5, 201, 203–5, 217–27, 338; Lynch, *Spain under the Habsburgs*, pp. 38, 78, 80, 87, 92–3, 95–7, 100; McNeill, *The Rise of the West*, pp. 580, 618–22, 639; Savory, "Safavid Persia," pp. 398, 400–1, 403, 406; Tilly, *Coercion, Capital, and European States*, pp. 31, 41, 78, 86–7, 161–2, 171; Wallerstein, *The Modern World-System*, vol. 1, pp. 165, 171, 174–5, 178–9; Wolf, *Europe*, p. 35.

9 Cameron, *The European Reformation*, pp. 20–37, 108–10, 151–5, 219–23; Downing, *The Military Revolution*, p. 163; Inalcik, "Rise of the Ottoman Empire," p. 329; Lynch, *Spain under the Habsburgs*, pp. 98–100; Vale, "Courts and Cities," p. 283–302.

10 Cameron, *The European Reformation*, pp. 285–6; Downing, *The Military Revolution*, pp. 161–2, 164–8; Tilly, *Coercion, Capital, and European States*, p. 156; Wallerstein, *The Modern World-System*, vol. 1, p. 232.

11 Abu-Lughod, *Before European Hegemony*, p. 20; Downing, *The Military Revolution*, pp. 216, 225–6; Inalcik, "Rise of the Ottoman Empire," pp. 330, 337; Lynch, *Spain under the Habsburgs*, pp. 177, 190–1, 204, 208, 216–17, 233–5, 237–41, 244–5, 247, 278, 287, 294, 296–7, 300–1, 303, 305–8, 327, 344–5; Tilly, *Coercion, Capital, and European States*, pp. 55, 90, 162; Wallerstein, *The Modern World-System*, vol. 1, pp. 185–6, 197, 201, 203–8, 209.

12 Abu-Lughod, *Before European Hegemony*, p. 93; Downing, *The Military Revolution*, pp. 74–8, 106–12, 170–9, 232–4; Guenée, *States and Rulers*, pp. 172–87; McNeill, *The Rise of the West*, pp. 580–1, 678–9.

13 McNeill, *The Rise of the West*, pp. 640–5.

14 Downing, *The Military Revolution*, pp. 44–8; McNeill, *The Rise of the West*, pp. 645–9.

15 Braudel, *Civilization and Capitalism*, p. 396; McNeill, *The Rise of the West*, pp. 606, 608–11; Tilly, *Coercion, Capital, and European States*, pp. 140–1; Wallerstein, *The Modern World-System*, vol. 1, pp. 313–17.

## Chapter 6   The Findings and their Implications for the Americas

1 Anderson, *Passages from Antiquity to Feudalism*; Frank and Gills, "Five Thousand Year World System," p. 23; Cameron, *The European Reformation*, pp. 20–33, 302; Chirot, "The Rise of the West"; Collins, *Weberian Sociological Theory*, pp. 9–10, 49, 76; Denley, "The Mediterranean," pp. 229–37; McNeill, *The Rise of the West*, pp. 579, 585; Weber, *General Economic History*.
2 Mann, *The Sources of Social Power*, vols 1 and 2.
3 Spengler, *The Decline of the West*.
4 Comte, *Religion of Humanity*; Hegel, *The Phenomenology of Mind*.
5 Anderson, *Passages from Antiquity to Feudalism*; Anderson, *Lineages of the Absolutist State*; Porter, *War and the Rise of States*.
6 Collins, *Weberian Sociological Theory*, pp. 9–10; Denley, "The Mediterranean," pp. 266–70; Lang, *Conquest and Commerce*; McNeill, *The Rise of the West*, pp. 491, 555–66, 660; Spybey, *Social Change, Development and Dependency*, pp. 66–7.

# References

Abu-Lughod, Janet L., *Before European Hegemony: The World System AD 1220–1350*. New York: Oxford University Press, 1989.

Anderson, Perry, *Passages from Antiquity to Feudalism* (1974). London: Verso, 1978.

—— *Lineages of the Absolutist State*. London: New Left Books, 1974.

Barber, Richard, *The Reign of Chivalry*. New York: St Martin's Press, 1980.

Barkey, Karen, *Bandits and Bureaucrats: The Ottoman Route to State Centralization*. Ithaca and London: Cornell University Press, 1994.

Bendix, Reinhard, *Kings or People: Power and the Mandate to Rule*. Berkeley: University of California Press, 1978.

Bloch, Marc, *Feudal Society*. Chicago: University of Chicago Press, 1961.

Braudel, Fernand, *Capitalism and Material Life 1400–1800*. New York: Harper and Row, 1973.

—— *Civilization and Capitalism, 15th–18th Century*, vol. 1: *The Structures of Everyday Life: The Limits of the Possible*. New York: Harper and Row, 1981.

Bright, Charles, and Susan Harding (eds), *Statemaking and Social Movements: Essays in History and Theory*. Ann Arbor: University of Michigan Press, 1984.

Brown, Thomas, "The Transformation of the Roman Mediterranean, 400–900." In *The Oxford History of Medieval Europe*, ed. George Holmes, 1–58. Oxford: Oxford University Press, 1992.

Brundage, Burr, *Empire of the Inca.* Norman: University of Oklahoma Press, 1963.

—— *Two Earths, Two Heavens: An Essay Contrasting the Aztecs and the Incas.* Albuquerque: University of New Mexico Press, 1975.

Bullough, D. A., *Carolingian Renewal: Sources and Heritage.* Manchester: Manchester University Press, 1991.

Burke, Victor Lee, "The Rise of Europe," *Humboldt Journal of Social Relations* 20 (1994): 1–30.

Cameron, Euan, *The European Reformation.* Oxford: Clarendon Press, 1991.

Chambers, James, *The Devil's Horsemen: The Mongol Invasion of Europe.* London: Cassell, 1988.

Charanis, Peter, "The Byzantine Empire in the Eleventh Century." In *A History of the Crusades,* vol. 1: *The First Hundred Years,* ed. Marshall W. Baldwin, general editor, Kenneth M. Setton, 177–219. Madison: University of Wisconsin Press, 1969.

Chase-Dunn, Christopher, and T. D. Hall (eds), *Core/Periphery Relations in Precapitalist Worlds.* Boulder: Westview, 1991.

Chirot, Daniel, "The Rise of the West," *American Sociological Review* 50 (1985): 181–95.

Claster, Jill, *The Medieval Experience, 300–1400.* New York: New York University Press, 1982.

Collins, Randall, *Weberian Sociological Theory.* Cambridge: Cambridge University Press, 1986.

Comte, Auguste, *Religion of Humanity: Subjective Synthesis, or Universal System of the Conceptions Adapted to the Normal State of Humanity* (1856). London: Routledge, 1891.

de Beauvoir, Simone, *The Second Sex.* New York: Vintage Books, 1952.

de Hartog, Leo, *Genghis Khan: Conqueror of the World.* New York: St Martins Press, 1989.

Denley, Peter, "The Mediterranean in the Age of the Renaissance, 1200–1500." In *The Oxford History of Medieval Europe,* ed. George Holmes, 222–76. Oxford: Oxford University Press, 1992.

Dobb, Maurice, *Studies in the Development of Capitalism.* London: Routledge, 1946.

Downing, Brian, *The Military Revolution and Political Change: Origins of Democracy and Autocracy in Early Modern Europe.* Princeton: Princeton University Press, 1992.

Duggan, Anne, *Thomas Becket: A Textual History of His Letters.* Oxford: Clarendon Press, 1980.

Duncalf, Frederic, "The Councils of Piacenza and Clermont." In *A History of the Crusades,* vol. 1: *The First Hundred Years,* ed.

Marshall W. Baldwin, general editor, Kenneth M. Setton, 220–52. Madison: University of Wisconsin Press, 1969.

—— "The First Crusade: Clermont to Constantinople." In *A History of the Crusades*, vol. 1: *The First Hundred Years*, ed. Marshall W. Baldwin, general editor, Kenneth M. Setton, 253–79. Madison: University of Wisconsin Press, 1969.

Engineer, Asgharali, *The Origin and Development of Islam: An Essay on its Socio-Economic Growth*. Bombay: Orient Longman, 1980.

Finer, S. E., "State and Nation Building in Europe: The Role of the Military." In *The Formation of National States in Western Europe*, ed. Charles Tilly, 84–163. Princeton: Princeton University Press, 1975.

Fossier, Robert, *Peasant Life in the Medieval West*. New York: Blackwell, 1988.

Frank, André Gunder, *Dependent Accumulation and Underdevelopment*. New York: Monthly Review Press, 1979.

Frank, André Gunder, and Barry K. Gills, "The Five Thousand Year World System: An Interdisciplinary Introduction," *Humboldt Journal of Social Relations* 18.1 (1992): 1–80.

Franzius, Enno, *History of the Byzantine Empire: Mother of Nations*. New York: Funk and Wagnalls, 1967.

Garraty, John. A., and Peter Gay (eds), *The Columbia History of the World* (1972). New York: Harper and Row, 1984.

Gerberding, Richard A., *The Rise of the Carolingians and the Liber Historiae Francorum*. Oxford: Clarendon Press, 1987.

Giddens, Anthony, *Capitalism and Modern Social Theory: An Analysis of the Writings of Marx, Durkheim and Max Weber*. Cambridge: Cambridge University Press, 1971.

—— *The Constitution of Society: Outline of the Theory of Structuration*. Cambridge: Polity Press; Berkeley: University of California Press, 1984.

—— *The Nation-State and Violence*, vol. 2 of *A Contemporary Critique of Historical Materialism*. Cambridge: Polity Press; Berkeley: University of California Press, 1985.

Given, James, *State and Society in Medieval Europe*. Ithaca: Cornell University Press, 1990.

Guenée, Bernard, *States and Rulers in Later Medieval Europe*. Oxford: Blackwell, 1985.

Haussig, Hans Wilheim, *A History of Byzantine Civilization*. New York: Praeger, 1971.

Hegel, Georg, *The Phenomenology of Mind* (1807). London: Allen and Unwin, 1961.

Held, David, *Political Theory and the Modern State*. Cambridge: Polity Press; Stanford: Stanford University Press, 1989.

Hodges, Richard, and David Whitehouse, *Mohammed, Charlemagne and the Origins of Europe: Archaeology and the Pirenne Thesis*. London: Duckworth, 1983.

Holmes, George (ed.), *The Oxford History of Medieval Europe*. Oxford: Oxford University Press, 1992.

Holt, P. M., Ann K. S. Lambton, and Bernard Lewis (eds), *The Cambridge History of Islam*, vol. 1: *The Central Islamic Lands*. London: Cambridge University Press, 1970.

Hourani, Albert, *A History of the Arab Peoples*. Cambridge: Belknap Press of Harvard University Press, 1991.

Howorth, Henry H., *History of the Mongols: From the Ninth to the Nineteenth Century*, part 1: *The Mongols Proper and the Kalmuks*. New York: B. Franklin, 1876.

Huntington, Samuel, *Political Order in Changing Societies*. New Haven: Yale University Press, 1968.

—— "The Clash of Civilizations?" *Foreign Affairs* 72.3 (1993): 22–49.

Imber, Colin, *The Ottoman Empire 1300–1481*. Istanbul: Isis Press, 1990.

Inalcik, Halil, "The Rise of the Ottoman Empire." In *The Cambridge History of Islam*, vol. 1: *The Central Islamic Lands*, ed. P. M. Holt, Ann K. S. Lambton, and Bernard Lewis, 295–323. London: Cambridge University Press, 1970.

James, Edward, *The Franks*. New York: Blackwell, 1988.

—— "The Northern World in the Dark Ages, 400–900." In *The Oxford History of Medieval Europe*, ed. George Holmes, 59–108. Oxford: Oxford University Press, 1992.

Johnson, Edgar N., "The Crusades of Frederick Barbarossa and Henry VI." In *A History of the Crusades*, vol. 2: *The Later Crusades, 1189–1311*, ed. Robert Lee Wolff and Harry W. Hazard, general editor, Kenneth M. Setton, 87–122. Madison: University of Wisconsin Press, 1969.

Jones, E. L., *The European Miracle: Environments, Economies, and Geopolitics in the History of Europe and Asia*, 2nd edn. Cambridge: Cambridge University Press, 1987.

Jones, Gwyn, *A History of the Vikings*. London: Oxford University Press, 1973.

Jones, Robert, *The Great Reformation*. Downers Grove, Ill.: Inter Varsity Press, 1985.

Kann, Robert A., *A History of the Habsburg Empire 1526–1918*. Berkeley: University of California Press, 1974.

Kazancigil, A. (ed.), *The State in Global Perspective*. Brookfield, Vt: Gower, 1986.

Kennedy, Paul, *The Rise and Fall of the Great Powers: Economic Change and Military Conflict from 1500 to 2000*. New York: Random House, 1987.

Kinross, Lord, *The Ottoman Centuries: The Rise and Fall of the Turkish Empire*. London: Jonathan Cape, 1977.

Köprülü, M. Fuad, *The Origins of the Ottoman Empire*, trans. and ed. Gary Leiser. Albany: State University of New York Press, 1992.

Krueger, Hilmar C., "The Italian Cities and the Arabs before 1095." In *A History of the Crusades*, vol. 1: *The First Hundred Years*, ed. Marshall W. Baldwin, general editor, Kenneth M. Setton, 40–53. Madison: University of Wisconsin Press, 1969.

Lane, Frederic C., *Venice: A Maritime Republic*. Baltimore: Johns Hopkins University Press, 1973.

Lang, James, *Conquest and Commerce: Spain and England in the Americas*. New York: Academic Press, 1975.

Lasko, Peter, *The Kingdom of the Franks: North-West Europe before Charlemagne*. London: Thames and Hudson, 1971.

Le Goff, Jacques, *Medieval Civilization 400–1500*, trans. Julia Barrow. New York: Blackwell, 1988.

Lenski, Gerhard, and Jean Lenski, *Human Societies: An Introduction to Macrosociology*, 3rd edn. New York: McGraw-Hill, 1978.

Lewis, Bernard, "Egypt and Syria." In *The Cambridge History of Islam*, vol. 1: *The Central Islamic Lands*, ed. P. M. Holt, Ann K. S. Lambton, and Bernard Lewis, 175–230. London: Cambridge University Press, 1970.

Logan, Donald F., *The Vikings in History*. London: Hutchinson, 1983.

Lopez, Robert S., "The Norman Conquest of Sicily." In *A History of the Crusades*, vol. 1: *The First Hundred Years*, ed. Marshall W. Baldwin, general editor, Kenneth M. Setton, 54–67. Madison: University of Wisconsin Press, 1969.

Lynch, John, *Spain under the Habsburgs*, vol. 1: *Empire and Absolutism 1516–1598* (1964), 2nd edn. Oxford: Blackwell, 1981.

Mann, Michael, *The Sources of Social Power*, vols 1 and 2. Cambridge: Cambridge University Press, 1986 and 1993.

—— *States, War and Capitalism*. New York: Blackwell, 1988.

Marx, Karl, and Frederick Engels, *Collected Works*. New York: International Publishers, 1975.

Mayer, Hans Eberhard, *The Crusades*. New York: Oxford University Press, 1972.

McKitterick, Rosamond, *The Frankish Kingdoms under the Carolingians*. London: Longman, 1983.

McNeill, William H., *The Rise of the West*. Chicago: University of Chicago Press, 1968.

—— *Venice*. Chicago: University of Chicago Press, 1974.

Mills, C. Wright, *The Power Elite*. New York: Oxford University Press, 1956.

Morris, Rosemary, "Northern Europe Invades the Mediterranean, 900–1200." In *The Oxford History of Medieval Europe*, ed. George Holmes, 165–221. Oxford: Oxford University Press, 1992.

Painter, Sidney, "The Third Crusade: Richard the Lionhearted and Philip Augustus." In *A History of the Crusades*, vol. 2: *The Later Crusades, 1189–1311*, ed. Robert Lee Wolff and Harry W. Hazard, general editor, Kenneth M. Setton, 45–86. Madison: University of Wisconsin Press, 1969.

Parsons, Talcott, *The Structure of Social Action*. New York: McGraw-Hill, 1937.

Phillips, E. D., *The Mongols*. New York: Praeger, 1969.

Poggi, Gianfranco, *The Development of the Modern State*. Stanford: Stanford University Press, 1978.

Porter, Bruce D., *War and the Rise of the State: The Military Foundations of Modern Politics*. New York: Free Press, 1994.

Randers-Pehrson, Justine Davis, *Barbarians and Romans: The Birth of Europe, AD 400–700*. Norman: University of Oklahoma Press, 1983.

Read, Jan, *The Moors in Spain and Portugal*. Totowa, N.J.: Rowman and Littlefield, 1975.

Reynolds, Susan, *An Introduction to the History of English Medieval Towns*. Oxford: Clarendon, 1984.

Riché, Pierre, *The Carolingians: A Family Who Forged Europe*. Philadelphia: University of Pennsylvania Press, 1993.

Ridley, Jasper Godwin, *Statesman and Saint: Cardinal Wolsey, Sir Thomas More and the Politics of Henry VIII*. New York: Viking Press, 1983.

Rogers, Michael, *The Spread of Islam*. Oxford: Elsevier-Phaidon, 1976.

Romanides, John S., *Franks, Romans, Feudalism and Doctrine: An Interplay between Theology and Society*. Brookline, Mass.: Holy Cross Orthodox Press, 1982.

Saunders, John Joseph, *The History of the Mongol Conquests*. London: Routledge and Kegan Paul, 1971.

Savory, R. M., "Safavid Persia." In *The Cambridge History of Islam*, vol. 1: *The Central Islamic Lands*, ed. P. M. Holt, Ann K. S. Lambton, and Bernard Lewis, 394–429. London: Cambridge University Press, 1970.

Setton, Kenneth M. (general editor), *A History of the Crusades*, vol. 2: *The Later Crusades, 1189–1311*, ed. Robert Lee Wolff and Harry W. Hazard. Madison: University of Wisconsin Press, 1969.

Skocpol, Theda, *Protecting Soldiers and Mothers: The Political Origins of Social Policy in the United States*. Cambridge: Belknap Press of Harvard University Press, 1992.

Sorokin, Pitirim A., *Social and Cultural Dynamics*, 4 vols. New York: American Book Company, 1937–41.

Sourdel, D., "The Abbasid Caliphate." In *The Cambridge History of Islam*, vol. 1: *The Central Islamic Lands*, ed. P. M. Holt, Ann K. S. Lambton, and Bernard Lewis, 104–40. London: Cambridge University Press, 1970.

Spengler, Oswald, *The Decline of the West*. New York: Knopf, 1939.

Spuler, B., "The Disintegration of the Caliphate in the East." In *The Cambridge History of Islam*, vol. 1: *The Central Islamic Lands*, ed. P. M. Holt, Ann K. S. Lambton, and Bernard Lewis, 143–74. London: Cambridge University Press, 1970.

Spybey, Tony, *Social Change, Development and Dependency*. Cambridge: Polity Press, 1992.

Stafford, Pauline, *Queens, Concubines, and Dowagers: The King's Wife in the Early Middle Ages*. Athens: University of Georgia Press, 1983.

Straus, Barrie Ruth, *The Catholic Church*. New York: Hippocrene Books, 1987.

Tierney, Brian, and Sidney Painter, *Western Europe in the Middle Ages, 300–1475*. New York: Knopf, 1983.

Tilly, Charles, "Reflection on the History of European State-Making." In *The Formation of National States in Western Europe*, ed. Charles Tilly, 3–83. Princeton: Princeton University Press, 1975.

—— "War Making and State Making as Organized Crime." In *Bringing the State Back In*, ed. Peter Evans, Dietrich Rueschemeyer, and Theda Skocpol, 169–91. Cambridge: Cambridge University Press, 1985.

—— *Coercion, Capital, and European States AD 990–1990*. Cambridge, Mass.: Blackwell, 1990.

Toynbee Arnold, *A Study of History*, 10 vols. New York and London: Oxford University Press, 1934–54.

Turan, Osman, "Anatolia in the Period of the Seljuks and the Beyliks." In *The Cambridge History of Islam*, vol. 1: *The Central Islamic Lands*, ed. P. M. Holt, Ann K. S. Lambton, and Bernard Lewis, 231–62. London: Cambridge University Press, 1970.

Vaglieri, Laura Veccia, "The Patriarchal and Umayyad Caliphates." In *The Cambridge History of Islam*, vol. 1: *The*

*Central Islamic Lands*, ed. P. M. Holt, Ann K. S. Lambton, and Bernard Lewis, 57–103. London: Cambridge University Press, 1970.

Vale, Malcolm, "The Civilization of Courts and Cities in the North, 1200–1500." In *The Oxford History of Medieval Europe*, ed. George Holmes, 276–323. Oxford: Oxford University Press, 1992.

Van Cleve, Thomas C., "The Fifth Crusade." In *A History of the Crusades*, vol. 2: *The Later Crusades, 1189–1311*, ed. Robert Lee Wolff and Harry W. Hazard, general editor, Kenneth M. Setton, 377–428. Madison: University of Wisconsin Press, 1969.

Wallerstein, Immanuel, *The Modern World-System*, vols 1 and 2. New York: Academic Press, 1974 and 1980.

—— *The Capitalist World-Economy*. Cambridge: Cambridge University Press, 1979.

Weber, Max, *The Protestant Ethic and the Spirit of Capitalism* (1904–5). New York: Scribners, 1958.

—— *General Economic History* (1923), trans. Frank H. Knight. New York: Collier-Macmillan, 1961. Original from lectures 1919–20.

Whitton, David, "The Society of Northern Europe in the High Middle Ages, 900–1200." In *The Oxford History of Medieval Europe*, ed. George Holmes, 109–64. Oxford: Oxford University Press, 1992.

Wolf, Eric, *Europe and the People without History*. Berkeley: University of California Press, 1982.

Zolberg, A. R., "Strategic Interactions and the Formation of Modern States: France and England." In *The State in Global Perspective*, ed. A. Kazancigil. Brookfield, Vt: Gower, 1986.

# Index